ZAGATSURVEY®

2002/03

CHICAGO RESTAURANTS

Local Editor: Alice Van Housen

Local Coordinators: Carolyn McGuire and Jill Van Cleave

Editor: Daniel Simmons

Published and distributed by
ZAGAT SURVEY, LLC
4 Columbus Circle
New York, New York 10019
Tel: 212 977 6000
E-mail: chicago@zagat.com
Web site: www.zagat.com

Acknowledgments

We thank Bill Rice, Brenda and Earl Shapiro, Laura Levy Shatkin and Tom Van Housen for their assistance.

This guide would not have been possible without the hard work of our staff, especially Betsy Andrews, Deirdre Bourdet, Reni Chin, Larry Cohn, Griff Foxley, Jessica Gonzalez, Diane Karlin, Natalie Lebert, Mike Liao, Dave Makulec, Donna Marino, Laura Mitchell, Rob Poole, Robert Seixas, Yoji Yamaguchi and Sharon Yates.

Contents

What's New

Despite ominous forecasts after September 11 and a slow-down in tourism this past winter, Chicago's restaurants have enjoyed an encouraging spring – and things are already heating up for the summer. Here's what's new:

Opening Gambits: Ambitious newcomers included Erawan Royal Thai, Kevin, mk North, Spring and Mi Sueño, Su Realidad, as well as upscale chains Napa Valley Grille and Roy's. Haute hotel dining is hot, with The Lobby and Shanghai Terrace premiering in The Peninsula and Wave in the W Chicago Lakeshore. Noteworthy neighborhood debuts included Andersonville's Jin Ju; Bucktown's Piece; Lakeview's Orange, Prego and Twist; Ukrainian Village's Fortunato; and Uptown's Magnolia Café.

Coming Attractions: By press time, Geno Bahena will have launched another mouthful-monikered Mexican (Apaxtleco), and coming soon to River North are a Bob Chinn's Crab House, Fogo de Chão and SushiSamba. The South Loop awaits Jerry Kleiner's French bistro and upscale Chinese, while American brasserie One North and the first city Krispy Kreme launch late summer in the Loop.

Chef Shuffle: Prominent chef peregrinations included the migration of Grant Achatz from The French Laundry in California to Trio after Shawn McClain sprang for Spring. Bernard Laskowski left Bin 36 to join Michael Kornick at mk; Kelly Courtney left MOD.; Todd Downs parked at Park Avenue Cafe; John Hogan found a happy home at Keefer's; and Gioco landed the promising Corcoran O'Connor.

Makeovers, Do-Overs & Just Plain Overs: Some good ideas got better, and some ill-fated ones got new life. North Pond and Spago remodeled; cushy RL went American; the down-scaled Vong's Thai Kitchen was born of Vong; and Fahrenheit morphed into Como. And we set down our forks to mark the passing of the original Bistrot Zinc, Blackhawk Lodge, Echo, Grace, Hubbard Street Grill, Hudson Club, Lakeview Supper Club, Maiz, Rudi's Wine Bar & Cafe and Villa Kula.

Value Propositions: Many developments bode well for consumers' wallets, including an apparent cap on upward-spiraling prices and a slew of creative promotions to lure us from our cocoons. Some bars are serving better-than-bar food, some better spots are serving bar menus and some notable chefs are delving into lower-priced concepts (e.g. Eric Aubriot's Tournesol and Susan Goss' recently opened West Town Tavern). The upshot? Chicago's average meal cost came in at a reasonable $29.29.

Chicago, IL
July 2, 2002

Alice Van Housen

About This Survey

For 24 years, Zagat Survey has reported on the shared experiences of diners like you. Here are the results of our *Chicago Restaurant Survey*, covering some 992 restaurants. This marks the 17th year we have covered restaurants in Chicago.

By regularly surveying large numbers of avid local restaurant-goers about their collective dining experiences, we hope to have achieved a uniquely current and reliable guide. For this book, nearly 2,400 people participated. Since the participants dined out an average of 2.8 times per week, this *Survey* is based on roughly 348,000 meals annually.

Of our surveyors, 52% are women, 48% men; the breakdown by age is 12% in their 20s, 24% in their 30s, 20% in their 40s, 25% in their 50s and 19% in their 60s or above. We thank each and every one of these surveyors – this book is really theirs.

Of course, we are especially grateful to our editor, Alice Van Housen, a freelance food writer and editor, and our coordinators, *Chicago Tribune* travel writer and editor Carolyn McGuire and cookbook author and food consultant Jill Van Cleave.

To help guide our readers to Chicago's best meals and best buys, we have prepared a number of lists. See Most Popular (page 9), Top Ratings (pages 10–15) and Best Buys (page 16). To assist the user in finding just the right restaurant for any occasion, without wasting time, we have also provided 45 handy indexes and have tried to be concise.

As companions to this guide, we also publish *America's Top Restaurants* and *Top U.S. Hotels, Resorts & Spas* as well as *Zagat Surveys* and Maps to more than 70 other markets around the world. Most of these guides are also available on mobile devices and at **www.zagat.com**, where you can also vote and shop.

To join our next *Chicago Survey* or any of our other upcoming *Surveys*, you can register at zagat.com. Each participant will receive a free copy of the resulting guide when it is published.

Your comments, suggestions and even criticisms of this guide are also solicited. There is always room for improvement with your help. You can contact us at chicago@zagat.com or by mail at Zagat Survey, 4 Columbus Circle, New York, NY 10019. We look forward to hearing from you.

New York, NY
July 2, 2002

Nina and Tim Zagat

Key to Ratings/Symbols

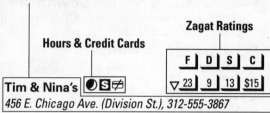

Name, Address & Phone Number

Zagat Ratings

Hours & Credit Cards

	F	D	S	C
Tim & Nina's ◐ [S] ≠	▽ 23	9	13	$15

456 E. Chicago Ave. (Division St.), 312-555-3867

◪ Hordes of "unkempt" U of C students have discovered this "never-closing" "eyesore", which "single-handedly" started the "deep-dish sushi pizza craze" that's "sweeping the Windy City" like a lake-effect storm; "try the eel-pepperoni-wasabi-mozzarella pie" – "it's to die for" (or from) – but bring cash, since "T & N never heard of credit cards or checks."

Review, with surveyors' comments in quotes

Restaurants with the highest overall ratings and greatest popularity and importance are printed in CAPITAL LETTERS.

Before each review a symbol indicates whether responses were uniform ■ or mixed ◪.

Hours: ◐ serves after 11 PM
[S] open on Sunday

Credit Cards: ≠ no credit cards accepted

Ratings: Food, Decor and Service are rated on a scale of **0** to **30.** The Cost (C) column reflects our surveyors' estimate of the price of dinner including one drink and tip.

F Food	D Decor	S Service	C Cost
23	9	13	$15

0–9 poor to fair
10–15 fair to good
16–19 good to very good
20–25 very good to excellent
26–30 extraordinary to perfection
▽ low response/less reliable

For places listed without ratings or a cost estimate, such as an important **newcomer** or a popular **write-in,** the cost is indicated by the following symbols.

I $15 and below
M $16 to $30
E $31 to $50
VE $51 or more

Most Popular

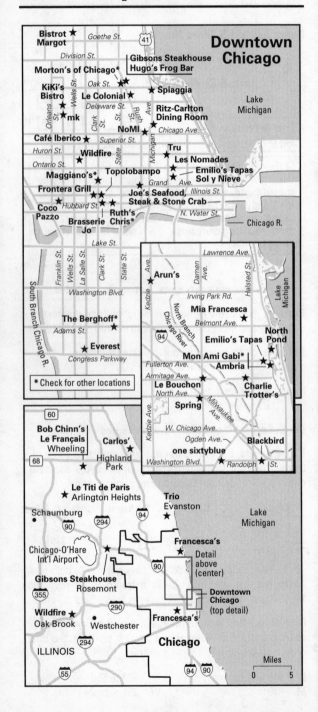

Downtown Chicago

Bistrot Margot ★
Goethe St.
41
Division St.
Gibsons Steakhouse
Hugo's Frog Bar
Morton's of Chicago*
Oak St.
KiKi's Bistro
Le Colonial ★
Spiaggia ★
mk
Delaware St.
Ritz-Carlton Dining Room
NoMI
Chicago Ave.
Café Iberico ★
Superior St.
Tru ★
Wildfire ★
Les Nomades ★
Huron St.
Ontario St.
Emilio's Tapas
Sol y Nieve ★
Maggiano's*
Topolobampo
Grand Ave.
Frontera Grill
Joe's Seafood, Steak & Stone Crab
Illinois St.
Coco Pazzo ★
Hubbard St.
Brasserie Jo
Ruth's Chris*
N. Water St.
Chicago R.
Lake St.
Lake Michigan

Wells St.
Orleans
Clark St.
State St.
Rush
Michigan Ave.

Lawrence Ave.
Arun's ★
Irving Park Rd.
Mia Francesca ★
Belmont Ave.
Emilio's Tapas
North Pond
Mon Ami Gabi*
Ambria ★
Fullerton Ave.
Charlie Trotter's
Armitage Ave.
Le Bouchon ★
North Ave.
Spring ★
W. Chicago Ave.
Ogden Ave.
Blackbird
one sixtyblue
Washington Blvd.
Randolph St.

Kedzie Ave.
Damen Ave.
North Branch
Chicago River
Halsted St.
94
Milwaukee Ave.
Lake Michigan

Washington Blvd.
Franklin St.
Wells St.
La Salle St.
Clark St.
State St.
The Berghoff*
Adams St.
Everest ★
Congress Parkway
*Check for other locations
South Branch Chicago R.

60
Bob Chinn's
Le Français
Wheeling
Carlos'
Highland Park
68
Le Titi de Paris ★
Arlington Heights
Trio ★
Evanston
Schaumburg
294
94
Francesca's ★
Chicago-O'Hare Int'l Airport
Detail above (center)
90
Downtown Chicago (top detail)
Gibsons Steakhouse
Rosemont
355
Wildfire ★
Oak Brook
290
Westchester
Francesca's ★
Chicago
ILLINOIS
294
55
94
90
Miles
0   5
Lake Michigan

www.zagat.com

Most Popular

Each of our reviewers has been asked to name his or her five favorite restaurants. The spots most frequently named, in order of their popularity, are:

1. Tru	21. Coco Pazzo
2. Charlie Trotter's	22. Trio
3. Ambria	23. Le Bouchon
4. Everest	24. Bob Chinn's Crab House
5. mk	25. North Pond
6. Frontera Grill	26. NoMI
7. Mon Ami Gabi	27. Joe's Seafood, Steak & Crab
8. Les Nomades	28. Hugo's Frog Bar
9. Gibsons Steakhouse	29. Le Français
10. Wildfire	30. Berghoff, The
11. Topolobampo	31. Café Iberico
12. Spiaggia	32. Le Colonial
13. Blackbird	33. Le Titi de Paris
14. Spring	34. Francesca's
15. Maggiano's Little Italy	35. Emilio's Tapas
16. Ritz-Carlton Dining Room	36. Ruth's Chris
17. Arun's	37. Mia Francesca
18. Carlos'	38. one sixtyblue
19. KiKi's Bistro	39. Bistrot Margot
20. Morton's of Chicago	40. Brasserie Jo

It's obvious that many of the restaurants on the above list are among Chicago's most expensive, but if popularity were calibrated to price, we are certain that a number of other restaurants would join the above ranks. Given the fact that both our surveyors and readers love to discover dining bargains, we have added a list of 80 Best Buys on page 16. These are restaurants that give real quality at extremely reasonable prices. They are the places where you'll find Chicagoans and their families on Sunday nights or, for that matter, on any day when they are not on expense account.

Top Ratings

Top lists exclude restaurants with low voting.

Top 40 Food Rankings

28	Seasons		Frontera Grill
	Les Nomades		Retro Bistro
	Ritz-Carlton Dining Room	25	Blackbird
	Charlie Trotter's		302 West
	Le Titi de Paris		D & J Bistro
	Carlos'		Avenues
	Le Français		Salbute
	Trio		Courtright's
27	Ambria		Gibsons Steakhouse
	Tru		Joe's Seafood, Steak & Crab
	Everest		Le Vichyssois
	Tallgrass		Printer's Row
	Spiaggia		Naha
	Les Deux Gros		Le Bouchon
	Topolobampo	24	Barrington Country Bistro
	Gabriel's		one sixtyblue
	Arun's		Ritz-Carlton Café
26	mk		Café Spiaggia
	Spring		Coco Pazzo
	Morton's of Chicago		Seasons Café

Top Food by Cuisine

American (New)
28 Seasons
 Charlie Trotter's
26 mk
 Spring
25 Blackbird

American (Regional)
24 Crofton on Wells
23 Meritage Cafe & Wine Bar
22 Prairie
 Zinfandel
21 Soul Kitchen

American (Traditional)
24 Ritz-Carlton Café
 Seasons Café
23 Lawry's The Prime Rib
 Walker Bros.
 Bongo Room

Asian
23 NoMI
 Le Colonial
 Yoshi's Café
 Catch 35
21 Red Light

Barbecue
21 Twin Anchors
20 Robinson's No. 1 Ribs
 Merle's Smokehouse
 Smoke Daddy*
 Carson's Ribs

Cajun/Creole
20 Heaven on Seven
 Wishbone
19 Davis Street Fishmarket
 Pappadeaux Seafood
 Dixie Kitchen & Bait Shop

Chinese
23 Hong Min
22 Phoenix
21 Emperor's Choice
20 Shine & Morida
 Ben Pao

Eclectic/International
24 Stained Glass Wine Bar
23 Room, The
21 Jane's
 Deleece
 She She

---

* Tied with restaurant directly above it

French (Bistro)
26 Retro Bistro
25 D & J Bistro
Le Bouchon
24 Barrington Country Bistro
Froggy's French Cafe

French (Classic)
28 Le Titi de Paris
27 Les Deux Gros
25 Le Vichyssois
24 Oceanique
La Petite Folie

French (New)
28 Les Nomades
Ritz-Carlton Dining Room
Carlos'
Le Français
Trio

Greek
23 Costa's
20 Santorini
Parthenon
Pegasus
Greek Islands

Hamburgers
21 Pete Miller's Steakhouse
19 Boston Blackie's
18 R.J. Grunt's
P.J. Clarke's
Twisted Spoke

Hot Dogs
22 Superdawg Drive-In
21 Wiener's Circle
19 Gold Coast Dogs
17 Fluky's

Indian
22 Tiffin
20 Viceroy of India
Gaylord India
Klay Oven
Indian Garden

Italian
27 Spiaggia
Gabriel's
24 Café Spiaggia
Coco Pazzo
Va Pensiero

Japanese
24 Mirai Sushi
Sushi Wabi
23 Bob San
Sushi Naniwa
Kuni's

Mediterranean
25 Avenues
Naha
22 Shallots
Lucca's
21 Tizi Melloul

Mexican
27 Topolobampo
26 Frontera Grill
25 Salbute
24 Cafe 28
23 Ixcapuzalco

Nuevo Latino
22 Mas
Nacional 27
21 Otro Mas
18 Mambo Grill

Pizza
21 Lou Malnati's Pizzeria
Pizza D.O.C.
Pizzeria Uno
20 Original Gino's East
Chicago Pizza & Oven Grinder

Seafood
25 Joe's Seafood, Steak & Crab
24 Oceanique
Atlantique
Hugo's Frog Bar
Nick's Fishmarket

Spanish/Tapas
23 Mesón Sabika
22 Café Iberico
21 Emilio's Tapas
20 Cafe Ba-Ba-Reeba!
19 Tapas Barcelona

Steakhouses
26 Morton's of Chicago
25 Gibsons Steakhouse
24 Ruth's Chris
Chicago Chop House
Las Tablas

Top Food

Thai
27 Arun's
22 Thai Pastry
21 Vong's Thai Kitchen
19 Star of Siam
18 P.S. Bangkok

Vegetarian
19 Reza's
18 Chicago Diner
    Blind Faith Café
16 Heartland Cafe
14 Slice of Life/Hy Life

Top Food by Special Feature

Breakfast*
23 Walker Bros.
22 Original Pancake House
21 Ina's
20 John's Place
    Lou Mitchell's

Brunch
28 Seasons
    Ritz-Carlton Dining Room
26 Frontera Grill
24 Caliterra Bar & Grille
    Park Avenue Cafe

Business Dining
28 Seasons
    Les Nomades
    Ritz-Carlton Dining Room
    Charlie Trotter's
    Le Titi de Paris

BYO
24 Las Tablas
23 Hong Min (Chinatown)
    Room, The
    Tre Kronor
22 Thai Pastry

Hotel Dining
28 Seasons
    Four Seasons
    Ritz-Carlton Dining Room
    Ritz-Carlton
    Trio
    Homestead
27 Ambria
    Belden Stratford
25 Gibsons Steakhouse
    Doubletree

Late Dining
25 Gibsons Steakhouse
24 Hugo's Frog Bar
23 Hong Min (Chinatown)
    Rosebud Steakhouse
22 Superdawg Drive-In

Meet for a Drink
26 mk
    Frontera Grill
25 Gibsons Steakhouse
    Joe's Seafood, Steak & Crab
    Naha

Newcomers/Rated
28 Kevin**
26 Spring
    Shanghai Terrace**
23 mk North
22 Keefer's

Newcomers/Unrated
    Fortunato
    Magnolia Café
    Masck
    Roy's
    Tournesol

Worth a Trip
28 Le Titi de Paris
    Arlington Heights
    Carlos'
    Highland Park
    Le Français
    Wheeling
    Trio
    Evanston
27 Tallgrass
    Lockport

---

* Other than hotels
** Low votes

Top Food by Location

Andersonville/Edgewater
- **24** Atlantique
  Francesca's
- **23** Pasteur
  Room, The
- **20** Tomboy

Bucktown
- **25** Le Bouchon
- **24** Café Absinthe
- **23** Meritage Cafe & Wine Bar
  Margie's Candies
  Cafe Matou

Chinatown
- **23** Hong Min
- **22** Phoenix
- **21** Emperor's Choice
- **19** Penang

Gold Coast
- **27** Spiaggia
- **25** Gibsons Steakhouse
- **24** Café Spiaggia
  Hugo's Frog Bar
- **23** Le Colonial

Lakeview/Wrigleyville
- **24** Cafe 28
  Mia Francesca
- **23** Yoshi's Café
  erwin, an american cafe
- **22** Matsuya

Lincoln Park/DePaul
- **28** Charlie Trotter's
- **27** Ambria
- **24** North Pond
  Las Tablas
  Aubriot

Little Italy/University Village
- **24** Francesca's
- **23** Chez Joel
- **22** Rico's
- **21** Tufano's Vernon Park Tap
  Tuscany

Loop
- **27** Everest
- **24** Entre Nous
  Nick's Fishmarket
- **23** Catch 35
  Vivere

Market District
- **24** one sixtyblue
  Sushi Wabi
- **23** Rushmore
- **22** La Sardine
- **21** Marché

Near North
- **28** Seasons
- **26** Morton's of Chicago
- **25** Avenues
  Joe's Seafood, Steak & Crab
- **24** Seasons Café

River North
- **27** Topolobampo
- **26** mk
  Frontera Grill
- **25** Naha
- **24** Coco Pazzo

Streeterville
- **28** Les Nomades
  Ritz-Carlton Dining Room
- **27** Tru
- **24** Ritz-Carlton Café
  Caliterra Bar & Grille

Suburban North
- **28** Carlos'
  Trio
- **27** Gabriel's
- **24** Froggy's French Cafe
  Va Pensiero

Uptown/Lincoln Square
- **22** Thai Pastry
- **21** Pizza D.O.C.
  La Bocca della Verità
  She She
- **19** Andies

West Loop
- **25** Blackbird
- **23** Nine
- **22** Carmichael's Steak House
- **20** Lou Mitchell's
  Wishbone

Wicker Park
- **26** Spring
- **24** Mirai Sushi
- **23** MOD.
  Bob San
  Bongo Room

Top 40 Decor Rankings

27 Spiaggia
Ritz-Carlton Dining Room
Everest
Tru
Seasons
26 Ambria
NoMI
Charlie Trotter's
Signature Room at the 95th
Les Nomades
Le Français
RL
Avenues
Seasons Café
25 Courtright's
Tizi Melloul
Entre Nous
Trio
Nine
302 West

Spring
Pump Room
Carlos'
120 Ocean Place
Le Titi de Paris
North Pond
Tallgrass
24 mk
Le Colonial
Atwood Cafe
Ritz-Carlton Café
Café Spiaggia
Arun's
Naha
Topolobampo
Lovells of Lake Forest
one sixtyblue
Gabriel's
23 Zealous
Vivere

Outdoors

Athena
Green Dolphin Street
Kamehachi
Meritage Cafe & Wine Bar
NoMI
Pegasus

Puck's at the MCA
Smith & Wollensky
South Gate Cafe
Tavern on Rush
Thyme
Topo Gigio Ristorante

Romance

Ambria
Café Absinthe
Chez Joel
Everest
Geja's Cafe
Gioco
KiKi's Bistro

Le Bouchon
Le Colonial
Spring
302 West
Tizi Melloul
Twelve 12
Va Pensiero

Rooms

Blackbird
Le Colonial
Marché
Nine
NoMI
North Pond
one sixtyblue

RL
Spiaggia
Spring
Tizi Melloul
Tru
Wave
Zealous

Views

Cité
Everest
Jackson Harbor Grill
Lobby, The
Mill Race Inn
NoMI

Oak Terrace
Riva
Seasons
Signature Room at the 95th
Spiaggia
Tasting Room, The

Top 40 Service Rankings

28 Charlie Trotter's
Ritz-Carlton Dining Room
Trio
Everest
27 Tru
Seasons
Le Français
Les Nomades
Ambria
Carlos'
Le Titi de Paris
Tallgrass
26 Gabriel's
Spiaggia
Arun's
25 Avenues
Seasons Café
Topolobampo
Spring
mk

24 302 West
Entre Nous
Froggy's French Cafe
Morton's of Chicago
Ritz-Carlton Café
Courtright's
Joe's Seafood, Steak & Crab
23 Gibsons Steakhouse
Va Pensiero
D & J Bistro
Stained Glass Wine Bar
Cafe Pyrenees
Le Vichyssois
NoMI
Bistro Banlieue
Nick's Fishmarket
Printer's Row
Les Deux Gros
Retro Bistro
Hugo's Frog Bar

Best Buys

Top 40 Bangs for the Buck

List derived by dividing the cost of a meal into its ratings.

1. Superdawg Drive-In	21. Cafe Nordstrom
2. Margie's Candies	22. Chicago Flat Sammies
3. Potbelly Sandwich Works	23. Nuevo Leon
4. Fluky's	24. Leo's Lunchroom
5. Wiener's Circle	25. Moody's Pub
6. Gold Coast Dogs	26. Nookies
7. Walker Bros.	27. Tre Kronor
8. Salt & Pepper Diner	28. Ann Sather
9. Original Pancake House	29. 5 Boroughs Deli
10. Artopolis Bakery & Cafe	30. Corner Bakery
11. Sarkis Grill	31. Cosí
12. Breakfast Club	32. Zoom Kitchen
13. Penny's Noodle Shop	33. Toast
14. Billy Goat Tavern	34. Taza
15. Orange	35. Cross-Rhodes
16. Johnny Rockets	36. Lucky Platter
17. Manny's Coffee Shop	37. Kitsch'n on Roscoe
18. Lou Mitchell's	38. Russell's Barbecue
19. Chipotle Mexican Grill	39. Tempo
20. Bongo Room	40. My Pie Pizza

Other Good Values

Addis Abeba	Joy Yee's Noodle Shop
Amitabul	La Cazuela Mariscos
Andies	Lem's BBQ
Army & Lou's	Lincoln Noodle House
Athenian Room	Lou Malnati's Pizzeria
Bite	LuLu's Dim Sum & Then Sum
BJ's Market & Bakery	Lutz Cafe & Pastry Shop
Chicago Diner	Noon-O-Kabab
Cold Comfort Cafe & Deli	Pasta Palazzo
Dell Rhea's Chicken Basket	Red Lion Pub
Edna's	Ruby of Siam
El Nandu	San Soo Gap San
Ethiopian Diamond	Seoul Dook Bae Gee
Flying Chicken	Silver Seafood
Gladys Luncheonette	Thai Little Home Cafe
Hashalom	Thai Pastry
Hilary's Urban Eatery	Twisted Spoke
Hot Doug's	Udupi Palace
Izalco	Uncommon Ground
Jang Mo Nim	Victory's Banner

Restaurant Directory

Chicago

F | D | S | C

Abril ◐ **S** 17 | 13 | 16 | $17
2607 N. Milwaukee Ave. (bet. Kedzie Ave. & Logan Blvd.), 773-227-7252
◪ Paisanos are polarized over this Logan Square "Mex cafe", so it's your call whether it offers "authentic", "tasty" food, "congenial" service and a "good bang for your peso", or just "typical" South-of-the-border fare slung by "rude" servers in a "shabby" space; respondents agree, however, that the "mega-margaritas" are "fantastic"; N.B. the kitchen stays open till 3 AM on weekends.

Addis Abeba **S** 20 | 11 | 16 | $16
3521 N. Clark St. (bet. Addison St. & Newport Ave.), 773-929-9383
■ "Adventurous palates" head to Wrigleyville for "Chicago's best Ethiopian" dining – "authentic", "slyly spicy" and "a bargain", to boot; the "friendly" service can be "slow at times", but "you get to eat with your hands" (staffers wear T-shirts bearing the international symbol for 'no flatware'), "a fun experience" that enlivens the otherwise "sparse", "non-glamorous atmosphere."

Adobo Grill **S** 19 | 18 | 18 | $29
1610 N. Wells St. (North Ave.), 312-266-7999
■ Surveyors swoon for the "magnificent margaritas and godly guacamole" "made tableside" at this "hip" Old Town two-year-old where the "inventive", "eclectic" fare "is some of the freshest in town"; it can get so "noisy" that you might have to "forget conversation", but with "personable" servers and a "fun atmosphere", the "see-and-be-seen" crowd doesn't seem fazed in the least.

Akai Hana ▽ 25 | 15 | 22 | $21
848 N. State St. (Chestnut St.), 312-787-4881
3223 W. Lake Ave. (Skokie Blvd.), Wilmette, 847-251-0384 **S**
■ "In-the-know" folks "go" to these Gold Coast and North Suburban "real Japanese" "favorites" for "reliable" "and affordable" "fine food" including a "wide range of appetizers" and "fresh" "bargain sushi that doesn't taste like a bargain"; "always mobbed", they feature "cheerful decor and staff" and a "kid-friendly", "family atmosphere", though there are beer and wine for the big folks.

A La Turka **S** 18 | 18 | 20 | $22
3134 N. Lincoln Ave. (Belmont Ave.), 773-935-6447
■ The "nicest-ever" servers are "thankful you came" to this "charming" Lakeview Turkish with an "authentic

feel" behind its "blah storefront"; "for the best experience", "sit on the floor at the rotating tables" to enjoy the "exotic" food, which is also a "great value"; P.S. young turks appreciate that "the belly dancer is neither old nor fat."

Albert's Café & Patisserie S   19 | 18 | 18 | $19 |
52 W. Elm St. (bet. Clark & Dearborn Sts.), 312-751-0666
■ "Indulge" in "old-world charm" at this "quaint" and "conservative" Gold Coast cafe/bakery that's a bastion of "the Left Bank in Chicago"; with "good food" (including "excellent pastries") and "consistent quality and service", it's "pleasant" for a "breakfast with a European feel", a "casual" lunch, a "ladies' brunch" or a "great break from Michigan Avenue" shopping.

Always Thai   ∇ 18 | 11 | 16 | $16 |
1825 W. Irving Park Rd. (bet. Ashland & Damen Aves.), 773-929-0100
◪ "Always a reliable choice", this Lakeview Thai is a "find" for "tasty, fresh food" ("try the chive dumplings") at "reasonable prices", even if the "menu is limited"; since its "less-than-stimulating decor" is "nothing to write home about", many view it as a "great take-out option."

Amarind's S   ∇ 20 | 14 | 17 | $22 |
6822 W. North Ave. (Oak Park Ave.), 773-889-9999
◪ Siam-savvy surveyors say it's "well worth a long trip" to this "artistic" Thai newcomer on the border of Oak Park and Chicago, where a "dedicated chef" creates "fine cuisine", including "offbeat selections"; foes feel, though, that "the food is the only thing that shines", saying service can be uneven and the decor "depressing."

AMBRIA   27 | 26 | 27 | $68 |
Belden Stratford Hotel, 2300 N. Lincoln Park W. (Belden Ave.), 773-472-5959
■ "No superlative is enough" to convey the "polished" "excellence" of Lettuce Entertain You's "pure luxe" Lincoln Park "grande dame", a "romantic" "special-occasion" favorite "suited for classicists" (the "dress code's enforced . . . yay!"); it's "always a divine experience" "worth every dollar" thanks to chef-owner Gabino Sotelino and chef de cuisine Anselmo Ruiz's "fabulous" New French fare, an "outstanding sommelier", "servers [who] appear as if by magic" and an atmosphere of "hushed elegance."

American Girl Place Cafe S   13 | 23 | 21 | $23 |
American Girl Pl., 111 E. Chicago Ave. (bet. Michigan Ave. & Rush St.), 312-943-9400
◪ A "must-see" "fantasy" for young ladies from "5 to 105", this "amusing" "theme restaurant" on the Mag Mile is a "sweet place to take your little princess and her doll", as the poppet playmates "are catered to" with their own

"special seating and dishware"; be warned, though, that most "boys are entirely bored" by the proceedings and "no one goes for" the "marginal", "production-line" food.

American Smokehouse S   ▽ 16 15 17 $20
66 W. Main St. (Rte. 12), Lake Zurich, 847-726-2272
☒ Cowpokes are conflicted about this "cozy" Northwest Suburban rib joint: some say it's "smokin'", with "simple", "straightforward comfort food" and "a good selection of side dishes" that "restore faith" among BBQ boosters; others complain of "average food" such as "dried-out ribs" "served at tepid temperatures" and "service that needs work", claiming "all the hype is just smoke."

Amitabul S   ▽ 19 9 16 $14
6207 N. Milwaukee Ave. (Nagle Ave.), 773-774-0276
■ Vegetarians and even some "steak lovers" laud the "healing qualities" of this "unique Korean vegan" on the Northwest Side", "a welcome departure from the typical" and "one of the best options" for "fresh and spicy" animal-free cuisine that's "not dressed up like it's got meat in it"; the ambiance may be (pardon the allusion) "bare-bones", but it's got a "peaceful vibe."

Andies S   19 16 17 $19
5253 N. Clark St. (Berwyn Ave.), 773-784-8616 ◗
1467 W. Montrose Ave. (Greenview Ave.), 773-348-0654
■ A "favorite" pair of "local quickies", these two Middle Eastern–Meds serve up "big menus" of "inexpensive", "healthy" food with enough "variety for everyone's tastes", including "lots of options for vegetarians"; both offer a "laid-back" "neighborhood" atmosphere, but most say the "Clark Street location has the nicer room" (as well as live jazz at Sunday brunch and on Monday nights).

Angelina Ristorante S   20 18 20 $25
3561 N. Broadway (Addison St.), 773-935-5933
☒ Nestled behind a "quaint storefront" "in the Boys Town area", this "ol' reliable" delivers "substantial" and "tasty" (if "somewhat predictable") Southern Italian fare, including "delicious" "fresh pastas", served by a "staff that gets to know you by name"; though "romantics" rate it "cute" and "cozy", expansive eaters warn that the "comfortable interior feels a touch claustrophobic when crowded."

Anna Maria Pasteria S   18 15 18 $22
3953 N. Broadway (Irving Park Rd.), 773-929-6363
■ Pasta-loving pen pals praise this "solid, basic Italian" as the "mama's kitchen" of Lakeview for its "big portions" of "traditional, consistently good" "stick-to-your-ribs" "home cooking" served "at reasonable prices" by a "friendly" staff in a "charming" "storefront" setting; P.S. no longer just a "great BYO" spot, it now serves beer and wine.

Ann Sather 🅂　　　　　17　13　17　$14
929 W. Belmont Ave. (Sheffield Ave.), 773-348-2378
3411 N. Broadway (Roscoe St.), 773-305-0024
5207 N. Clark St. (Foster St.), 773-271-6677
Ann Sather Café 🅂
3416 N. Southport Ave. (Roscoe St.), 773-404-4475
1448 N. Milwaukee Ave. (North Ave.), 773-327-9522
■ This expanding family of "solid Swedish" spots has been a Chicago "constant over the years", best beloved for its "mind-blowing", "sinful" cinnamon rolls, hearty "hangover" breakfasts and "cheap", "tasty, old-fashioned" eats; the "people-watching is a show" and the "friendly" staffers act "like they've known you all your life", so expect "long waits" on "crowded weekends."

Antico Posto 🅂　　　　　20　20　20　$27
Oakbrook Center Mall, 118 Oakbrook Ctr. (Rte. 83),
Oak Brook, 630-586-9200
■ Even "from a distance you can smell the [scent of] garlic" wafting from this Lettuce Entertain You outpost in the Western Suburbs; "surprisingly good for a mall restaurant", it boasts "comfortable tables" and "melt-in-your-mouth" "Italian staples" served by an "aware" staff in a "warm", "sedate" atmosphere; as suggested by the "racks that greet you when you walk in", there's also a "great wine program."

Arco de Cuchilleros 🅂　　　　18　14　16　$22
3445 N. Halsted St. (bet. Addison & Belmont Aves.),
773-296-6046
■ Tapas tasters graze upon "lots of little nibbly things" at this Boys Town "best-kept secret", "especially in summer", when they can be sampled on the "wonderful garden-oasis" "patio in back" rather than at one of the "tables crammed into" the "small", "unassuming" interior; either way, wash them down with "excellent sangria" or a "great margarita."

Army & Lou's 🅂　　　　▽ 20　14　21　$16
422 E. 75th St. (King Dr.), 773-483-3100
■ Though most "Lincoln Park flannel-shirt frat boys are too chicken to come on down", Southern-savvy surveyors "get to this" "inexpensive and dependable" "diner-type" destination on the Far South Side for "fantastic soul food"; it's "not for dieters", but trenchermen "die for" the "catfish (yow!)" or "down-home chitterlings" ("wow!") and always "save room for" the "great peach cobbler."

Art of Pizza, The 🅂　　　　－ － － I
3033 N. Ashland Ave. (Nelson St.), 773-327-5600
The "excellent stuffed pizza" at this Lakeview purveyor represents "a solid pie" to critics who comprehend the aesthetics of dough, sauce and toppings; owner Art (pun intended) Shabez prides himself on providing "fresh, well-

prepared" 'za – "as well as delicious chicken parmesan, lasagna and salads" – and "great service" to the patrons who pack the "few tables" and stools in his "tiny place."

Artopolis Bakery & Cafe 🅂   20 | 19 | 19 | $15
306 S. Halsted St. (Jackson St.), 312-559-9000
■ "Fast food with class", "flair and taste" is on the "creative menu" at this "upscale Greektown cafe and bakery" that's "great for grazers", since it's "lighter and fresher than your mainstay" Hellenic eatery; fans "love the artopita" sandwiches, "amazing soups" and "delicious pastries", and "friendly service" adds to the "good vibe" of its "light and airy" space; P.S. it's "easy on the wallet" too.

ARUN'S 🅂   27 | 24 | 26 | VE
4156 N. Kedzie Ave. (bet. Belle Plaine & Berteau Aves.), 773-539-1909
■ Showcasing Arun Sampanthavivat's "culinary genius", this "intimate" and "beautiful" Albany Park "haute" Thai "temple" "satisfies all the senses" with "superior" service and "one aphrodisiac after another"; "set aside a full evening" for the "leisurely" (and obligatory) $85 prix fixe menu, as "each of the 12 courses is a treat" "to eat and behold", featuring "artistic presentations" and a "gradual escalation of spice levels."

a tavola   22 | 19 | 22 | $36
2148 W. Chicago Ave. (bet. Hoyne Ave. & Leavitt St.), 773-276-7567
■ Though "it's small", many judge this "gem" of a Northern Italian in Ukrainian Village the "gnumber-one spot for gnocchi" that "melts in your mouth" – just one of the "pricey pastas" on its "limited menu" of "simple, elegant" fare offered in an "unusually intimate" and "serene dining" room; with "terrific service" from a staff that "cares enough to get it right", it "often surprises and always delights."

Athena ◗🅂   20 | 20 | 18 | $24
212 S. Halsted St. (Adams St.), 312-655-0000
■ "In the heart of Greektown", this "good establishment" is a "favorite" for its "solid" Athenian "standards" and "consistent service"; still, some say "the main attraction here" is "fun outdoor dining in the summer", since the "lovely patio" not only "rocks" with "great city views" but also offers a breather from the "hubbub like a Mykonos windmill" generated within by the "boisterous" clientele and "chatty waiters."

Athenian Room 🅂   18 | 10 | 17 | $16
807 W. Webster Ave. (Halsted St.), 773-348-5155
■ "Greektown comes to Lincoln Park" at this "diner-ish" (some say "dump"-ish) "neighborhood institution", a "dependable" and "nostalgic" favorite for its "terrific

chicken" Kalamata and an "easy stop for a gyro" or a "reliably good burger" (they serve American dishes too), all at "bargain prices" that add to the "value."

Atlantique S | 24 | 20 | 23 | $40
5101 N. Clark St. (bet. Carmen & Foster Aves.), 773-275-9191
■ Most mariners consider this Andersonville seafooder a prize "catch" for its "imaginative", "beautiful presentations" of "fine, fresh fish" and other "well-prepared" delights from the deep (chef-owner "Jack Jones is a genius!"), complemented by a "thoughtfully assembled" wine list; the "civilized", "softly lit" room with an "ocean motif" affords "intimate", "leisurely" dining, abetted by "on-the-ball" service from a "friendly staff."

Atwater's S | ▽ 19 | 23 | 21 | $37
Herrington Inn, 15 S. River Ln. (State St.), Geneva, 630-208-7433
◪ A "small dining room" of "understated elegance" "with a view" of the "lovely Fox River" "makes the drive worthwhile" to this "upscale" West Suburban New French–American set in the recently remodeled and expanded Herrington Inn; "knowledgeable servers" enhance the experience, though the "imaginative menu" strikes world-weary wayfarers as "a bit too pricey" and sometimes "disappointing."

Atwood Cafe S | 21 | 24 | 20 | $32
Hotel Burnham, 1 W. Washington St. (State St.), 312-368-1900
■ A "shining star on State Street", this "exquisite" "architectural gem" within the "beautifully restored" Hotel Burnham serves "cozy" American "comfort food", garnering praise for its "famous pot pies" and "divine bread pudding"; it's "a hot spot for a Loop lunch" ("if you can snag a table"), "a favorite place for tea" "after a Field's excursion" and "a great location for pre-theatre dining"; P.S. "big windows" afford "great people-watching."

Aubriot S | 24 | 18 | 23 | $50
1962 N. Halsted St. (Armitage Ave.), 773-281-4211
◪ "Bravo!" boom boosters of this "charming" "Lincoln Park gem" and its eponymous owner Eric Aubriot, a "talented" "chef's chef" whose "lovely", "clean presentations" and "exciting", "inventive mix of original and traditional" French cuisine are backed by "outstanding service"; critics, however, cite a "stark atmosphere" that "lacks warmth" and "small portions" from a "pricey" bill of fare with "as many misses as hits."

Aurelio's Pizza S | 18 | 12 | 16 | $15
Centennial Plaza, 1455 W. Lake St. (Lombard Rd.), Addison, 630-889-9560
18162 Harwood Ave. (183rd St.), Homewood, 708-798-8050
19836 Wolf Rd. (La Porte Rd.), Mokena, 708-478-0022
(continued)

(continued)
Aurelio's Pizza
601 E. 170th St. (Cottage Grove Ave.), South Holland,
708-333-0310
■ Pie-faces fawn over this chain of "family-favorite"
suburban staples (especially the "flagship Homewood"
location) and its "authentic Chicago-style pizza", praising
everything from the "sweet", "tomatoey sauce" to the
"thin-and-crispy crust" (its "Super Six [selection] is an
institution"); so what if the "typical decor" is "nothing
special"? – you can always "order for delivery."

Avenue Ale House ◑ S   ▽ 15 | 18 | 15 | $21
825 S. Oak Park Ave. (bet. Harrison & Jackson Sts.), Oak Park,
708-848-2801
■ West Suburban sports fans give a "thumbs-up" to this
"friendly neighborhood" "bar/restaurant" year-round –
"in summer" they "like the rooftop cafe" with its "skyline
views", "in winter it's a cozy spot for dinner" and anytime
it's a "place to watch the game" or hear some "ok bands"
while chowing down on a "good burger" or other "typical
bar food" and chugging one of their 70-plus beers.

AVENUES S   25 | 26 | 25 | $70
Peninsula Chicago, 108 E. Superior St. (bet. Michigan Ave. &
Rush St.), 312-573-6754
■ It's "high-end all the way" at this "perfect! perfect!
perfect!" Peninsula hotel venue, a Near Norther with a
New French–Med "seafood-intensive" menu compliments
of chef Gerhard Doll; expect "mighty-fine fine dining" in
a "posh, proper" and perhaps just a soupçon "snobby"
setting (the "gold color scheme is apt" given the "top
prices"), where an "outstanding" staff "gives it their all."

Babaluci Italian Eatery S   18 | 15 | 16 | $23
2152 N. Damen Ave. (Webster Ave.), 773-486-5300
1001 W. Golf Rd. (bet. Gannon Dr. & Higgins Rd.),
Hoffman Estates, 847-843-3663
■ City or suburb, this pair of Italian sisters is a "sure thing"
for "big portions" of "great", "basic stuff to fill you up", all
"at a decent price"; what's "fun" and "funky" for some might
be "a little noisy" for others, but either way the "festive
ambiance" is "good for large groups"; N.B. the Bucktown
branch features live jazz on weekends.

Bacaro da Nino S   ▽ 25 | 18 | 22 | $31
405 Sheridan Rd. (Waukegan Ave.), Highwood, 847-432-7168
■ A "find" for North Suburbanites seeking "a refreshing
change", this Highwood two-year-old specializes in
"excellent Northern Italian with a Venetian flair", including
a "nice variety of flavorful seafood entrees, risottos and
pastas"; the truly devoted declare "Venice-born chef"-
owner "Maurizio Fonda is a genius", and his staff ensures

that "everyone is made welcome"; P.S. you can enjoy patio dining in warm weather.

Bacchanalia S⌀   22 15 22 $27
2413 S. Oakley Ave. (bet. 24th & 25th Sts.), 773-254-6555
▣ "Thankfully un-trendy", this Heart of Italy "oldie but goodie" is a "traditional" "Italian neighborhood spot" where "garlic is king" and the "homestyle cooking" (such as "great chicken Vesuvio") is as "real" as the "generous" staff; there are a few complaints, however, about "tight quarters" that some say are "in need of updating" and a "cash-only" policy that credit-card carriers find "a pain."

Bacino's   17 12 14 $17
75 E. Wacker Dr. (Michigan Ave.), 312-263-0070 S
2204 N. Lincoln Ave. (Webster Ave.), 773-472-7400 S
118 S. Clinton St. (Adams St.), 312-876-1188
Bacino's Trattoria S
36 S. La Grange Rd. (Ogden Ave.), La Grange, 708-352-8882
1504 N. Naper Blvd. (Ogden Ave.), Naperville, 630-505-0600
Ravinia Plaza, 15256 S. La Grange Rd. (153rd St.), Orland Park, 708-403-3535
■ In the "best deep-dish" campaign of Chicago's pizza wars, allies admire this chain for "awesome stuffed" pies that are "really loaded", like the signature "healthy spinach option"; there's also "good" "cheesy" flat 'za and other "standard Italian fare", but "inconsistent service" and "modest surroundings" draw some barbs; N.B. at press time, the Wacker location was closed for renovation.

Bagel, The S   ∇ 23 16 21 $15
3107 N. Broadway St. (bet. Belmont Ave. & Diversey Pkwy.), 773-477-0300
Old Orchard Shopping Ctr., 50 Old Orchard Ctr. (Old Orchard Rd.), Skokie, 847-677-0100
■ A taste of "New York in Lakeview" and the Northern Suburbs, these "traditional delis" – part of "a dying breed" – "delight diners" with a "wide variety" of "some of the best Jewish food around" (including "good bagels" and "great matzo ball soup"); rapacious reviewers report that "huge servings" make it "the place to go for an eatfest."

Balagio   – – – E
19917 S. La Grange Rd. (Pleasant Hill Rd.), Frankfort, 815-469-2204 S
18042 Martin Ave. (Ridge Rd.), Homewood, 708-957-1650
"Sophisticated" for the Southwest Suburbs, these sister spots are "reliable dining choices" cradling "kitchens that produce consistently good-quality", "huge portions" of "great" Italian food, served in a "friendly" manner within "gorgeous" interiors featuring "beautiful frescoes"; N.B. at press time, plans were afoot for a future branch in La Grange.

Bandera 🅂   19 | 18 | 18 | $26

535 N. Michigan Ave., 2nd fl. (bet. Grand Ave. & Ohio St.),
312-644-3524

■ The "great smell" of "excellent rotisserie chicken" draws "crowds" to this "consistent and comforting" Streeterville American offering Mag Mile views and "hearty, affordable" fare with "Southwest flair" (raves for the "great jalapeño cornbread"); daters approve of the "cave-like", "sexy" atmosphere and nightly "live jazz" (except Sundays), though certified city-dwellers suggest it's "a touch of the suburbs on Michigan Avenue."

Bangkok 🅂   ▽ 19 | 15 | 16 | $17

3542 N. Halsted St. (Addison St.), 773-327-2870

◪ Partisans praise this "somewhat cramped" Wrigleyville "nook" known for its "good takeout" and "authentic" Siamese spices as "one of the more creative Thais in the city", but naysayers note "lots of competition" in the field and claim "there is better" to be found than its "predictable" entrees or "adequate all-you-can-eat [lunch] buffet"; still, most agree it "will do in a pinch."

Bangkok Star 🅂   ▽ 20 | 14 | 19 | $17

1443 W. Fullerton Ave. (bet. Ashland & Southport Aves.),
773-348-8868

■ "Cheap and consistently good", the Thai fare at this Lincoln Park "favorite" comes "as spicy as you want it", but timid tasters be warned that the "authentic cuisine may leave you wanting more Americanized dishes"; visually oriented sorts sigh it's "too bad" the "simple decor" "isn't better"; P.S. "good for large groups", it accepts reservations for parties of six and up.

Bank Lane Bistro   ▽ 16 | 16 | 17 | $29

670 Bank Ln. (bet. Deer Path & Westminster Rds.),
Lake Forest, 847-234-8802

◪ This "pleasant" North Suburban boîte decorated with "imposing Parisian posters" strikes surveyors as a bit "erratic", with New American and French "bistro-type food" that's sometimes "satisfying" but sometimes not, service that swings from "good" to just "fair" and an interior that some find "romantic" but others call "uncomfortable."

Bar Louie ●🅂   14 | 13 | 14 | $18

1321 W. Taylor St. (Loomis St.), 312-633-9393
3545 N. Clark St. (Addison St.), 773-296-2500
47 W. Polk St. (Dearborn St.), 312-347-0000
123 N. Halsted St. (Randolph St.), 312-207-0500
1704 N. Damen Ave. (bet. North Ave. & Willow St.), 773-645-7500
226 W. Chicago Ave. (Franklin St.), 312-337-3313
1520 Sherman Ave. (Grove St.), Evanston, 847-733-8300
22 E. Chicago Ave. (Washington St.), Naperville,
630-983-1600

(continued)
Bar Louie's
913 N. Milwaukee Ave. (Lake Cook Rd.), Wheeling, 847-279-1199
Louie on the Park ◐ [S]
1800 N. Lincoln Ave. (Clark St.), 312-337-9800
◪ "Late-night" Louie lovers find "big fun" at the "many locations" of this "dependable chain" of "noisy", "upbeat" "hipster and yupster hangouts" and swear they're "not just for getting smashed" in, thanks to "above-average bar food"; others say they serve "middling pub grub", "forgot about service as they expanded" and are "too smoky."

Barn of Barrington [S] 16 19 17 $32
1415 S. Barrington Rd. (¼ mi. north of Dundee Rd.), Barrington, 847-381-8585
◪ Its "memorable setting" is the main draw of this "dated" Northwest "Suburban eatery" in a "pretty" "antique-filled barn", not its "sometimes disappointing service" or menu of "good" but "uninspired" Traditional American dishes; still, "blue hairs" and spring chickens alike "go for the Sunday champagne brunch", one reason this "landmark" has "staying power."

BARRINGTON COUNTRY BISTRO [S] 24 21 22 $36
Foundry Shopping Ctr., 700 W. Northwest Hwy. (Hart Rd.), Barrington, 847-842-1300
■ "Inventive" and "unfailingly excellent", this "great French bistro" in a "relaxing country setting" is "worth a drive" to the Northwest Suburbs for its "delicious" and "authentic" food, including "delightful rabbit and osso buco"; "owners Jean-Pierre and Denise [Leroux] make it feel like home", and the "first-rate" "waiters' knowledge" about the "extensive wine list" is an added "thrill."

Basta Pasta [S] 18 16 18 $25
6733 Olmsted Ave. (Northwest Hwy.), 773-763-0667
◪ "Don't eat for two days before" a visit to this "lively", "high-decibel" Edison Park "neighborhood spot" "where the fun" and "good Southern Italian food" "come in troughs", the "friendly" staff really "works hard" and "the price is right"; it's a place "for eaters, not nitpicky diners" of the sort who might snort 'basta!' about such "basic" fare and "nothing-fancy" ambiance.

BD's Mongolian Barbeque [S] 15 13 15 $17
3330 N. Clark St. (bet. Belmont Ave. & Roscoe St.), 773-325-2300
■ "Design your own dinner" at this "festive" stir-fry smorgasbord in Wrigleyville, where you "choose your own ingredients" from "many options" then hand them off to a "stand-up comedian cook" who sets them a-sizzling on the "communal wok"; the servers may be "inexperienced", but "they want you to have fun" – and "kids love it."

Becco d'Oro [S] 21 | 20 | 20 | $41

Radisson Hotel & Suites, 160 E. Huron St. (St. Clair St.), 312-787-1300

■ Fans of this "distinctive" Streeterville Italian in the Radisson Hotel & Suites say it's "better than its more pretentious competitors" thanks to a "talented" and "accommodating chef" who turns out "superior pasta" and other "imaginative" fare "prepared with love"; a "refined" interior and "great service" make for "an exceptional experience" that should "impress the most demanding clients"; P.S. "sit outside on a warm summer night."

Bella Notte [S] 21 | 16 | 19 | $27

1372 W. Grand Ave. (Noble St.), 312-733-5136

■ There's "always a doggy bag" after a visit to this "old-style" Near West "gem" with "reliable service" and a "*Sopranos*-like supper-club" feel; "gargantuan portions" of "can't-lose specials" and other "consistently good", "straight-on" Southern Italian selections made with "fresh, flavorful and tasty ingredients" draw raves, despite the "cramped dining room."

Benihana of Tokyo [S] 18 | 17 | 20 | $31

Fitzpatrick Hotel, 166 E. Superior St. (Michigan Ave.), 312-664-9643

747 E. Butterfield Rd. (bet. Highland Ave. & Meyers Rd.), Lombard, 630-571-4440

1200 E. Higgins Rd. (Meacham Rd.), Schaumburg, 847-995-8201

150 N. Milwaukee Ave. (Dundee Rd.), Wheeling, 847-465-6021

◪ Go for "dinner and a show" to this Japanese teppanyaki chain known for "communal tables", a "convivial" vibe and "great antics" from "tableside chefs" who "cook to entertain"; though the "theme-park" concept may be "a bit hackneyed", locals say it's "not just for tourists" but "for groups" or a "family night out"; the downside: expect to "leave smelling like stir-fry."

Ben Pao [S] 20 | 23 | 20 | $28

52 W. Illinois St. (Dearborn St.), 312-222-1888

◪ Lettuce Entertain You's River North outpost for lotus-eaters draws a "Ben wow!" for "sinfully sensual decor" and a "unique", "chic Chinese" menu that's "not authentic but awesome" nonetheless; fans give a "pow!" to the "terrific" black-pepper scallops, "fabulous cherry bomb shrimp", "peppy staff" and "cool cocktails", even if the disappointed denounce the place as "gimmicky" and "uneven."

BERGHOFF, THE 19 | 19 | 19 | $22

17 W. Adams St. (bet. Dearborn & State Sts.), 312-427-3170

O'Hare Int'l Airport, Concourse C (I-90), 773-601-9180 [S]

■ "Great Wiener schnitzel" scarfers are "always looking for an excuse to go to this "indestructible" Loop "landmark", a "sentimental favorite" for "solid German" fare and house-brewed beer served amid "old-world" "wood-paneled glory"; regulars report that "half the fun" is the "consistently surly" "100-year-old waiters" – "you can't get any more Chicago" than this; N.B. the O'Hare outpost has a lighter cafe menu.

Best Hunan S
17 | 14 | 18 | $20

Hawthorn Fashion Sq., 700 N. Milwaukee Ave. (Rte. 60), Vernon Hills, 847-680-8855

■ "Despite the strip-mall feel", this "traditional Chinese" in the Northwest Suburbs has some surveyors swearing it's still aptly named, with "good", "fresh, reliable" fare such as "spicy crispy chicken" and a staff that "treats you like family"; another bonus: you "can get Peking duck without ordering in advance."

Bêtise, A Bistro on the Lake S
19 | 21 | 20 | $33

Plaza del Lago, 1515 Sheridan Rd. (Lake Ave.), Wilmette, 847-853-1711

◪ Bistro-goers battle it out over this informal French "serving a North Shore clientele" in the Plaza del Lago shopping center near, though not *on*, Lake Michigan (would-be water-watchers will want to watch elsewhere); pros praise the "warm" and "charming" decor, "considerate service", "reliable entrees" and "specials [that] are really special"; cons cavil that it's "somewhat pricey", "predictable" and "pedestrian."

Biaggio's S
20 | 18 | 18 | $30

10296 S. 78th Ave. (west of Harlem Ave.), Palos Hills, 708-237-1050

■ The "chef is not afraid of garlic" at this South Suburban Italian offering "high quality standards" and "obliging" service in a "homey" setting; pugilism proponents are pleased to report having "met Muhammad Ali while dining on linguine" – no tall tale since The Champ's "charming daughter" Rasheda Ali-Walsh is co-owner; P.S. though the Downtown branch has closed, "another will soon open in Orland Park."

Bice Grill S
18 | 18 | 18 | $28

154 E. Ontario St. (bet. Michigan Ave. & St. Clair St.), 312-664-1474
Northbrook Court Mall, 2124 Northbrook Court Mall (Lake Cook Rd.), Northbrook, 847-272-9003

■ "If you can't afford Bice, try the next best" thing advise Grill-goers who groove on the "good, solid" and "price-worthy" Northern Italian fare at these Streeterville and North Suburban little sisters that are "adjacent" to their "big brothers"; they're "good spots for a casual", "light dinner" and "great for local workers" in search of a "quick", albeit "crowded, lunch."

Bice Ristorante S
| 20 | 20 | 19 | $39 |

158 E. Ontario St. (bet. Michigan Ave. & St. Clair St.),
312-664-1474
Northbrook Court Mall, 2124 Northbrook Court Mall
(Lake Cook Rd.), Northbrook, 847-272-9003

☑ Taken "all together", the "friendly staffers", "trendy" "Eurotrash clientele", "mouthwatering menu" and "great wine selection" at these Streeterville and North Suburban Northern Italians (offspring of a prolific Milanese mamma) make for what most call a "satisfying" experience; "many tempting choices" are served in settings of "considerable style", though some still say this "sophisticated" pair is "not worth the high tariff" and "falls short of its pretense."

Big Bowl S
| 18 | 17 | 17 | $20 |

60 E. Ohio St. (Rush St.), 312-951-1888
159 W. Erie St. (bet. La Salle Blvd. & Wells St.),
312-787-8297
6 E. Cedar St. (State St.), 312-640-8888
215 Parkway Dr. (Deerfield Rd.), Lincolnshire, 847-808-8880
1950 E. Higgins Rd. (Rte. 53), Schaumburg, 847-517-8881

☑ Bowled-over boosters declare "the bowl is, in fact, big", as are the "big food and big fun", at this "Americanized" Asian chain of "always lively" "fast-food heavens"; the "noodles are great" and you can "get things the way you want them" at the stir-fry bars, but bummed bowlers say they strike out with "dependable but uninspired" fare.

Billy Goat Tavern ⊉
| 14 | 11 | 13 | $10 |

430 N. Michigan Ave. (Wacker Dr.), 312-222-1525 ◐ S
3516 N. Clark St. (Addison St.), 773-327-4361 S
330 S. Wells St. (Van Buren St.), 312-554-0297
309 W. Washington Blvd. (Franklin St.), 312-899-1873
1535 W. Madison St. (Ogden Ave.), 312-733-9132 S
O'Hare Field Terminal 1, Concourse C, Gate 18 (I-90),
773-462-9368 S

■ The Goats are multiplying thanks to the success of the "under-the-city" original on lower Michigan, "a Chicago icon ('nuff said)" whose gruff staffers were the inspiration for *SNL*'s famed "cheezborger, cheezborger, cheezborger" skit; "bring antacid" for the "cheap hangover food" at this "real guys' place" where "lack of decor *is* the decor"; N.B. cash only.

Biloxi Grill S
| 20 | 17 | 18 | $27 |

313 E. Liberty St. (Main St.), Wauconda, 847-526-2420

☑ "Great Southern cooking" is on the menu at this "rustic" Northwest Suburban home of "mouthwatering pecan-crusted catfish", "tasty BBQ" and "berry cobbler to die for" served up by a "friendly" staff; detractors declare the fare "sometimes great, sometimes not so great" and say "get a table by the window" for "good views" of Bang's Lake, as otherwise "the atmosphere is lacking."

Bin 36 ◐ [S] 21 | 21 | 19 | $38

339 N. Dearborn St. (bet. Kinzie St. & Wacker Dr.), 312-755-9463

◪ Oenophiles enjoy this "hopping" River North "shrine to wine" where "fanciful, flirtatious" flights flank "swank" New American dishes on an "awesome tasting menu"; the "airy, bright" space is "hip without the gotta-wear-black attitude", and the "knowledgeable" staff "guides without pushing"; still, some are sour on the "stark" decor and "deafening din"; N.B. the Food rating may not reflect a mid-*Survey* chef change.

Bistro Banlieue [S] 24 | 22 | 23 | $36

44 Yorktown Convenience Ctr. (bet. Butterfield Rd. & Highland Ave.), Lombard, 630-629-6560

■ "A hint of Paris in the [Western] Suburbs", this French "bistro *magnifique*" offers "comforting food" "bountifully plated with taste to match"; the "understated" digs are "cozy" despite the "bizarre" "strip-mall location", and the "accommodating" staff provides "super service"; P.S. calorie- or cost-conscious customers will appreciate that they "offer entrees in two sizes."

Bistro Marbuzet [S] 23 | 21 | 19 | $38

7600 W. Madison St. (Des Plaines Ave.), Forest Park, 708-366-9090

■ The "West Suburban crowd" savors a "taste of the city" at Jack Jones' "elegant French" and New American bistro, an "unexpected find for Forest Park" where "healthy portions" of "innovative, delicious food" get "stylish presentations" in a "lovely setting"; even those who say the "unpolished" "service needs to catch up" to the clever cuisine concede it's unquestionably "friendly."

Bistro 110 ◐ [S] 21 | 20 | 19 | $35

110 E. Pearson St. (bet. Michigan Ave. & Rush St.), 312-266-3110

■ There's an air of "joie de vivre" at this "bustling" Near North bistro that's "very French in a very American (friendly) way"; "known for wood-roasted dishes" and "awesome garlic", it's "always a safe bet" in a "great location for shoppers" just "off the Mag Mile", even if some respondents reckon it's "past its prime"; P.S. the "Sunday jazz brunch" is a "favorite."

BISTROT MARGOT [S] 21 | 20 | 20 | $35

1437 N. Wells St. (Schiller St.), 312-587-3660

■ A "bit of Paris" in Old Town, this "romantic", "bustling bistro" is the "*parfait*" place for "a good honest meal" of "authentic" French fare with "suave service"; in fact, some supporters who're "sorry it's been discovered" by the "lively" "crowds" choose to forgo its "cramped" interior – "like dining in a phone booth with 50 of your closest friends" – in favor of its sidewalk cafe.

Bistrot Zinc S
19 | 20 | 19 | $31 |

1131 N. State St. (bet. Cedar & Elm Sts.), 312-337-1131

■ Now soloing since its Southport sibling's shuttering, this "solid" State Street staple with a "genuine" French bistro feel is prized for its "always-charming" atmosphere, as well as "traditional and consistent fare" like "wonderful *poulet grand-mère*"; not only will it "tide you over until your next trip to Europe", but it's also "reasonably priced for the Gold Coast."

Bistro Ultra S
20 | 17 | 20 | $30 |

2239 N. Clybourn Ave. (Webster Ave.), 773-529-3300

◪ A "happy find" "hidden" in the Clybourn corridor, this "intimate" bistro beckons with "personable service", a "diverse wine list" and chef Juan Hurtado's "consistently good" (if "limited") menu of French fare at "fair prices"; though many applaud it for "avoiding getting sucked into trendiness", skeptics are "not sure what the fuss is about" and say there's "nothing distinctive" about its "small space."

Bite ●S
∇ 18 | 12 | 13 | $14 |

1039 N. Western Ave. (Cortez St.), 773-395-2483

■ "Great for a cheap date", this "hip" Humboldt Park Eclectic "with a funky beat" plates "unpretentious" eats that are "a cut above fast food"; still, some slam the "spotty service" and say the decor "could use a bump", since a "high number of body piercings per server" isn't everyone's idea of ambiance; P.S. it's "BYO, baby!"

BJ's Market & Bakery S
∇ 22 | 12 | 19 | $13 |

8734 S. Stony Island Ave. (87th St.), 773-374-4700

■ "Forget your diet and go" for "tasty" "home cooking" served "cafeteria-style" "from the Southern kitchen" of this soulful Far South Sider, favored more for its "small prices" and "the most heavenly, awe-inspiring piece of catfish you'll ever eat" than the "nothing-fancy" decor.

BLACKBIRD
25 | 19 | 23 | $48 |

619 W. Randolph St. (bet. Desplaines & Jefferson Sts.), 312-715-0708

■ "Wear black" within the "white surroundings" of this "see-and-be-scene" West Loop New American where "brilliant" chef Paul Kahan takes you on "a wonderful journey of amazing flavors" and "knowledgeable" servers "match the food" with "great wine selections"; "go with people you like", though, "because you'll be squeezed in tight" in a "minimalist" room that strikes some as "elegantly stark", others as "antiseptic."

Black Duck Tavern & Grille S
14 | 16 | 14 | $26 |

1800 N. Halsted St. (Willow St.), 312-664-1801

◪ Some say this Lincoln Park American is "more of a bar than a restaurant" thanks to "crowds" of "singles" in search of "eye candy", while others opine it's "becoming a real neighborhood place" and a "nice" "post-Steppenwolf spot"; either way, most agree the "fair-to-good food" from a "menu that's going in too many directions" "could be better" and "is secondary to the scene."

Blind Faith Café **S**   18 | 13 | 16 | $17
525 Dempster St. (Chicago Ave.), Evanston,
847-328-6875
☑ Evanston's "veggie heaven" is "true to the faith", luring "a beautiful following" of "dedicated vegetarians" and "people with special dietary needs" with "innovative", "eclectic" fare that converts claim "even meat lovers will love"; still, a few heretics harrumph that the "homey" environment is a bit "bare-bones" and the "sincere", "groovy crew" is sometimes "spacey."

Bluefin   ▽ 19 | 14 | 18 | $29
1952 W. North Ave. (Milwaukee Ave.), 773-394-7373
☑ Schools of thought swim separately on whether the "creative preparations" from the "mainly sushi menu" at this Bucktown Japanese are "artistic" or "strange, but they work" fans say, thanks to fin fare so "amazingly fresh" it's "still gasping"; critics carp that the "nice" but "forgetful" servers aren't always on a roll and claim the room "looks like a warehouse."

Bluepoint Oyster Bar **S**   19 | 18 | 18 | $37
741 W. Randolph St. (Halsted St.), 312-207-1222
☑ Despite its location "in landlocked Chicago", this Market District shellfish haven has a "great variety" of "expensive-but-worth-it oysters and clams", "huge shrimp and crab legs" and other "good seafood"; the "dark", "cozy" room is "classy and relaxing" to some seafarers, though others warn it's "not for a quiet night"; P.S. landlubbers who detest the denizens of the deep may dig the "excellent steaks."

BOB CHINN'S CRAB HOUSE **S**   21 | 13 | 18 | $33
393 S. Milwaukee Ave. (Dundee Rd.), Wheeling,
847-520-3633
☑ If you're "in the mood for raucousness" and "awesome" seafood, "join the herd" of Northwest "Suburbanites" and "tourists" who "stampede" this "big, noisy barn" seating 650; though the "good mai tais" "help with the wait", many "don't care for being" "shuffled, seated, served and shown the door" and wonder "why the crowds" "line up"; N.B. at press time, a Downtown opening was pending.

Bob San **◑S**   23 | 20 | 20 | $34
1805 W. Division St. (Wood St.), 773-235-8888
■ Specializing in "top-notch, fresh sushi" that's "some of the best in the city", this Wicker Park "hipster" hawks "delicious" "Japanese cuisine matched" with a "fantastic

wine list"; restaurateur Bob Bee, "the owner, makes you feel at home", and his "friendly" staff provides "fast service" in a "funky" setting with a "great vibe"; P.S. it's "open late."

Bogart's Charhouse 🖪   15   15   14 $27
18225 Dixie Hwy. (183rd St.), Homewood, 708-798-2000
17344 Oak Park Ave. (171st St.), Tinley Park, 708-532-5592
🖪 South and Southwest Suburban boosters of these "decent family steakhouses" with a "catchy name" and "semblances of Bogie" throughout say "get there early" to avoid "long waits" for a "real deal" on slabs so "huge" they're practically a "side of beef"; the "disappointed" are "at a loss to understand their popularity", humphing that this is not the beginning of a beautiful friendship.

Bone Daddy ◗🖪   16   13   16 $20
551 N. Ogden Ave. (Grand Ave.), 312-226-6666
🖪 Expect "smoky ribs and a smoky bar" at this Near West Twisted Spoke spin-off that fans call the "daddy of all comfort-food spots" for its "tasty dry-rub" varieties ("not the 'fall-off-the-bone' type") and "good pulled-pork BBQ" at "bargain" prices; those who "expected more" declare the "unimaginative food" "just ok" and add "once was enough."

Bongo Room 🖪   23   18   17 $16
1470 N. Milwaukee Ave. (Honore St.), 773-489-0690
■ Surveyors serve up a staggering stack of superlatives for the "delicious" "gourmet pancakes" and "unique omelets" at this "breakfast favorite", an "inventive yet consistent" Wicker Park American that's "so good it should be cloned"; there's "always" a "trendy crowd" hanging around "for a seat" in the "hip, flaky" space, so "be prepared to wait and wait" ("it's worth it"); N.B. the kitchen closes at 2:30 PM.

Boston Blackie's   19   13   17 $17
164 E. Grand Ave. (St. Clair St.), 312-938-8700 🖪
120 S. Riverside Plaza (bet. Adams & Monroe Sts.),
312-382-0700
405 Lake Cook Rd. (Waukegan Rd.), Deerfield, 847-418-3400 🖪
Hubbard Woods Plaza, 73 Green Bay Rd. (Scott St.),
Glencoe, 847-242-9400 🖪
🖪 Many folks' "burger of choice" graces the grills of this Streeterville "hamburger saloon" and its three younger brothers, all of whom "do well at what they set out to do" – serve "bar food with class", such as "tender chicken sandwiches" and "good salads", at "cheap prices"; still, some say they "lack atmosphere", especially the original Grand Avenue outpost with its "depressing" "'70s" decor.

BRASSERIE JO 🖪   21   21   20 $35
59 W. Hubbard St. (bet. Clark & Dearborn Sts.), 312-595-0800
🖪 "All you need is the Eiffel Tower" to complete the "authentic Parisian experience" at this "true brasserie"

in River North, where there's "always an 'up' feeling"; "legendary chef" Jean Joho fashions "French comfort food" with an "Alsatian influence, something different from the standard", though curmudgeons claim it's "not as special as Jo thinks"; still, many midday *mangeurs* are "sorry they've closed for lunch."

Breakfast Club, The 🗲⊘　　20　13　17　$13
1381 W. Hubbard St. (Noble St.), 312-666-3166
■ Join the clubbers who "crawl out of bed and go" to this Near West "neighborhood treasure" in a "crowded" but "cute pink cottage" for "good, honest" "Traditional [American] breakfast food" "and plenty of it", such as "wonderful French toast" and "great omelets"; factor in "friendly", "fast-paced" service and it's definitely "worth the hunt"; N.B. there's lunch too, but no dinner.

Brett's Café Americain 🗲　　20　16　19　$26
2011 W. Roscoe St. (Damen Ave.), 773-248-0999
☑ When not in the kitchen crafting "elevated comfort food", chef-owner Brett Knobel might be found "chatting with customers" at this "eclectic" New American in Roscoe Village; supporters savor her "elegant twist on brunch" and "heavenly baked goods", saying this "fine" "sleeper" "should be busier" despite decor that's a trifle "tired" and service that seesaws between "amiable" and "brusque."

Bricks ◗🗲　　19　14　18　$17
1909 N. Lincoln Ave. (Wisconsin St.), 312-255-0851
■ The "awesome", "creative" thin-crust pizza with "gourmet ingredients" (like "good BBQ chicken" and "pureed artichoke sauce") "melts in your mouth" at this "small, dark" "subterranean gem" in Lincoln Park, where "accommodating service" means "crowded" can be "fun"; P.S. the "young crowd loves it" and dubs it "da bomb."

Bruna's Ristorante 🗲　　21　15　19　$26
2424 S. Oakley Ave. (24th Pl.), 773-254-5550
■ "*Buono, buono, buono!*" shout supporters of the "simply prepared" "classic Italian dishes" at this "charming" "family-run" Heart of Italy "neighborhood standby" that makes "you feel like an old friend"; though some say the "homey" interior "needs a face-lift", regulars "love" that this "blast from the past" "hasn't changed in years."

Bubba Gump Shrimp Co. 🗲　　13　14　15　$23
Navy Pier, 700 E. Grand Ave. (Lake Shore Dr.), 312-252-4867
☑ Aptly "located at Navy Pier", this "kid-friendly" *Gump*-themed seafooder serves up "lots of fried stuff" in a "cute" nautical room or "outdoor dining" space that's "fun" for "people-watching"; but grumps who grumble the "concept is lame" feel "Forrest would frown" at this "tourist trap's" "chain food, chain ambiance" and "gimmicky service."

Buca di Beppo S
16 | 19 | 18 | $23

2941 N. Clark St. (bet. Oakdale & Wellington Aves.),
773-348-7673
90 Yorktown Shopping Ctr. (bet. Butterfield Rd. & Highland Ave.),
Lombard, 630-932-7673
15350 S. 94th Ave. (159th St.), Orland Park, 708-349-6262
604 N. Milwaukee Ave. (Lake Cook Rd.), Wheeling,
847-808-9898

☑ "Come hungry and expect noise" at these "crazy, cozy, kitschy" and "crowded" chain outposts where the "campy" "conglomerations of memorabilia" look "like an Italian grandmother's house exploded"; portions are so "huge" "you could open a shelter" with the leftovers, but purists posit that quantity and "lots of garlic" can't compensate for "unimaginative", "blah" dishes.

Bukhara S
18 | 16 | 16 | $25

2 E. Ontario St. (State St.), 312-943-0188

☑ Fans of this Near North Indian say it's "worth fighting for parking" to sample its "yummy curry chicken and naan", especially for the "good lunch buffet" that's a "deal"; nevertheless, nabobs of negativity natter there's "nothing unusual" about the "average" food, "disappointing" service and "too-dark decor."

BUtterfield 8 ●S
– | – | – | E

713 N. Wells St. (Superior St.), 312-327-0940

Restaurateur Demetri Alexander star-69s that classic Liz-Taylor-as-classy-call-girl flick with this River North reinvention of his former Lola's space (with Savarin sandwiched briefly between); the glam factor runs high (lit Plexiglas floor, white leather and butter-yellow velvet appointments), and the cuisine harks back to haute American fare of yore (chilled tomato juice, turtle soup, beef Wellington, chicken Kiev) accompanied by cocktails coyly called 'Pillow Talk' and 'Hollywood Swinger.'

Cab's Wine Bar Bistro S
▽ 20 | 20 | 21 | $35

430 N. Main St. (Duane St.), Glen Ellyn, 630-942-9463

■ Life is a Cabernet at this "romantic" "class act" in the Western Suburbs, a "pleasant place" where it's "great to try a flight" from the "excellent [Cab-focused] wine list" thanks to "knowledgeable servers" whose "good recommendations" will help you "pair" "sophisticated selections" with "interesting choices" from its "consistently good" New American menu; all in all, it's "a lucky find that you'll want to share with friends."

Café Absinthe S
24 | 21 | 21 | $40

1954 W. North Ave. (Damen Ave.), 773-278-4488

■ Bucktown's "favorite" "hidden gem" is "still hip", but "at least you can get in now" ("if you can find the door", that is) to savor the "fresh take on interesting ingredients" of its "consistently creative" "but not too froufrou" seasonally changing New American menu; conversationalists comment that it can be "noisy", but canoodling "couples" covet the "clandestine" quality of its "intimate, dark" digs.

Cafe Ba-Ba-Reeba! [S] 20 20 18 $27

2024 N. Halsted St. (bet. Armitage & Fullerton Aves.), 773-935-5000

◪ There's "something on the menu for everyone" at Lincoln Park's "tasty" tapas "pioneer", a Lettuce Entertain You Spanish "favorite" that's remained "a constant over the years" as a "fun place" to visit "with friends" or "a date" (as long as you don't mind "long waits" and "little elbow room"); still, the jaded jab it's "lost steam" to the competition.

Café Bernard [S] 20 17 19 $32

2100 N. Halsted St. (Dickens Ave.), 773-871-2100

■ "One of the oldest" in town, this "humble", "homey" bistro on a "quiet little corner" in Lincoln Park may still be "unknown" to some, "but it's not unloved" by the "habitués" who haunt it; owner "Bernard [LeCoq] cares about every plate" of "classic", "reasonably priced" French fare "going out of" his "consistent" kitchen, though some wish he'd concern himself with the "quaint", somewhat "tired" decor.

Cafe Bolero [S] ▽ 19 14 17 $21

2252 N. Western Ave. (south of Fullerton Ave.), 773-227-9000

■ For "easy Cuban eating" (a cuisine "not readily found in Chicago"), this "lively" Bucktown "neighborhood spot" run by "friendly owners" is "exceptionally good", including "tropical" "favorites" like "fantastic ceviche"; you get "so much for so little" that "a meal can be had on appetizers alone", and this place was serving "mojitos long before they became drink of the year."

Cafe Central [S] 21 18 21 $32

455 Central Ave. (Green Bay Rd.), Highland Park, 847-266-7878

■ This "lovely, casual" "little sister" of the "famous Carlos'" is a North Suburban natural for "huge plates" of "hearty", "dependable bistro food" that's "well worth trying" and "reasonably priced"; "hands-on owners" "Carlos and Debbie [Nieto] consistently" ensure a "good experience" within a "charming" "Parisian interior" that's "comfortable" to some, a bit "cramped" to others; P.S. save room for the "excellent desserts."

CAFÉ IBERICO ◐ [S] 22 17 17 $23

739 N. La Salle Blvd. (bet. Chicago Ave. & Superior St.), 312-573-1510

■ Regulars report this "hopping" "hangout" in River North is "jammed solid for a reason" – namely, "delicious Spanish tapas" "as they were meant to be", except perhaps for the "large portions" ("no tiny ones here!") at "reasonable prices" that make for "good value"; the "to-die-for sangria" makes the "long waits" "worth it", but the "great energy" generated by the "pulsing crowd" can be "ear-splitting."

Café La Cave S   22 | 23 | 22 | $43

2777 Mannheim Rd. (bet. Higgins Rd. & Touhy Ave.), Des Plaines, 847-827-7818

■ "Fall in love" at this "old-line Continental" O'Hare-area "expense-accounter" that "still has class" and "deserves its good reputation"; whether you "dine in the cave" (a "romantic simulated" grotto) or formal dining room (a "great throwback" to a more "elegant" time), you'll find tables "well spaced" "for a proposal", "social dinner or client" tête-à-tête and "rich cuisine" like "excellent Dover sole" and "must-have bananas Foster."

Café Le Loup S   ∇ 18 | 14 | 17 | $26

3348 N. Sheffield Ave. (bet. Belmont Ave. & Roscoe St.), 773-248-1830

◪ Windy Cityites wolf down "good bistro fare" at this "family-run" Lakeview "casual French" whose "small", "quirky", "cozy quarters" feature lupine "prints" and posters; while all agree it's "economical", hecklers howl about "uninspiring food", "enthusiastic but eccentric service" and a "so-so inside" area, preferring the "great patio that's heated in winter."

Café Luciano S   19 | 19 | 20 | $28

871 N. Rush St. (Chestnut St.), 312-266-1414
2676 Green Bay Rd. (bet. Central Ave. & Isabella St.), Evanston, 847-864-6060

◪ "Solid Italian comfort food" is the draw at this duo of "intimate cafes", "favorites with locals" who call them "dependable" for "consistent quality", "friendly service" and "comfortable" environs; the "unimpressed", though, find the "not-very-inventive menu" a bit "old-fashioned" and "ordinary"; P.S. speaking of "pedestrian", the Gold Coast branch's sidewalk seating affords "great people-watching."

Cafe Matou S   23 | 20 | 22 | $36

1846 N. Milwaukee Ave. (bet. Armitage & North Aves.), 773-384-8911

■ "Serene and satisfying", this "under-appreciated" bistro "sleeper" on the fringe of Bucktown is "wonderful by all available standards", offering an "adventurous menu" of "French food well prepared" by chef Charlie Socher, an "excellent wine list" and "outstanding service" in a "modern yet charming" space; its "low profile" and "secluded" location help it "keep a good clientele."

Cafe Nordstrom S   19 | 17 | 17 | $15

Nordstrom, 55 E. Grand Ave. (Michigan Ave.), 312-464-1515
10 Oakbrook Ctr. (bet. Butterfield & Spring Rds.), Oak Brook, 630-571-2121

(continued)
Cafe Nordstrom
*Woodfield Shopping Ctr., 6 Woodfield Shopping Ctr.
(bet. Higgins Rd. & Rte. 53), Schaumburg, 847-605-2121
Old Orchard Ctr., 77 Old Orchard Shopping Ctr. (bet. Golf Rd. &
Skokie Blvd.), Skokie, 847-677-2121*
■ "Get stoked to go shopping" at these "classy" yet
"casual" cafes that are "fun on the run" and "a welcome
relief from bad mall food", offering up a "fast and healthy"
assortment of Eclectic "pick-me-up" fare with "great
children's selections"; not only are these "shoppers'
heavens" "perfect for a mother and daughter after a huge
spree", but "guys like them" too.

Cafe Pyrenees 23 | 18 | 23 | $37
*River Tree Court Mall, Rte. 60 & Milwaukee Ave. (Rte. 21),
Vernon Hills, 847-918-8850*
■ "Don't tell" Downtown dwellers about this "culinary
treasure in a strip mall" say selfish West Suburbanites
who call this "classic French" bistro "a real find" for its
"artfully prepared" fare ("every meal is excellent"); despite
their best efforts, savvy city surveyors have discovered
that its "delicious food" and "gracious" service more than
make up for its "unlikely setting."

Cafe Selmarie ▣ 19 | 15 | 17 | $18
*4729 N. Lincoln Ave. (bet. Giddings St. & Western Ave.),
773-989-5595*
▣ "Is it a great bakery that serves" "good food", or is it a
"good" New American "restaurant with a great bakery
attached"? query quibblers confused by this "quaint"
Lincoln Square "dessert mecca"; still, with goodies "worthy
of a trip to the gym", sweet-toothed surveyors suggest you
"decide for yourself"; P.S. it's also a "nice place" to "meet
a friend for lunch" or a "yummy Sunday brunch."

CAFÉ SPIAGGIA ▣ 24 | 24 | 23 | $39
980 N. Michigan Ave., 2nd fl. (Oak St.), 312-280-2750
■ Not only is this "high-style" Mag Mile Italian eatery
"terrific" for a shopping break, respondents report it's also
"more fun" and "personal" than its "serious big brother,
Spiaggia", offering the "same kitchen" (though a "different
menu") "and same view for less money"; Tony Mantuano's
"top-notch" food is "beautifully presented", and the
"attentive servers" provide "great service" within an
"elegant", "conversation-friendly atmosphere."

Café 36 ▣ 24 | 20 | 22 | $39
22 Calendar Ct. (La Grange Rd.), La Grange, 708-354-5722
■ Find "France in La Grange" at this "West Suburban
heaven" of a French bistro whose "creative" menu of
"outstanding" food (including "interesting selections
of game") "never disappoints", and whose "charming"

staff offers "professional service"; though the thrifty think
it's a little "pricey for the area", most say "the extra dollars
are well worth it."

Cafe 28 🆂　　　　　　　24 | 17 | 20 | $25
1800 W. Irving Park Rd. (Ravenswood Ave.),
773-528-2883
■ Latin lovers laud this "locationally challenged" Lakeview
Cuban-Mexican, a "little place with a big kick" where
"fabulous flavors burst" from "creative dishes, making for
exciting and satisfying" dining; though you'll be "treated
like family" at the "innovative [Sunday] brunch", some
advise that you "avoid the weekend crowds", saying it's
becoming "too popular" and "loud"; P.S. don't miss the
"fun drink list."

California Pizza Kitchen 🆂　　　16 | 13 | 16 | $18
52 E. Ohio St. (bet. Rush St. & Wabash Ave.),
312-787-6075
Water Tower Pl., 845 N. Michigan Ave., 7th fl. (bet. Chestnut &
Pearson Sts.), 312-787-7300
Oakbrook Center Mall, 551 Oakbrook Ctr., 2nd level (Rte. 83),
Oak Brook, 630-571-7800
Woodfield Village Green, 1550 E. Golf Rd. (Meacham Rd.),
Schaumburg, 847-413-9200
◪ The "creative spin" on "designer pizza" at these "busy"
city and suburban outposts of a national chain is "never
a bummer" to aficionados of their "excellent topping
combinations"; naysayers find them "noisy" and "nothing
special", but however you slice it they're "dependable"
"places for kids where adults can still eat well."

Caliterra Bar & Grille ●🆂　　24 | 21 | 22 | $43
Wyndham Hotel, 633 N. St. Clair St. (Erie St.),
312-274-4444
■ "Brilliant chef" John Coletta keeps a "careful eye" on the
"consistently inventive" Californian-Italian cuisine at this
"undiscovered gem" in Streeterville, where his "seasonal
obsession" results in "monthly menus offering great
variety"; the "beautiful room" is so "quiet and civilized"
some swear you'll "forget it's in a hotel"; "good views",
"down-to-earth" service and an "awesome brunch"
complete the picture.

Calypso Cafe 🆂　　　　　　19 | 17 | 17 | $23
Harper Ct., 5211 S. Harper Ave. (53rd St.), 773-955-0229
■ "Don't forget to bring your sunscreen" to this "upbeat"
Hyde Park Caribbean where an "inventive" menu offers
"authentic fare from the islands" like "good jerk chicken
wings" and "sweet plantains" at a "great bang for the
buck"; escapists "never feel rushed" in the "smart, bright"
room, a "one-of-a-kind place" that's especially "fun" "on
a cold, snowy day."

Campagnola [S] 24 20 22 $40

815 Chicago Ave. (Main St.), Evanston, 847-475-6100

■ "Affable" chef-owner Michael Altenberg "continues to amaze" at this two-tier Italian in the North Suburbs where the "creative yet refined cuisine" showcases "top-shelf organic ingredients" that are "fresh! fresh! fresh!" and the "intelligent staff" provides "sincere hospitality"; surveyors split over the duo of dining levels – some like the "rustic first floor", others "prefer the more-expensive upstairs" that features "excellent-value tasting dinners."

Cannella's on Grand [S] 18 12 19 $29

1132 W. Grand Ave. (May St.), 312-433-9400

◪ Fans of Steven Cannella's defunct digs on Wells Street and West Huron are still relishing the "rebirth of an old favorite"; like its old-guard Italian predecessors, this "friendly" two-year-old "Grand Avenue restaurant" is known for "large portions" of "good hearty food" at "reasonable prices", though cutting-edge culinary critics complain the fare's as "ordinary" as the "decor is bland."

Cantare [S] ▽ 22 21 21 $40

200 E. Chestnut St. (Mies van der Rohe Way), 312-266-4500

■ A relatively "new favorite" for "tasty [Northern] Italian off the Mag Mile", this "lesser-known" sophomore sibling of Volare is a "friendly" Streeterville spot that's "a calamari- and tiramisu-free zone" thanks to "master chef" Edward Leonard's "creative" interpretations of "classic" dishes; as part of the "good service", they've recently started to do some tableside cooking.

Cape Cod Room [S] 22 22 22 $45

Drake Hotel, 140 E. Walton St. (Michigan Ave.), 312-787-2200

◪ "Savor a trip down memory lane" at this Streeterville "landmark" "in the Drake" Hotel, a "stiff-upper-lip" "old-school seafood" spot (you "can't beat the oysters" and "awesome bookbinder soup") with a "dark" "New England" atmosphere; the experience is "expensive but worth it" to fans but "pricey" to those who say it's "lost its luster"; N.B. jackets are preferred at dinner.

Capital Grille [S] 23 23 22 $46

633 N. St. Clair St. (Ontario St.), 312-337-9400

■ Streeterville's "sophisticated steakhouse" is a "carnivore heaven" replete "with cigars" and "testosterone", where "high-quality beef" and "lobsters the size of Trident submarines" make for "great power lunches" as well as "expense-account" dinners; yes, "it's a chain, but it feels local" say capital-ists who compliment its "classy", "clubby atmosphere" and appreciate the "A-1 treatment" from its "top-notch" staff.

CARLOS' S
28 | 25 | 27 | $68

429 Temple Ave. (Highwood Ave.), Highland Park, 847-432-0770

■ "Worth the drive at twice the distance", this North Suburban veteran is "always a sure bet" for "a special night out" thanks to "outstanding", "palate-pleasing" New French cuisine that's so "dependably wonderful" devotees "dream about" it; "invisible attention" from a "stellar staff" overseen by "superb hosts Carlos and Debbie Nieto" is another hallmark of its "small and comfortable" room; P.S. the "great wine list" boasts 1,500 bottles.

Carlucci S
20 | 20 | 19 | $35

250 Marriott Dr. (Milwaukee Ave.), Lincolnshire, 847-478-0990
6111 N. River Rd. (Higgins Rd.), Rosemont, 847-518-0990

☑ Cronies say these "old-fashioned" "Italian restaurants for Italians" in the Northwest Suburbs are "always reliable" for "well-prepared" fare, though some dubious diners are "disappointed" by what they deem "ordinary" output and call them "pricey for pasta"; still, the River Road sibling is a "good place to meet a friend passing through O'Hare."

Carmichael's Chicago Steak House S
22 | 20 | 21 | $38

1052 W. Monroe St. (bet. Morgan St. & Racine Ave.), 312-433-0025

■ To fans, the "terrific cuts" "rank with the best" at this "unpretentious" West Loop "steak-and-cigar stop" in a "good location" near the United Center, a "great before-the-game place" where you might just "catch" sight of a few "celebrity locals and athletes"; "it feels like everyone knows your name" within its "cavernous but comfortable" confines, though some prefer the "super outside seating."

Carmine's S
20 | 18 | 18 | $34

1043 N. Rush St. (bet. Bellevue Pl. & Cedar St.), 312-988-7676

☑ "Plentiful" portions of "tasty" "true Italian food" lure the loyal to this "reliable Rosebud" restaurant, a "popular hangout" in a part of the Gold Coast cards have christened the "Viagra triangle"; it's a "place to be seen" ("go early to avoid long waits"), with "great people-watching" and "fabulous alfresco dining", "weather permitting", though wafflers wonder "what's the hype about?"

Carson's Ribs S
20 | 13 | 17 | $26

5970 N. Ridge Ave. (Clark St.), 773-271-4000
612 N. Wells St. (Ontario St.), 312-280-9200
200 N. Waukegan Rd. (bet. Deerfield & Lake Cook Rds.), Deerfield, 847-374-8500
5050 N. Harlem Ave. (Foster Ave.), Harwood Heights, 708-867-4200

☑ "Still the standard" to many, these city and suburban BBQ "classics" give you an "honest slab at an honest price", with "meaty", "macho ribs" that are "consistently tender" and served in "artery-clogging abundance" (though some prefer the "awesome pork chops"); still, the quarrelsome question the "frayed decor", quipping "the setting of natural Formica is perfect for takeaway."

Catch 35 S   23 | 21 | 21 | $39 |
Leo Burnett Bldg., 35 W. Wacker Dr. (bet. Dearborn & State Sts.), 312-346-3500
■ "Interesting preparations" of "Asian-influenced" seafood "subtly enhanced by light sauces" make for the "freshest catch in the Loop" at this "unique", "contemporary" spot where a "personable and knowledgeable" staff helps patrons navigate the "vast menu"; a "favorite" "for business lunches" and tête-à-têtes of "the well-heeled", it's also "well-situated for Goodman Theater"–goers.

Cerise S   ▽ 21 | 21 | 19 | $46 |
Le Méridien Hotel, 520 N. Michigan Ave., 5th fl. (Grand Ave.), 312-645-1500
☑ "One of the best restaurants no one seems to know about", this "upscale" Near North bistro "hidden" in the Le Méridien Hotel is "hard to find" but "worth the search" say fans of its French-Med fare; foes of this "fledgling" one-year-old feel the "disappointing service" "needs work."

Charlie's Ale House S   15 | 15 | 15 | $19 |
1224 W. Webster Ave. (Magnolia Ave.), 773-871-1440
Navy Pier, 700 E. Grand Ave. (Lake Shore Dr.), 312-595-1440
☑ "The '60s live on" at these "cozy" pubs; sure, they may be "more bar than restaurant" and "could benefit from an expanded menu", but they're "good" for "a brew and a burger", as well as other "decent", "traditional" American "bar food"; besides, folks "love the beer garden" at the DePaul location and the Navy Pier branch's "fun patio."

CHARLIE TROTTER'S   28 | 26 | 28 | VE |
816 W. Armitage Ave. (Halsted St.), 773-248-6228
■ Possessed of a "perfectionist's zeal", chef-owner Charlie Trotter "overlooks no detail" at this "world-class" Lincoln Park New American "innovator", "an epicurean's idea of heaven" where "creative cooking", "a well-chosen wine list", "flawless service" (rated No. 1 in our *Survey*) and "lovely atmosphere" add up to an "exhilarating", "one-of-a-kind culinary experience"; N.B. regarding rampant rumors of Charlie leaving Chicago behind – will he trot or will he not? – he says not.

Cheesecake Factory S   20 | 18 | 17 | $22 |
John Hancock Ctr., 875 N. Michigan Ave., lower level (Chestnut St.), 312-337-1101 ●
Woodfield Mall, 53 Woodfield Rd. (Plum Grove Rd.), Schaumburg, 847-619-1090

(continued)

(continued)
Cheesecake Factory
*Old Orchard Ctr., 374 Old Orchard Ctr. (Skokie Blvd.), Skokie,
847-329-8077*
☑ "The menu is almost as long as the wait" at these
"cavernous" city and suburban chainsters, each a "guilty
pleasure" where the "giant portions" of "consistently
good" American fare just might "leave no room for" the
"decadent" and "dreamy cheesecakes" (it's "hard to pick
just one flavor"); still, some fuddy-duddies frown about the
"fantasy" decor and the "smiley" staffers who "can't keep
up with the tourists."

Chef's Station S   ▽ 26 | 21 | 22 | $33
*Davis Street Metra Station, 915 Davis St. (Church St.),
Evanston, 847-570-9821*
■ Though it's "hard to find your way" to the "unexpected
location" of this "easy-to-overlook" North Suburban "under
the train tracks" in Evanston's historic "Davis Street Metra
Station", those who do report it's "a top-quality surprise"
that gives the "gourmet treatment" to "innovative" New
American dishes at "reasonable prices"; "great service"
and a tasting menu that's "a steal" add to the appeal; P.S.
beer and wine only.

Chez François   – | – | – | M
14 S. Third St. (State St.), Geneva, 630-262-1000
Born in Spain but raised in France, aptly named chef-owner
François Sanchez has opted for nurture over nature,
transforming his former West Suburban tapas restaurant,
Granada, into this new Southern French bistro with earthy
regional specialties – a representative signature dish is
duck breast and duck ravioli with red cabbage in a red-
wine-and-fig sauce – served in a colorful dining room that
evokes the sensuous, sunny Gallic countryside.

Chez Joel S   23 | 20 | 22 | $36
1119 W. Taylor St. (Racine Ave.), 312-226-6479
■ A "surprisingly good" "French gem" set "amid all the
red-sauce Italians" in Little Italy, this "always-pleasing"
"standout" of a bistro offers "food prepared with care and
skill" in a "low-key", "homey" environment that some say is
a bit too "cozy" thanks to "tables crammed" "so close you
dine with your neighbors" – no wonder the claustrophobic
covet an "outdoor summer seat" in the "great garden."

Chicago Chop House S   24 | 19 | 22 | $44
60 W. Ontario St. (bet. Clark & Dearborn Sts.), 312-787-7100
☑ "Here's the beef" brags the brotherhood of "good ol'
boys", "big-city movers and shakers" and "conventioneers"
who descend upon the "dark" dining rooms of this River
North "Chicago landmark", a "classy" steak-and-chop
shop known for "great meat" "without all the pretension";

a word to the wise: "if you want a little quiet, ask to be seated upstairs", as the "first-floor piano bar is raucous."

Chicago Diner S　　18　13　16　$16
3411 N. Halsted St. (Roscoe St.), 773-935-6696
581 Elm Pl. (bet. 1st & 2nd Sts.), Highland Park, 847-433-1228
☑ "Interesting" and "inventive" flesh-free fare ranging from "healthy tofu stir-fries" to "delicious 'meat' dishes (without the meat)" that "even a carnivore would love" have fans fawning over these "casual" Wrigleyville and Suburban North "vegetarian nirvanas"; still, the "loveless" complain of "bland results" and "hole-in-the-wall" surroundings.

Chicago Firehouse Restaurant S　19　21　19　$36
1401 S. Michigan Ave. (14th St.), 312-786-1401
☑ Expect no alarms at this "dignified" South Loop pioneer in an "authentic two-story firehouse", as the only thing "smokin'" is the "hearty American fare" ("move over, mom!") served either in its "quiet, civilized" dining rooms or on its "lovely patio"; some wet blankets, though, say it's "a little expensive" for this "neighborhood-in-progress"; N.B. the Food rating may not reflect a recent chef change.

Chicago Flat Sammies S　16　12　13　$12
163 E. Pearson St. (Michigan Ave.), 312-664-2733
■ "When shopping on Michigan Avenue", "snack"-ers stop into this "crowded" Streeterville Lettuce Entertain You spot in the historic Pumping Station for a "quick", "cheap lunch" of "surprisingly good" "gourmet-ish fast food" such as the eponymous "flavorful sandwich", "good salads and flatbread" pizzas and "excellent milkshakes."

Chicago Kalbi ❶S　－　－　－　M
3752 W. Lawrence Ave. (Hamlin Ave), 773-604-8183
Though relatively unknown, this Northwest Sider is an "excellent place for Korean BBQ" where "friendly service" outshines the plain decor; the namesake dish – marinated ribs wrapped with rice and bean paste in a lettuce leaf – is especially "fun" when you "cook it yourself" using "fresh ingredients" over a wood-fired tabletop grill; P.S. "get a private room."

Chicago Pizza & Oven Grinder Co. S⇥　20　16　16　$19
2121 N. Clark St. (bet. Dickens & Webster Aves.), 773-248-2570
☑ A "great twist on the typical pizzeria", this "affordable" Lincoln Park "classic" has been serving up "unique sandwiches" and "amazing pizza pot pies" ("an upside-down treat") since '72; doubters dismiss the latter as "bizarre" and "not really" 'za and ponder the propriety of its "unorganized waiting list" that "isn't written down"; P.S. "cash only."

CHIC Cafe S　　　　21　14　18　E

Cooking and Hospitality Institute of Chicago,
361 W. Chestnut St. (Orleans St.), 312-873-2032
■ "Students cook and serve" at this River North BYO under
the auspices of the Cooking and Hospitality Institute of
Chicago, where "guinea pigs" gladly gather for an "ever-
changing" and "always surprising" Eclectic–Contemporary
French prix fixe menu that's not only a "delicious" "delight"
but an "excellent value" as well (lunches are just $15 ,
while dinners are only $25), even though "you're really
eating someone's homework."

Chief O'Neill's Pub S　　　　18　20　17　$19

3471 N. Elston Ave. (Addison St.), 773-583-3066
■ Denizens of this "wonderfully friendly" "local pub"
on the Northwest Side claim you'll "leave with an Irish
accent", so "authentic" are its "cute atmosphere" (with a
"great beer garden") and "generous portions" of "hearty",
"traditional" fare – from "burgers and brew" to "fantastic
fish 'n' chips"; curmudgeonly crawlers, however, call the
food a bit "bland" ("pass the salt" "and pepper").

Chilpancingo S　　　　23　21　20　$36

358 W. Ontario St. (Orleans St.), 312-266-9525
■ "Holy mole!" exclaim enthusiasts of "Frontera Grill
alum" Geno Bahena's "festive and lively" River North
sophomore ("sister of Ixcapuzalco" and the new Mi
Sueño, Su Realidad) where "sophisticated", "creative
regional Mexican cuisine" is paired with "sexy straight-up
margaritas" or pours from an "outstanding wine list"; the
"exotic" space features "authentic" folk art and "vivid
paintings that reflect the vivid flavors", including "works
by the chef-owner" himself.

Chinn's 34th St. Fishery S　　　　21　13　18　$29

3011 W. Ogden Ave. (bet. Fender Ave. & Naper Blvd.), Lisle,
630-637-1777
☑ You "must go early for a table", as there's "almost always
a wait" at this West Suburban seafooder serving "a whole
lotta fresh fish" and "garlic-butter rolls to die for" at
"reasonable prices"; critics concede it's "not as crowded
as Bob Chinn's" Crab House, its Wheeling cousin, but
complain that its "smaller" setting is just as "noisy" and
"needs better decor."

Chinoiserie S⊅　　　　20　12　15　$26

509 Fourth St. (Linden Ave.), Wilmette, 847-256-0306
☑ Champions cheer this North Suburban Eclectic-Asian as
"a mixed marriage that works", praising the "creative"
interplay of "interesting Chinese and French" influences in
its "mouthwatering" fare; dissenters dismiss the menu,
though, as an "inauthentic" and "odd mixture" that's "pricey
for a casual restaurant", adding the service is "earnest"

but "disjointed" and the decor is "disappointing"; P.S. it's "BYO" and "cash only."

Chipotle Mexican Grill   15 | 11 | 13 | $11

2256-58 N. Orchard Ave. (bet. Clark & Halsted Sts.), 773-935-6744 🅂

3181 N. Broadway (Belmont Ave.), 773-525-5250 🅂

2000 N. Clybourn Ave. (Cortland St.), 773-935-5710 🅂

316 N. Michigan Ave. (bet. Water St. & Wacker Dr.), 312-578-0950 🅂

1166 N. State St. (Division St.), 312-654-8637 🅂

291 E. Ontario St. (Fairbanks Ct.), 312-587-7753 🅂

10 E. Jackson Blvd. (State St.), 312-566-0308

711 Church St. (bet. Orrington & Sherman Aves.), Evanston, 847-425-3959 🅂

601 N. Martingale Rd. (bet. Higgins Rd. & Woodfield Mall Dr.), Schaumburg, 847-517-8670 🅂

5373 Touhy Ave. (Niles Center Rd.), Skokie, 847-763-1580 🅂
Additional locations throughout the Chicago area

🖾 Amigos who approve of this McDonald's-owned Mexican chain say it serves "good fast food" in the form of "cheap", "healthy" "throw-pillow-size burritos" made from "fresh ingredients" "you choose yourself" (plus "knock-your-socks-off margaritas"); desperados dismiss them, though, as "bland", "gringo-style" "McBurritos" and slam the "stark" "warehouse" surroundings.

Christophe   ▽ 25 | 23 | 24 | $43

111 N. Main St. (Crystal Lake Ave.), Crystal Lake, 815-444-0374

■ A haven of "excellent" "city dining" "in the far [Northwest] Suburbs" (about 50 miles from Downtown Chicago), this "small, up-and-coming" New American "in Crystal Lake" offers "superior" French-influenced fare and "excellent service" in an "intimate atmosphere" of hardwood floors, exposed brick and vintage Parisian posters.

Cielo 🅂   ▽ 19 | 22 | 19 | $34

Omni Chicago Hotel, 676 N. Michigan Ave., 4th fl. (Huron St.), 312-944-7676

■ "Everything about this fine restaurant is understated" – including its "hidden" location on the fourth floor of Near North's Omni Chicago Hotel – but undaunted acolytes advise it's worth seeking out for its "high-quality" New American and Northern Italian fare and "stately", "modern" room with a "great ceiling" graced by an "awesome" trompe l'oeil sky mural and "huge windows" offering "fantastic views of bustling Michigan Avenue."

Cité 🅂   18 | 23 | 19 | $59

Lake Point Tower, 505 N. Lake Shore Dr., 70th fl. (bet. Grand Ave. & Illinois St.), 312-644-4050

🖾 High atop Lake Point Tower, this celestial 70th-story Streeterville stalwart draws raves for its "romantic" room and one of the "best views in Chicago" ("although you pay for it"); the starry-eyed say its "excellent" New French–American menu and "great service" add up to an "exquisite night on the town", though the earthbound earmark the "food good but" "overpriced" and the servers "snooty."

Clark Street Bistro S
19 15 18 $29

2600 N. Clark St. (Wrightwood Ave.), 773-525-9992

☑ "For a romantic dinner", supporters say "you should not miss" this Lincoln Park bistro (big brother to Chez Joel) that satisfies with a "consistently good", if "not ground-breaking", Northern "Italian and French combo" menu offered in a "homey, relaxed atmosphere"; nevertheless, naysayers knock the "unusual Moroccan-accented decor" and a few servers with "attitude."

Clubhouse, The S
19 21 19 $30

Oakbrook Center Mall, 298 Oakbrook Ctr. (Rte. 83), Oak Brook, 630-472-0600

☑ Though it's closed its onsite golf pro shop, Oak Brook's "trendy" yet "classy" "meet market" is still a sweet spot thanks to new owners; members of the gallery consider it "a club I'd actually join", with "great people-watching" and "generous portions" of Traditional American fare in a "good-looking", "high-energy setting"; holdouts hint the "manly" meals are "good but inconsistent" and favor the "quieter upstairs" over the "noisy" main floor.

Club Lucky S
19 18 18 $26

1824 W. Wabansia St. (bet. Ashland & Damen Aves.), 773-227-2300

☑ Mixing "martinis and meatballs" for a "young, hip crowd", this "swinging" "supper club" "led the Bucktown restaurant surge" a decade ago and is still serving Southern Italian "comfort food" ("nothing fancy – just good, large portions") in a setting that's a "retro throwback to the '40s and '50s"; still, "long waits" have some gamblers trying their luck at "plenty of better places."

Cochon Sauvage S
▽ 22 19 20 $39

1060 College Ave. (President St.), Wheaton, 630-784-8015

☑ Hog-wild Western Suburbanites "can't believe" this "great bistro" is "tucked away in Wheaton", yet there it is – a "wonderful find" for "excellent French cuisine" that's not as rustic as the name would imply"; still, not everyone "can't wait to go again", as some squeal about "inconsistent service" and grunt that it's "not as good as Les Deux Gros", its Glen Ellyn littermate.

COCO PAZZO S
24 22 23 $42

300 W. Hubbard St. (Franklin St.), 312-836-0900

■ "It feels like Italy" at this "polished" "NYC import" in River North where the "top-of-the-line" Northern Italian cuisine combines "innovative choices with classic favorites" ("chef Tony Priolo is a master of risotto"); "beautiful lighting" enlivens the "warm atmosphere" of its "handsome" "loft space", and "mature service" means it's "always outstanding" for "personal entertaining" or a "power lunch."

Coco Pazzo Cafe S   22 | 20 | 21 | $33

Red Roof Inn, 636 N. St. Clair St. (Ontario St.), 312-664-2777

■ "The 'crazy chef' is right on target" at Streeterville's "more casual", "more affordable" "version of Coco Pazzo" (restaurateur Pino Luongo's popular River North eatery), where the "beautiful people" congregate for "inventive" Northern Italian "comfort food" in a "relaxed", "European setting" complete with some of the "best outdoor dining" in town.

CoCoRo/East Restaurant   ∇ 20 | 14 | 18 | $30

668 N. Wells St. (bet. Erie & Huron Sts.), 312-943-2220

☑ Shabu-shabu seekers and sushi searchers are split over this "small and comfortable" River North Japanese: some swear the fare is "authentic", "fresh and delicious", while others find it "disappointing"; service remarks are similarly skewed, ranging from regrettably "rushed" to favorably "fast"; nevertheless, everyone agrees there's a "nice selection of sakes."

Cold Comfort Cafe & Deli S   ∇ 18 | 12 | 12 | $11

2211 W. North Ave. (Leavitt St.), 773-772-4552

☑ "No more trips to the kosher deli in the suburbs" for some thanks to this "quaint" and (name notwithstanding) "cozy" spot set in a Bucktown building that dates to 1886; a "well-kept secret" for "mouthwatering sandwiches" to take out or eat in, and "killer breakfasts", it's a "fun place" featuring a "friendly staff" that "tries hard" – still, some surveyors say it "needs more waiters."

Como S   – | – | – | E

695 N. Milwaukee Ave. (Huron St.), 312-733-7400

In a nod to their famed, now-defunct Como Inn, the Marchetti family has revived the name for a new generation at this old-guard Italian on the Near West site of their former Fahrenheit; the menu reads like a roll call of classic pasta, meat and chicken dishes, and the updated loftlike space sports creamy walls, a draped ceiling with chandelier and canopied booths, with a patio for warm-weather dining.

Convito Italiano S   19 | 15 | 17 | $23

Plaza del Lago, 1515 Sheridan Rd. (north of Lake Ave.), Wilmette, 847-251-3654

☑ "Always yummy" to loyalists, this North Shore market and trattoria is a "great spot" for "simple", "reliable" Italian fare that's "less than cutting-edge but still a fine meal"; contrarians who're convinced it's become "complacent" cite "basic decor" and "service [that] can be a little cold" as reasons to "pick up a picnic" or "bring home dinner."

Copa Cubana S   ▽ 19 | 17 | 19 | $23

224 S. Main St. (bet. Jackson & Jefferson Sts.), Naperville, 630-983-2672

☑ "For something a little different", a "swelling crowd" of Naperville natives coos over the "creative" yet "authentic" Cuban fare at this "real gem" located in a former laundromat that's now a "fun, festive" brick-and-stucco room flecked with vintage photos of Havana; some dissidents declare that they're "not crazy about the food" but wonder "where else can you get plantains in the [Western] Suburbs?"

Cornelia's Restaurant S   19 | 18 | 19 | $29

750 W. Cornelia Ave. (bet. Broadway & Halsted St.), 773-248-8333

■ Gone is the "kitschy name" of this former 'Roosterant' in Boys Town, and with it the chicken-centric focus and farm-implement motif; what remains is a "sweet date place" for couples (including some of the "Will & Grace" variety) where they "take great care" with "innovative" Italian dishes and American "comfort food" like "nice pork chops"; P.S. certain "spotlighted artworks" on the walls are for sale.

Corner Bakery   17 | 13 | 13 | $13

1121 N. State St. (Cedar St.), 312-787-1969 S
676 N. St. Clair St. (Erie St.), 312-266-2570 S
516 N. Clark St. (Grand Ave.), 312-644-8100 S
Field Museum, 1400 S. Lake Shore Dr. (opp. Soldier Field Stadium), 312-588-1040 S
Market Bldg., 140 S. Dearborn St. (Marble Pl.), 312-920-9100
360 N. Michigan Ave. (bet. Wacker Dr. & Water St.), 312-236-2400 S
Goodman Theatre, 56 W. Randolph St. (Dearborn St.), 312-346-9492 S
224 S. Michigan Ave. (Adams St.), 312-431-7600 S
Sears Tower, 233 S. Wacker Dr. (Adams St.), 312-466-0060
175 Old Orchard Ctr. (bet. Golf Rd. & Skokie Blvd.), Skokie, 847-933-1555 S
Additional locations throughout the Chicago area

☑ "Proving fast food can be good", this expanding chain of "quick pick-me-up stops" draws crowds of "carb lovers" with its "relatively healthy" menu of "consistently good sandwiches, pizzas, breads and pastries"; critics complain of "assembly-line" fare and "confusing, chaotic, cafeteria-style ordering", contending they're "not as special" now that "there's one on every corner."

Cosí   15   14   12 $13
57 E. Grand Ave. (Rush St.), 312-321-1990 **S**
116 S. Michigan Ave. (bet. Adams & Monroe Sts.),
312-263-6595 **S**
203 N. La Salle Blvd. (Lake St.), 312-368-4400
230 W. Washington St. (Franklin St.), 312-422-1002 **S**
1200 N. State Pkwy. (Division St.), 312-266-7125 **◗S**
25 E. Hinsdale Ave. (Garfield Ave.), Hinsdale,
630-654-5033 **S**
1101 N. Lake St. (Harlem Ave.), Oak Park,
708-524-8412 **S**
☑ Though this "corporate" chain offers "many choices" of "unique salads" as well as "creative sandwiches" on "delicious bread", raters resent paying "NYC prices" ("it should be called 'Costlí'") for what some call "forgettable food" and add "too bad they don't have the service thing down"; N.B. some locations offer an expanded dinner menu served by waiters.

Costa's **S**   23   21   22 $28
340 S. Halsted St. (Van Buren St.), 312-263-9700
1 S. 130 Summit Ave. (Roosevelt Rd.), Oakbrook Terrace,
630-620-1100
■ A Greek chorus of connoisseurs cries "*opa!*" for these "favorite" Gemini twins, together rated "the best" in our *Survey* for their nationality's cuisine; whether dining at the "elegant Greektown" Castor "or the West Suburban" Pollux, expect these brothers to deliver a "welcoming atmosphere" "as charming as Athens", with "savory" "upscale" specialties presented on "white tablecloths" by "knowledgeable" servers.

COURTRIGHT'S **S**   25   25   24 $49
8989 S. Archer Ave. (Willow Springs Rd.), Willow Springs,
708-839-8000
■ You'll "feel like you're at your rich uncle's house" when visiting this "elegant yet exceedingly comfortable" New American retreat, a "'downtown' spot in the Southwest Suburbs" whose "high quality standards", "amazing wine cellar" and "beautiful" "parklike" "setting on the [Cook County] Forest Preserve" "complement its wonderful" cuisine; N.B. the Food rating may not reflect the recent arrival of executive chef Michael Tsonton.

Cousin's **S**   18   15   14 $18
2833 N. Broadway (Diversey Pkwy.), 773-880-0063
☑ The "delicious aromas" of "flavorful", "familiar Med" favorites "with an exotic Turkish twist" prompt the faithful to "grab a floor pillow" at this "comfy", "vegetarian-friendly" Lakeview spot, the sole survivor of an erstwhile North Side trio; still, "friendly but haphazard service" that can be "painfully slow" has doubters declaring they "wouldn't recommend that [their] cousins go there."

Crab Street Saloon ◐ [S] – – – M

1061 W. Madison St. (Aberdeen St.), 312-433-0013

It's ok to put your elbows on the table at this West Loop Maryland-style seafooder where nautical ephemera and a vintage bar create a fishy saloon feel; East Coasters won't find the piles of hard-shells they crave, but king crab legs, shrimp and three varieties of oysters daily (with burgers and fried chicken for landlubbers) are ample consolation; N.B. there's a free United Center shuttle service.

Crawdaddy Bayou [S] 14 19 17 $24

412 N. Milwaukee Ave. (bet. Dundee & Lake Cook Rds.), Wheeling, 847-520-4800

◩ A "raucous" "party every day", this "crazy Cajun" in the Northwest Suburbs serves up "hot stuff" like BBQ shrimp that has some Chicagoans saying it's "the most fun you can have this side of New Orleans"; other Yankees yammer that its "marginal" bayou bites are as "inauthentic" as its "kitschy" ersatz-swamp setting, adding "Emeril wouldn't set foot in" this "imitator."

Creole ▽ 18 15 18 $20

(fka Club Creole)

226 W. Kinzie St. (bet. Franklin & Wells Sts.), 312-222-0300

◩ Some are "amazed anyone finds" this River Norther behind the Merchandise Mart, but "classic Creole and Cajun" cravers know they can get "a pretty good fix" within its "fun atmosphere"; still, what some say are "solid Louisiana flavors" the "disappointed" discount as "inauthentic"; N.B. the Food rating does not reflect a post-*Survey* shift toward Southern comfort food.

Crofton on Wells 24 20 22 $45

535 N. Wells St. (bet. Grand Ave. & Ohio St.), 312-755-1790

■ "Suzy can cook" say "fine-dining" fans who "go often to Crofton" to "treasure" the "adventure" of its "creative" eponymous chef-owner's "excellent" Regional American fare; the "minimalist" decor of this "quiet haven" in River North strikes some as "sleek" and "romantic", but others deem the "drop-ceiling"-ed digs a bit "dull" and wish "she would pretty up the place."

Cross-Rhodes [S] ≠ 19 9 17 $14

913 Chicago Ave. (Main St.), Evanston, 847-475-4475

■ Scholars of "classic cheap Greek" give extra credit to this "reliably good" North Suburban offering "comfort food" like "great gyros, chicken and fries at great prices"; "fast service" from a "friendly" crew makes it a "favorite family place" despite a decidedly "no-frills atmosphere" that has some saying "don't bother eating in"; speaking of credit, cancel the cards 'cause it's "cash only."

Cru Wine Bar & Café ◗ S   17 | 19 | 16 | $26
888 N. Wabash Ave. (Delaware Pl.), 312-337-4001
☒ Swirl-and-sippers say a "vino paradise" awaits at this "totally Euro", "hip-and-comfortable" Gold Coaster that's "mostly for nibbles" and "great flights" of wine; the "cozy and classy" atmosphere "with chandeliers and couches" makes it a "nice" "place for a date" or "to meet after work for drinks", but off-put oenophiles object to "sporadic service" and call it "average for the price."

Cucina Bella S   18 | 17 | 19 | $27
543 W. Diversey Pkwy. (bet. Clark St. & Hampden Ct.), 773-868-1119
Cucina Bella Osteria & Wine Bar S
1612 N. Sedgwick Ave. (North Ave.), 312-274-1119
☒ These 'beautiful kitchens' in Old Town and Lincoln Park are each a "homey" "neighborhood place to meet friends" over "so much" "authentic Italian" food you'll have "enough for seconds", though detractors damn with faint praise, labeling the fare "pretty good"; if you can't get a reservation to "sit at the chef's table", "bring your dog and sit outside."

Cullen's Bar & Grill S   – | – | – | M
3741 N. Southport Ave. (bet. Addison St. & Irving Park Rd.), 773-975-0600
"Small and often crowded", this American version of a "classic Irish pub" in Lakeview is "popular with the bar crowd" for its "great atmosphere", expansive patio and "good food and drink" including "homespun meatloaf and mashed potatoes", "great onion rings" and, of course, Guinness; it's also a "fun" pre- or post-play stop for stage-struck visitors to owner-impresario Michael Cullen's adjacent Mercury Theater.

Cyrano's Bistrot & Wine Bar   21 | 20 | 20 | $34
546 N. Wells St. (Ohio St.), 312-467-0546
■ "Roxanne would approve" of the "good, honest French cooking" "done right" "without breaking the bank" at this "funky but chic" bistro boasting "comfortable" environs that are "surprisingly quaint" for River North; headed by a "warm and friendly" "husband-and-wife team" (chef Didier Durand and wine cellar master Jamie Pellar), the "polite staff" will "make you feel right at home."

Cy's Crab House S   16 | 14 | 16 | $26
3819 N. Ashland Ave. (Grace St.), 773-883-8900
933 N. Milwaukee Ave. (Lake Cook Rd.), Wheeling, 847-279-1700
☒ Those with "a taste for crab" can't concur on this city and suburban duo: some say they're "nice", "family-oriented" places where you "can go in jeans" for a "great value on fresh seafood" and "Middle Eastern side dishes"; others yawn "ho-hum", admitting that the "fair" fare will

do "in a pinch" but dinging the "disappointing service" and dismissing the decor as "lacking."

Czech Plaza [S] ≠ ▽ 20 | 9 | 21 | $15

7016 W. Cermak Rd. (Home Ave.), Berwyn, 708-795-6555

◪ Czech out the "big portions" of "simple, tasty, rib-sticking" "Bohemian" dishes (some for "less than a sawbuck") recalling "grandma's good food" at this "old-world" outpost in the Western Suburbs; the service is "quick and no-nonsense", but most warn "don't go for the ambiance 'cause there ain't any"; P.S. another "problem: they don't accept credit cards."

D & J BISTRO [S] 25 | 21 | 23 | $35

First Bank Business Ctr., 466 S. Rand Rd. (Rte. 22), Lake Zurich, 847-438-8001

■ Allies who "have never had a bad meal" at this Northwest Suburban spot applaud its "authentic" French bistro "comfort food prepared in an upscale way"; "urban sophistication with rural charm" makes it "feel like Paris despite the strip-mall" setting, and if it's a little "crowded", it may be because the "consistency is excellent" and the "price is right."

Dave & Buster's ◐ [S] 12 | 14 | 13 | $20

1030 N. Clark St. (bet. Maple & Oak Sts.), 312-943-5151

1155 N. Swift Rd. (bet. Army Trail Rd. & Lake St.), Addison, 630-543-5151

◪ "Fun is key" at these Gold Coast and Suburban Northwest outposts of a national chain of "family places" whose "mass appeal" is gazillions of games; still, arcade-ians who berate the "blah bar food" "wish the chow was as good as" (and not just "a break from") the "entertaining" trivial pursuits; as is, some say "it's hard to believe anyone without kids would set foot" in them.

Dave's Italian Kitchen [S] 18 | 13 | 17 | $17

1635 Chicago Ave. (bet. Church & Davis Sts.), Evanston, 847-864-6000

■ "An Evanston tradition", this "college haunt" is a "bargain" in a "basement", with "good Italian fare" like "satisfying pastas and thin-crust pizzas" at "1960s prices"; the decor is "nothing fancy" and "noisy students" can make it "hard to have a conversation" here, but fans find it so "quirky and endearing" that some are shouting "Dave, open one in Chicago!"

David's Bistro [S] ≠ ▽ 28 | 20 | 25 | $34

Norwood Plaza, 623 N. Wolf Rd. (Central Ave.), Des Plaines, 847-803-3233

■ A "small storefront" in the Northwest Suburban Norwood Plaza strip mall is home to this "chef-owned" bistro where the eponymous David Maish gives "excellent presentation"

to the "outstanding", "innovative" and reasonably priced
French-American cuisine on his "unique menu"; with a
"friendly" staff and a cozy dining room replete with
"beautiful wood walls" of bird's-eye maple and red oak,
it's "a great hideaway."

Davis Street Fishmarket S 19 15 17 $25
501 Davis St. (Hinman Ave.), Evanston, 847-869-3474
☑ "Happy faces" hint at the "chaotic fun" of Evanston's
"seafood lover's heaven", which afishionados say is
"always spot-on" for its "large selection" of "fresh" fin
food with Cajun-Creole flare and "fabulous oyster bar", all
offered in a "down-to-earth" "neighborhood atmosphere"
"reminiscent of the East Coast"; still, critics crab about
"long waits", "noise" and "spotty service."

Dearborn Diner S 12 13 14 $17
Hampton Inn & Suites, 449 N. Dearborn St. (Illinois St.),
312-755-0077
☑ "Much like its predecessor, Fog City" Diner, this two-
year-old in River North's Hampton Inn & Suites offers
"homey", "basic" American fare in a space made to
look "just like a '50s" greasy spoon; at best it's a "nice
change from fast food" and an "alternative to the high-end
restaurants in the neighborhood", but a bevy of bored
bobby-soxers laments that it's "lackluster all around."

Dee's Mandarin S 21 16 17 $23
1114 Armitage Ave. (Seminary Ave.), 773-477-1500
■ Good fortune for Lincoln Parkers – this "gourmet Chinese"
is "a bright spot" in the neighborhood for "flavorful,
generous servings" of "good but not flashy" Mandarin
cuisine and "fantastic Szechuan" specialties, all made from
"quality ingredients and unusual recipes" and "seemingly
lighter and healthier than" some competitors' fare; P.S.
there's "reliable carry-out" too.

Deleece S 21 17 20 $26
4004 N. Southport Ave. (Irving Park Rd.), 773-325-1710
■ "Deleece is always delish" declare devotees of the
"eclectic and tasty" New American cuisine prepared
"with culinary flair" and "smartly served" at this "casual"
Wrigleyville "restaurant that you'll wish was in *your*
neighborhood"; "filled with regulars", its "unassuming"
interior strikes many as "inviting" and "cozy", though a
few find its "decor lacking" and say it's "noisy" when
"crowded"; P.S. the Sunday "brunch is lovely."

Dell Rhea's Chicken Basket S 19 13 16 $16
645 Joliet Rd. (Frontage Rd.), Willowbrook, 630-325-0780
■ For a "nostalgic" "no-frills family dinner" of "fried
chicken the way it used to be", the faithful flock to this
"classic roadhouse" (circa 1946) in the Southwest Suburbs,

a "time warp that transports you" "back to the days of Route 66"; "hard to find but worth the search", it's a "favorite standby" that's "holding up after all these years."

Del Rio　　　　19 | 17 | 21 | $30
228 Green Bay Rd. (Rte. 22), Highwood, 847-432-4608
■ "You're never a stranger" at this North Suburban "classic", a "throwback to Highwood's yesteryears" where the kitchen reassures with "consistently good" "solid Italian cooking" supported by a "vast wine list" and delivered with "personal service" in a "crowded but fun" "atmosphere from the past"; "don't expect cutting-edge", just "rich" dining that's "old-fashioned, in a good way."

Dick's Last Resort 🖪　　　　12 | 13 | 13 | $20
River East Plaza, 435 E. Illinois St. (Lake Shore Dr.), 312-836-7870
🗷 Gluttons for punishment "wear old clothes" to this "dockside" Navy Pier "tourist place" (part of a "chain" that prides itself on having "no class whatsoever") to "get sloppy" over "messy BBQ" and seafood while enduring "obnoxious" barbs from a "deliberately insulting staff"; those who don't "like the abuse" or the "rowdy", "raunchy" revelry "stay away in droves", suggesting you "make it your last resort" as well.

Diosa Red 🖪　　　　▽ 19 | 22 | 19 | $36
3419 N. Clark St. (Sheffield Ave.), 773-880-0001
🗷 "A new level of fusion" is reached at this "cutting-edge" "eclectic" Asian in Wrigleyville where the "eye-candy" "servers clad in Suzy Wong dresses" make operatives "feel like 007" and the "fabulous hallucinogenic decor" has some seeing "too much red"; a duo of "adventurous" chefs – one Chinese, one French – turns out an "imaginative menu", though some say it's "pricey for the quality."

Dixie Kitchen & Bait Shop 🖪　　　　19 | 18 | 17 | $19
Harper Ct., 5225 S. Harper Ave. (53rd St.), 773-363-4943
825 Church St. (Benson Ave.), Evanston, 847-733-9030
■ Whether at the "Hyde Park haven" or the "Evanston eatery", these "cute" Soul sisters seduce with "abundant" portions of "tasty" Cajun, Creole and "Southern cuisine" ("love those fried green tomatoes") that "hit the spot" for most, though holdouts hint the food's "good for a fix but not like home cookin'"; either way, "you have to love" these "Dixie" chicks' "diverse clientele and servers."

Don Juan 🖪　　　　21 | 18 | 19 | $29
6730 N. Northwest Hwy. (bet. Devon & Touhy Aves.), 773-775-6438
Don Juan on Halsted 🖪 ⇗
1729 N. Halsted St. (bet. North & Willow Aves.), 312-981-4000
■ Though loyalists of the "original" "Edison Park location" swear it's "better" than its upstart sibling in Lincoln Park, the consensus is that "both are wonderful" thanks to

the "ultra-fresh, bright flavors" of Patrick Concannon's "innovative Mexican cuisine", not to mention the "fabulous margaritas"; also, the one-year-old "on Halsted" has the "bonus of a nice patio" and proximity to "the Steppenwolf and Royal George" theaters.

Don Roth's Blackhawk S 22 | 20 | 21 | $33 |
61 N. Milwaukee Ave. (Dundee Rd.), Wheeling, 847-537-5800
■ A steak-and-seafooder serving substantially the "same menu as 30 years ago", this "traditional, old-style" "Chicago classic" in the Northwest Suburbs is a "step back in time, but a pleasant one" "for meat lovers" thanks to a "consistent" kitchen serving up "no surprises"; the "kitschy spinning salad bowl" "may be a gimmick", but some consider it "worth the trip."

Don's Fishmarket & Tavern S 19 | 18 | 19 | $30 |
9335 Skokie Blvd. (south of Golf Rd.), Skokie, 847-677-3424
◪ North Suburban mariners maintain that this "local hangout" is a "worthwhile" "oldie but goodie" for "reliable seafood" "done every way you want", with "old-fashioned service", to boot; its dining room "draws" "value"-conscious "retired folk" with "early-bird specials", and the "limited menu" of its "casual, comfortable tavern" is also "a bargain"; still, some perceive the provender as "plain", "predictable" and "pedestrian."

Dover Straits S 21 | 19 | 20 | $30 |
1149 W. Golf Rd. (Gannon Dr.), Hoffman Estates, 847-884-3900
245 US Hwy. 45 (Rte. 83), Mundelein, 847-949-1550
■ These "always-dependable" Northwest Suburban seafood siblings are "traditional" "favorites" of a "generally older crowd" that "skips the fancy stuff" at other spots in favor of their "great early-bird" specials and "really good, basic fish menu", including "excellent Dover sole"; another "big plus" is their "dance floors with live bands" some nights (varies by location); those "into trying something new", though, may be "disappointed."

Dozu Sushi & Lobster S ▽ 19 | 19 | 17 | $35 |
100 E. Walton St. (bet. Michigan Ave. & Rush St.), 312-274-1000
■ Fans report that "some amazing food" can be found at this sophomore Gold Coast "BYO" Japanese seafooder, including "fab sushi" that's "fresh (and expensive)" and tanks teeming with lobsters (served steamed or stir-fried) that are so big you'll think they're "on steroids"; also, as the name suggests, the "elegant decor" and "beautiful" waterfalls are welcoming.

Duke of Perth S 17 | 17 | 18 | $17 |
2913 N. Clark St. (Oakdale Ave.), 773-477-1741
■ Lakeview locals feel "lucky to have" this Scottish-American pub "in the neighborhood"; it's "the real thing",

with "cozy, authentic decor" that makes you "feel like you're eating in Glasgow" and "celestial fish and chips" aided by a "good choice of UK ales" and an "amazing" selection of scotches; one complaint from the kilt-clad, though – it "should offer haggis!"

Du Yee S　　　　　　　▽ 21　11　21　$19
3203 N. Clark St. (Belmont Ave.), 773-549-5698

■ "Innovative preparations" from a "diverse menu" of Chinese, Japanese, Indonesian, Thai and Vietnamese dishes make this Lakeview Asian "a new favorite" for those few who've found it; not only are the dishes "well above average" and the prices "reasonable", but the staff "tries to please" – and apparently succeeds; N.B. the bar is limited to beer and wine only.

D'Vine Restaurant & Wine Bar S　18　16　18　$38
1950 W. North Ave. (Damen Ave.), 773-235-5700

◪ "Fun wine-pairing dinners" from a "creative" New French–New American menu and a "trendy" vibe render this Wicker Parker a "romantic date place", and it's also a "good spot for late-night" weekends thanks to a DJ spinning Brazilian jazz or ambient house tunes and a 2 AM kitchen closing Fridays and Saturdays; dissenters dismiss it as "pretentious", though, citing less-than-divine service from a "full-of-themselves staff."

Eclectic　　　　　　　▽ 21　18　19　$39
117 E. North Ave. (Main St.), Barrington, 847-277-7300

■ Set in a historic schoolhouse (the former site of the now-defunct Greenery), this – you guessed it – Eclectic eatery is considered "promising" by some and the "best newcomer" in the Northwest Suburbs by others; the "innovative chef" employs "various global influences" to create a "gourmet dining experience" in a "nice, intimate setting" where you can expect "personal attention."

Edelweiss Restaurant S　　▽ 21　20　20　$28
7650 W. Irving Park Rd. (Cumberland Ave.), Norridge, 708-452-6040

■ As Chicago's selection of traditional Teutonics shrinks, surveyors "in an oompah mood" give this "solid" "classic" a ratings boost for its "good German food" and service with "just enough schmaltz"; it's a "bit out of the way", but "if you like heavy" fare such as "great schnitzel" supplemented by an "excellent beer selection", there's no place better" in the Northern Suburbs.

Edna's S　　　　　　　　－ － － 　⏟
3175 W. Madison St. (Kedzie Ave.), 773-638-7079

The down-home Soul Food is just what you'd expect at this thirtysomething Far West diner that sports a long Formica counter and vinyl stools – the perfect setting for generous servings of hot homemade biscuits, fried chicken, stewed collard greens and ham hocks on rice, followed by pies and peach cobbler; N.B. no liquor is served.

Edwardo's [S] 18 | 11 | 14 | $16

2662 N. Halsted St. (1 block south of Diversey Pkwy.), 773-871-3400
1212 N. Dearborn St. (Division St.), 312-337-4490
521 S. Dearborn St. (bet. Congress Pkwy. & Harrison St.), 312-939-3366
1321 E. 57th St. (bet. Kenwood & Kimbark Aves.), 773-241-7960
904 W. Army Trail Rd. (County Farm Rd.), Carol Stream, 630-830-9600
6831 North Ave. (Grove Ave.), Oak Park, 708-524-2400
9300 Skokie Blvd. (Gross Point Rd.), Skokie, 847-674-0008
401 E. Dundee Rd. (east of Milwaukee Ave.), Wheeling, 847-520-0666

◪ Going "head to head" in a category crowded with "too many chains", this group gets its slice of the praise pie for "some of the best deep-dish pizzas around", especially the "great stuffed spinach" variety (with a "dandy thin-crust" version too), made with "all-natural" "fresh ingredients"; many addicts "always take out", though, as there's little to "no atmosphere"; N.B. alcohol service varies by location.

EJ's Place [S] 21 | 17 | 19 | $37

10027 Skokie Blvd. (Old Orchard Rd.), Skokie, 847-933-9800

◪ Lots of Northwest Suburban "locals" like this "steady" Italian steakhouse "related to Erie Cafe and Gene & Georgetti" through family (though all are separately owned), calling it "ideal" for its "great steaks and fresh fish" served in a "clubby", "cozy cabin atmosphere"; nevertheless, less laudatory participants pronounce it "pricey for Skokie" and pan a few worrisome "waiters with New York attitude."

Elaine ▽ 21 | 18 | 20 | $35

10 W. Jackson Ave. (Washington St.), Naperville, 630-548-3100

◪ Already "popular in the Western Suburbs", this "hip", "stylish" one-year-old set in a "lovely old house in Naperville" offers an "inventive American" menu by "hands-on" toque-owner Ted Cizma (opening chef of the much-lauded, late lamented Grace); with "so much potential", though, it's yet to live up to the high expectations of some surveyors who cite "ups and downs" in food and service.

Eli's the Place for Steaks [S] 21 | 18 | 21 | $42

215 E. Chicago Ave. (Michigan Ave.), 312-642-1393

◪ "Don't change a thing" say diehard fans of this "old-fashioned" Streeterville chop shop slicing "huge portions" of "top-notch" beef and "amazing cheesecake" in a "manly", "relaxed dining room" run by a staff that "treats you courteously"; still, a new generation grumbles it's "your father's idea of a steakhouse" that serves "yesteryear's food" and "needs a face-lift."

El Jardin 🖪   15 | 13 | 14 | $20

3335 N. Clark St. (bet. Addison St. & Belmont Ave.), 773-528-6775

☑ Surveyors say the "average food" at this "reliable" Wrigleyville Mexican pales in comparison to its "killer – and I mean killer – margaritas" ("what's in those, anyway?"), but at least its "brunch is the best hangover cure around", as long as you avoid its "great outdoor seating area", which can be "too loud and crowded even for the Cubs and college crowds."

El Nandu 🖪   ∇ 19 | 14 | 19 | $18

2731 W. Fullerton Ave. (bet. California & Fairfield Aves.), 773-278-0900

■ Fans fancy this "cozy" "haunt" in Logan Square for "el yummo" Argentinean fare such as "excellent beef", "delicious chimichurri dishes" and "great empanadas" washed down with "best-kept-secret sangria"; there's "not much for the vegetarians", but carnivores appreciate getting "good food for the dollar"; N.B. a guitarist spices up the night Thursday–Saturday.

El Presidente ◑🖪   ∇ 14 | 10 | 14 | $15

2558 N. Ashland Ave. (Wrightwood Ave.), 773-525-7938

☑ "Where else can you get *chilaquiles* at 3 AM on Xmas?" – so surveyors sum up the appeal of this "24-hour" spot serving "cheap" and "basic Mexican" fare on "busy Ashland Avenue" at the Northwest edge of Lincoln Park; still, the peevish protest about "run-of-the-mill" food and "vinyl decor" that amounts to "zero atmosphere."

EMILIO'S TAPAS 🖪   21 | 19 | 19 | $27

444 W. Fullerton Pkwy. (Clark St.), 773-327-5100
4100 W. Roosevelt Rd. (Manheim Rd), Hillside, 708-547-7177
EMILIO'S TAPAS SOL Y NIEVE 🖪
215 E. Ohio St. (bet. Fairbanks Ct. & St. Clair St.), 312-467-7177
EMILIO'S TAPAS LA RIOJA 🖪
230 W. Front St. (Wheaton Ave.), Wheaton, 630-653-7177

■ Each of Emilio Gervilla's tapas spots has its loyalists, but a quorum clamors for the "huge variety" of their "intensely flavored" and "authentically Spanish" "grazing goodies" (including "daily specials that yield tasty treasures"), all "reasonably priced" and served in "lively" yet "relaxing" settings that add up to "an utterly charming experience."

Emperor's Choice ◑🖪   21 | 13 | 18 | $24

2238 S. Wentworth Ave. (Cermak Rd.), 312-225-8800

☑ Though some would "prefer to keep this place a secret", word is out that this Chinatown "classic" Cantonese-

Mandarin offers "always-fresh" "Chinese seafood like no other" – including what some say is the "best Peking lobster" around – in a "noisy, authentic" atmosphere; the emperor's new naysayers, though, deem it "not so choice anymore" and decry the "dreary", "dated" decor.

Entre Nous S   24 | 25 | 24 | $53
The Fairmont Hotel, 200 N. Columbus Dr. (Wacker Dr.), 312-565-7997
■ Just between us, the Fairmont Hotel's remaining restaurant (Primavera has packed it in) is a "romantic", "elegant" destination for "superb" New American dining; patrons feel "graciously spoiled" by "impeccable service" in a "formal setting" offering "lots of classy comfort" and live entertainment some nights; N.B. the Food rating may not reflect a post-*Survey* chef change.

Erawan Royal Thai Cuisine S   ▽ 23 | 25 | 26 | $52
729 N. Clark St. (Superior St.), 312-642-6888
■ River North's "high-end" Siamese "newcomer" is "pricey but well worth it", considering the "quality ingredients and creative presentations" of its "super meals" from two menus (one traditional, the other "Thai-Western fusion"), both supported by a "terrific wine list"; the "elegant", "beautiful decor" and "polite service" also help ensure a "great night out"; N.B. both owner and chef are veterans of top-rated Arun's.

Erie Cafe S   21 | 19 | 22 | $39
536 W. Erie St. (Kingsbury St.), 312-266-2300
◪ "Now *this* is a steakhouse!" cry cronies of River North's cousin of Gene & Georgetti and EJ's Place (separately owned by members of one *famiglia*), an "old-school" spot "for schmoozing with clients and associates", where the "simple" Italian "man's food" is "top-quality", the service is "pro" and the location "looks like a movie set"; still, the "uninspired" say it "lacks charm."

erwin, an american cafe & bar S   23 | 21 | 23 | $36
2925 N. Halsted St. (Oakdale Ave.), 773-528-7200
■ "They care and it shows" at this "quiet charmer" in Lakeview, where chef-owner Erwin Drechsler's "deft touch" yields "outstanding" New American cuisine that's "uncomplicated" yet "sophisticated" and offered on "seasonal menus as varied as the Chicago weather", making it "worth many visits"; the "neighborhood feel" may "lack buzz" ("this isn't see-and-be-seen"), but it's "warm, cozy" and "without pretense."

ESPN Zone S   12 | 19 | 13 | $20
43 E. Ohio St. (Wabash Ave.), 312-644-3776
◪ Sideliners kick back at this "big, boisterous interactive-games" chain outpost in River North, calling it a "sports-

lovers' paradise" with American fare that's "better than the ballpark (and more fun)" and predicting you'll come away with a case of "tube envy from so many big TVs"; spoilsports say it's a "sensory-overload" "spectacle only", as the "typical" bar food is "better left to the tourists."

Ethiopian Diamond [S] ▽ 21 | 12 | 17 | $17

6120 N. Broadway (Glen Lake Ave.), 773-338-6100

■ When white-bread Midwesterners wish for "food like somebody *else's* mom used to make", they head to this "feisty", "fun" spot in Edgewater for "tasty and unique" Ethiopian dishes – including many "healthy vegetarian choices" – that are not only "authentic" and "spicy" (i.e. "not Americanized") but a "value" too; good thing, since the draw is definitely "not the decor."

Ethiopian Village [S] ▽ 14 | 10 | 15 | $17

(aka Ethio Cafe)

3462 N. Clark St. (bet. Cornelia & Newport Aves.), 773-929-8300

◪ This Wrigleyville restaurant may have two names, but it serves just one cuisine – "authentic Ethiopian"; the "communal eating" makes it "fun" "for a group", and its "interesting buffet" is a "good way to try this food" for first-timers (with lots of choices "for vegetarians"); nevertheless, many are "lukewarm" toward the "disappointing food."

EVEREST 27 | 27 | 28 | $74

One Financial Pl., 440 S. La Salle Blvd., 40th fl. (Congress Pkwy.), 312-663-8920

■ "Dress to the teeth and allow lots of time" for a "prime-dining" "splurge" at this "heavenly" "high-end" haven 40 floors above the Loop; chef Jean "Joho has the touch", turning out "breathtaking" New "French haute cuisine" with "an emphasis on Alsatian" flavors "backed" by an "amazing" "booklike wine list" and "superior service"; the "opulent" "safari" interior has detractors, but all are awed by its "stellar views."

Evergreen ◐ [S] – | – | – | M

2411 S. Wentworth Ave. (24th St.), 312-225-8898

More upscale than most of its neighbors on this stretch of Wentworth in Chinatown, this charming Cantonese-Mandarin standout is an evergreen favorite for Hong Su chicken and kung pao beef, along with a few seafood surprises like giant clams in black bean sauce, served on white tablecloths in a large and attractive room.

Ezuli ◐ [S] ▽ 20 | 16 | 16 | $22

1415 N. Milwaukee Ave. (Wood St.), 773-227-8200

■ Named after a Haitian love goddess, this "fun, electric place" in Wicker Park attracts worshipers with "wonderful Caribbean cuisine" such as "awesome jerk chicken", "piña colada bread pudding to die for" and other "flavorful", "interesting food"; the setting is "hip" and "trendy but not pretentious", and a "hostess dancing" to DJ music six nights a week adds to the "cool atmosphere."

Fadó Irish Pub S   13 | 19 | 14 | $21 |
100 W. Grand Ave. (Clark St.), 312-836-0066
☑ "Good times" are reported at this "fun" River North link in an Irish-themed "national chain" by fans who call it a "favorite watering hole" with "great music and decor", an "interesting" layout that "lends itself to socializing" and some "decent" "pub grub"; separatists say "go for the Guinness, not the food", claiming that the long-ago "authentic feel" is actually "manufactured for tourists."

Famous Dave's S   18 | 16 | 16 | $20 |
1631 W. Lake St. (½ mi. east of Hwy. 53), Addison, 630-261-0100
113 S. Western Ave. (south of Main St.), Carpentersville, 847-428-9190
Yorktown Ctr., 206B Yorktown Ctr. (Highland Ave.), Lombard, 630-620-6363
1126 E. Ogden Ave. (Burlington Ave.), Naperville, 630-428-3500
948 S. Barrington Rd. (Ramblewood Dr.), Streamwood, 630-483-2480
99 Townline Rd. (bet. Aspen & Deerpath Drs.), Vernon Hills, 847-549-9933
Additional locations throughout the Chicago area
☑ "Tasty" ribs are the business of this "fun, casual" "roadhouse" chain in the Northwest and West Suburbs (the Downtown location has been sold to and renamed by Isaac Hayes) where the tickled tell us the "finger-licking food" "done right at the right price" is "worth its weight in BBQ sauce"; the fickle find fault with the "formula" feel, "ordinary" output and "iffy" service.

Father & Son Pizza ◑S   17 | 13 | 16 | $19 |
2475 N. Milwaukee Ave. (Sacramento Blvd.), 773-252-2620
5691 N. Milwaukee Ave. (Markham Ave.), 773-774-2620
Marcello's ◑S
645 W. North Ave. (bet. Halsted & Larrabee Sts.), 312-654-2560
☑ These "informal" fraternal Logan Square and Northwest Side pizza-and-Italian places have partialists who prize their signature thin-and-crispy 'za and other "Italian food at value" prices, though panners pooh-pooh the product as "passable" and the pies as "just adequate"; similarly, some say Marcello's is a "good, inexpensive restaurant", while others say it's "trying to be upscale" but missing the mark.

Feast S   20 | 18 | 17 | $27 |
1616 N. Damen Ave. (North Ave.), 773-772-7100
■ Feasters fawn over this "hip" Bucktown New American, saying it's "a good local place that's just fancy enough"; chef Debra Sharpe brings "a touch of whimsy" to her "creative"

yet "down-home" fare, which is served up in an "inviting" and "funky atmosphere" – in short, "for both the eyes and the palate, the name says it all!"; P.S. there's "delightful" outdoor dining too.

Filippo's S
22 | 16 | 20 | $27

2211 N. Clybourn Ave. (Webster Ave.), 773-528-2211
■ Greedy gluttons are "glad no one knows this" "cozy" Clybourn Corridor Southern "Italian eatery", "one of the undiscovered treasures" in town that "carefully prepares" "terrific", "dependable" dishes, including "some of best pastas in Chicago"; a "friendly staff" and "comfortable prices" contribute to the "homey feeling"; P.S. the kitchen's "very accommodating with special requests."

Fireplace Inn, The ●S
18 | 16 | 17 | $26

1448 N. Wells St. (bet. North Ave. & Schiller St.), 312-664-5264
☑ It may be "nothing fancy", but loyalists nevertheless "love those ribs" at this Old Town BBQ "joint" that's been "packing them in like sardines" since 1969; a few firebrands grumble over "generic" grub, "dark" digs and "slow" service, but the "nice outdoor garden" and sports on TV help keep it a "neighborhood favorite."

5 Boroughs Delicatessen, The
16 | 10 | 14 | $12

738 N. Wells St. (bet. Chicago Ave. & Superior St.),
312-915-0188
☑ Dedicated defenders of this North River yearling insist it's a "Gotham"-style deli with "good corned beef", "bagels an East Coaster can respect" and "matzo ball soup that will cure the dead"; foes feel that it's "inauthentic" and "expensive", kvetching it's "more like NJ than NY."

Flat Top Grill S
18 | 14 | 15 | $19

319 W. North Ave. (Orleans St.), 312-787-7676
3200 N. Southport Ave. (Belmont Ave.), 773-665-8100
1000 W. Washington Blvd. (Carpenter St.), 312-829-4800
707 Church St. (bet. Orrington & Sherman Aves.), Evanston,
847-570-0100
726 Lake St. (Oak Park Ave.), Oak Park, 708-358-8200
☑ "Go hungry" and "choose your own fresh ingredients, then watch 'em cook it all up" at this "fun" (if "hectic") chain of Asian-American stir-fry stops where "lots of good choices" and a "helpful staff" allow inter-activists to be as "creative as they want"; flat-liners flame the "DIY" concept, claiming it "all tastes the same", but admit it's "a great place for kids."

Flavor S
– | – | – | M

6818 W. North Ave. (Oak Park Ave.), 773-889-3528
Westward-ho the wagons (or SUVs) to this Far West newcomer, a cozy and modestly priced New American that aims to please with a flavorful lunch menu of wraps,

salads and sandwiches, and signature dinner dishes such
as seared sea bass with shiitakes followed by dessert
'egg rolls' of cookie dough; a small BYO lounge welcomes
smokers, and garden dining is available.

Fluky's 🅂🚭   17 | 10 | 14 | $8 |
The Shops at Northridge, 520 N. Michigan Ave. (bet. Michigan &
Ohio Sts.), 312-245-0702
6821 N. Western Ave. (Pratt Blvd.), 773-274-3652
Lincolnwood Town Ctr., 3333 W. Touhy Ave. (McCormick St.),
Lincolnwood, 847-677-7726
3061 Dundee Rd. (Landwehr Rd.), Northbrook, 847-272-9215
◪ Canine critics give "two paws up" to the "hot dogs from
heaven" served at these fast food "fixtures" where faithful
followers "bow [wow] in homage" to a "classic" "dawg"
"done right" as well as "good grilled onions and fries" and
"a not-so-bad chicken-breast sandwich" too; connoisseurs
snarl they're "not real contenders."

Flying Chicken 🅂   ⎯ | ⎯ | ⎯ | I |
3811 N. Lincoln Ave. (Wolcott Ave.), 773-477-1090
Though this Lincoln Square Colombian's specialty is
rotisserie chicken, the only flying those birds are doing is off
the plate, as are generous portions of oxtail or hen soup,
empanadas, churrascos and sides of yucca and plantains
that are worth a try; carryout may be your best bet, though,
since the bare-bones ambiance is somewhat lacking.

Fond de la Tour   23 | 23 | 23 | $47 |
40 N. Tower Rd. (bet. Butterfield & Meyers Rds.), Oak Brook,
630-620-1500
◪ Folks for whom "consistency counts" are fond of the
"traditional French" favorites on offer at this "elegant"
West Suburban bistro with "nice decor", "one of the few
untrendy gems left" where "the food and service remain so
special"; though some detractors dismiss it as "overpriced"
and "a bit dated", most say it's "an oldie but a goodie."

Fondue Stube 🅂   19 | 12 | 17 | $29 |
2717 W. Peterson Ave. (Fairfield Ave.), 773-784-2200
◪ People who pine to "play with their food" find "a
splendid change of pace from traditional dining" at this
"simple treasure" in Rogers Park with "fondue as good as
in Switzerland" and "friendly service" in a "quaint, cozy"
room; nonetheless, yet-to-be-impressed yodelers yell
"you'll need a Swiss bank account for what it charges"
and yawn that the decor "could do with an overhaul."

foodlife 🅂   17 | 15 | 14 | $16 |
Water Tower Pl., 835 N. Michigan Ave., mezzanine level
(bet. Chestnut & Pearson Sts.), 312-335-3663
◪ "More intriguing than the usual food court", this "fun"
"shopping stop" "at Water Tower" Place is a wonderland

of "choices, choices, choices", with 13 kitchens serving everything from Asian to Cajun to Italian to Mexican to Thai to all-American burgers and fries; the "cafeteria"-style setup makes it a "great place for on-the-run eating", though some say the "format is confusing" and "not cheap", warning "watch out for" the "automatic service charge" of 7.5 percent.

Fortunato ●〕S   – | – | – | E |
2005 W. Division St. (Damen Ave.), 773-645-7200
Chef-owner Jennifer Newbury's new Ukrainian Village venture explores an ingredient-driven approach to Italian hearth cooking, with a seasonal focus on organic vegetables, fresh-made pasta, and meat and seafood prepared within her glass-enclosed kitchen's wood-burning oven (and paired with native vinos); like the cuisine it serves, the stylish earth-toned dining room conjures the feel of the *campagna*.

Founders Hill
Restaurant & Brewery S   – | 16 | 16 | $20 |
(fka Founders Hill Brewing Co.)
5200 Main St. (Grove St.), Downers Grove, 630-963-2739
■ The "beer's the thing" at this West Suburban "hangout" "geared to the young drinking crowd" that is known for creating its own selection of "uniquely flavored" "specialty brews" on site; nevertheless, suds-swillers "hope" that "a recent change in ownership", a new chef (John Ayaleanos) in the kitchen and a "new" American menu will "improve" its culinary fortunes.

Four Farthings S   17 | 17 | 17 | $24 |
2060 N. Cleveland Ave. (bet. Dickens & Lincoln Aves.), 773-935-2060
■ "A second kitchen to many" folks in the Lincoln Park neighborhood, this "local joint" boasts a "comfortable pub atmosphere" and is "nicer than your typical bar", featuring "some high-end entrees" such as several "surf 'n' turf" selections that supplement its Traditional American menu of "great salads and burgers"; P.S. it's "especially great outdoors" on the "nice" 75-seat patio that "welcomes well-behaved dogs."

Fox & Obel Cafe S   ▽ 26 | 19 | 21 | $12 |
401 E. Illinois St. (McClurg Ct.), 312-379-0112
■ The "crowds are starting to show up" at this American cafe "in the upscale market" of the same name (located at the corner of McClurg Court in Streeterville) for "excellent light meals" including "fantastic soups", "great breads" and "delicious sandwiches prepared with fabulous ingredients", as well as "good" pastries and coffee; to some, it's the "best new quick-food" stop around for breakfast, lunch or dinner.

FRANCESCA'S AMICI 🆂   24   19   20 $31
174 N. York Rd. (bet. North Ave. & 2nd St.), Elmhurst,
630-279-7970

FRANCESCA'S BRYN MAWR 🆂
1039 W. Bryn Mawr Ave. (Kenmore Ave.), 773-506-9261

FRANCESCA'S BY THE RIVER 🆂
200 S. Second St. (Illinois St.), St. Charles, 630-587-8221

FRANCESCA'S CAMPAGNA 🆂
127 W. Main St. (2nd St.), West Dundee, 847-844-7099

FRANCESCA'S FIORE 🆂
7407 Madison St. (Des Plaines Ave.), Forest Park, 708-771-3063

FRANCESCA'S INTIMO 🆂
293 E. Illinois St. (bet. Bank Ln. & Western Ave.), Lake Forest,
847-735-9235

FRANCESCA'S NORTH
Northbrook Shopping Ctr., 1145 Church St. (Shermer St.),
Northbrook, 847-559-0260

FRANCESCA'S ON TAYLOR 🆂
1400 W. Taylor St. (Loomis St.), 312-829-2828

FRANCESCA'S TAVOLA 🆂
208 S. Arlington Heights Rd. (NW Hwy.), Arlington Heights,
847-394-3950

LA SORELLA DI FRANCESCA 🆂
18 W. Jefferson Ave. (bet. Main & Washington Sts.),
Naperville, 630-961-2706

■ 'Mama' Mia Francesca (Scott Harris' Wrigleyville
original) has spread her signature style – "frequently
changing" menus of "hearty", "creative" and "reasonably"
priced dishes from Rome and the surrounding areas of
Tuscany, Umbria and Lazio – throughout the city and
suburbs with her fast-growing group of "stylish" daughters,
"reliable" and "consistently lively" gals who set a "family-
yet-upscale" mood.

Francesco's Hole in the Wall 🆂⊘   24   16   21 $29
254 Skokie Blvd. (bet. Dundee & Lake Cook Rds.), Northbrook,
847-272-0155

☑ "A sauce slurper's symphony" resounds off the "bare
brick" walls of this "ridiculously tiny", "old-style" North
Suburban "hangout" serving "fantastic, homemade"
Southern Italian fare fans "dream about"; some wallflowers
wonder, though, if it's worth the "long wait" for a spot in
its "cramped quarters" and suggest you'll either "need
to know the owners" or "go at an unpopular hour" "to get
seated"; N.B. cash only.

Freddy's Ribhouse 🆂   _   _   _   M
1555 N. Sheffield Ave. (North Ave.), 312-377-7427
26 W. Hubbard St. (Dearborn St.), 312-863-7427
These rib-wrangling brothers tickle tasters with their "top-
tier BBQ at mid-tier prices", including "great babybacks"
and "crisp fries"; the Lincoln Park original features an

early-20th-century look while the River North sibling has more of a sports-bar feel, but both locations offer a "kid-friendly" atmosphere and parent-friendly libations ("try Freddy's lager!") as well as outdoor dining for that true, open-air barbecue experience.

Froggy's French Cafe   24   19   24 $36
306 Green Bay Rd. (Highwood Ave.), Highwood, 847-433-7080
■ "Authentic, simple French cooking" with a strong seafood focus from a "friendly and approachable" toque together with "casual but attentive service" from a "knowledgeable staff" and a "comfortable, earthy European" ambiance render this "dependable", "busy" bistro in the North Suburbs an "old favorite" of Francophiles; "try the chef's menu, an ever-changing sampler served in five courses."

FRONTERA GRILL   26   22   22 $34
445 N. Clark St. (bet. Hubbard & Illinois Sts.), 312-661-1434
■ "A Chicago legend and deservedly so", this River Norther (the more casual older brother of top-rated Topolobampo) is "the one that started it all", showing "what depth Mexican food can have" with "charming" chef-owner Rick Bayless' "world-class" "died-and-gone-to-heaven" creations; add in "an interesting variety" of "fabulous margaritas" and "great service" from a "professional staff" and it's no wonder "it can be nearly impossible to get in."

Furama 🖸   ▽ 17   10   13 $19
4936 N. Broadway (Argyle St.), 773-271-1161
2828 S. Wentworth Ave. (31st St.), 312-225-6888
🗹 "An excellent variety" of "reliable dim sum" is served "from numerous carts" seven days at week at this Uptown and Chinatown duo where a Cantonese-Mandarin "menu is also available"; still, some say the fare is "so-so" and take a dim view of the "slow service" and "old-looking decor."

GABRIEL'S   27   24   26 $51
310 Green Bay Rd. (Highwood Ave.), Highwood, 847-433-0031
■ "A most enjoyable evening" awaits at this "classic" New French–Italian on the North Shore where "sincerity is evident" in the "excellent presentation" of "top-notch", "terrific food"; the "creative" kitchen is overseen by "scrupulously attentive" "hands-on chef-owner" Gabriel Viti, and the "elegant but casual" dining room is staffed by "real professionals"; P.S. grape groupies gloat it has "one of the best wine lists" around.

Gale Street Inn 🖸   19   16   18 $25
4914 N. Milwaukee Ave. (Lawrence Ave.), 773-725-1300
935 Diamond Lake Rd. (bet. Rtes. 45 & 83), Mundelein, 847-566-1090
■ "Everyone makes you feel welcome" at this Suburban Northwest–Northwest Side American duo (unaffiliated for

14 years) known for "tender, tasty, meaty ribs" "you can cut with a spoon"; those who "make the trip to Jefferson Park" will find a "traditional" "supper-club" ambiance, while "beautiful views" of Diamond Lake greet guests of the Mundelein sibling, which recently moved across the street.

Gaylord India S | 20 | 14 | 19 | $23 |

678 N. Clark St. (Huron St.), 312-664-1700
555 Mall Dr. (Higgins Rd.), Schaumburg, 847-619-3300
■ Serving an "extensive menu" of "complex, exotic" and "authentic [Northern] Indian food" (and some Southern specialties) like "rich flavorful curries" "as good as on Devon" Street in Chicago's Little India, these "reliable" city and suburban subcontinentals are also prized for "friendly service"; P.S. the "bargain lunch buffets" offer "great choices and good value."

Geja's Cafe S | 22 | 22 | 21 | $38 |

340 W. Armitage Ave. (bet. Clark St. & Lincoln Ave.), 773-281-9101
■ For "something a little different", "take your honey" to this Lincoln Park fondue "favorite", a "rustic", "romantic getaway" where "it's fun to cook your" own "nice, leisurely meal" and sample an "adventurous wine list" while "live guitar music" "adds to the ambiance"; "plan to get your clothes dry-cleaned" afterward, though, as that "hot-oil smell" can cling (don't worry – it's "worth it").

Gene & Georgetti | 23 | 16 | 20 | $46 |

500 N. Franklin St. (Illinois St.), 312-527-3718
☑ "Forget the rest" say fans of River North's "old-time Chicago" "steakhouse saloon", a "famous" "institution" with a "men's club atmosphere" that opened in 1941 and just "gets better with age" thanks to "big slabs" of "great steaks (and they know it)" and "good service (if they know you)"; contrary carnivores claim it's become a "caricature of itself" and slam the "surly" staff and "run-down decor."

Genesee Depot S | 21 | 16 | 21 | $26 |

3736 N. Broadway (bet. Grace St. & Waveland Ave.),
773-528-6990
■ A Boys Town "BYO bargain", this "unpretentious" Traditional American established in 1974 is still chuggin' along, "nurturing" its regulars with "friendly service" and "yummy", "priced-right" fare that's "like home cooking for a special occasion"; the "rustic" dining room behind its "quaint storefront" may be "unpretentious", but it does offer a "nice", "homey atmosphere."

Giannotti Steak House S | 22 | 17 | 20 | $35 |

17 W. 400 22nd St. (bet. Midwest Rd. & Rte. 83),
Oakbrook Terrace, 630-833-2700
☑ "Try the eight-finger cavatelli" (the signature dish) advise aficionados of this "manly" Italian steakhouse situated in a

West Suburban strip mall; its traditional menu offers a trip back to a "lost era", when "good food" was "abundant", and its "nice bar" features "good [live] entertainment" most nights; still, faultfinders fret about "heavy" fare that's priced "on the high side for what you get."

GIBSONS STEAKHOUSE ●S   25 | 21 | 23 | $48

1028 N. Rush St. (Bellevue Pl.), 312-266-8999
Doubletree Hotel, 5464 N. River Rd. (bet. Balmoral & Bryn Mawr Aves.), Rosemont, 847-928-9900

◪ "To see and be seen", a "forty-something crowd" of "power brokers", "glitterati", "wanna-bes", "pinky ring"-ers and "major league ballplayers" packs this "exciting", "testosterone-filled hot spot" and "watering hole", an "expense-account heaven" for "A-1 martinis" and "obscene portions" of "excellent" "fresh meat"; those who find it a "noisy" "Gold Coast cliché" report its offshoot in "Rosemont is a little quieter."

Gilardi's S   21 | 21 | 21 | $31

23397 N. Rte. 45 (Rte. 21), Vernon Hills, 847-634-1811
■ "Consistently good", "classic Italian home cooking" lures loyalists to this Suburban Northwest "hidden treasure"; the "tranquil" and "romantic" setting is reminiscent of "going to a relative's" "neat old house" with a "great front porch", and the "friendly host and staff" "make you feel like a part of the family", helping make this a "nice place to go."

Gino's Steak House S   ∇ 21 | 17 | 20 | $33

16299 S. Wallace Ave. (163rd St.), Harvey, 708-331-4393
◪ Since 1950, this South Suburban steakhouse stalwart (a senior sibling of the Millennium Steaks & Chops shops) has been grilling up a "great bone-in steak" and other "honest, down-to-earth" fare in an "enjoyable" environment replete with the original stained-glass windows; those who find it not so genial, however, lament that it's "loud" and avow the victuals are merely "average."

Gioco S   21 | 21 | 19 | $40

1312 S. Wabash Ave. (13th St.), 312-939-3870
■ "The South Loop comes alive with good Italian food" proclaim partisans of this "pioneer" located "off the beaten path", where "great chef" Corcoran O'Connor creates cuisine that's "innovative" and "hearty" (if somewhat "expensive"), including some "standout specials"; the "ultra-chic", "inviting" atmosphere of its "fun" former-speakeasy setting includes a "cool bar" and "great patio seating in summer."

Giordano's S   18 | 11 | 14 | $17

5159 S. Pulaski Rd. (bet. Archer & 51st Sts.), 773-582-7676 ●
5927 W. Irving Park Rd. (Austin Ave.), 773-736-5553
310 W. Randolph St. (Franklin St.), 312-201-1441

(continued)
Giordano's
730 N. Rush St. (Superior St.), 312-951-0747
5311 S. Blackstone Ave. (53rd St.), 773-947-0200
500 Davis St. (Hinman Ave.), Evanston, 847-475-5000 ◖
Crest Creek Sq., 796 Royal St. George (Ogden Ave.),
Naperville, 630-717-6446
17 W. 280 W. 22nd St. (bet. Meyers & Midwest Sts.),
Oakbrook Terrace, 630-620-7979
Additional locations throughout the Chicago area
◪ This "casual" city and suburban chain draws its share of
supporters in Chicago's deep-dish derby with "impressive
stuffed pizzas" (and "good thin-crust" too, with a "wide
spectrum of toppings"); nevertheless, some 'za-lots claim
it's "inconsistent" and sneer that service "can be lacking."

Gladys Luncheonette ◖ S ⌿   ▽ 26 | 17 | 21 | $16
4527 S. Indiana Ave. (45th St.), 773-548-4566
◪ Ever since owner Gladys Holcomb arrived from Memphis
in the mid-'40s, this "traditional and homey" institution
in what some call a dicey section of Hyde Park has been
serving "Soul Food at its best" – from favorites like ham
hocks, catfish, collard greens and sweet potato pie to
more Yankee-challenging specialties like the curiously
complimented "awful good brains 'n' eggs."

Glen Ellyn Brewing Company S   16 | 16 | 17 | $24
433 N. Main St. (Duane St.), Glen Ellyn, 630-942-1140
◪ From a "decent menu (for a brewery)", this "pleasant"
West Suburban American offers a "simple but dependable"
assortment of "hearty food"; those who find the grub "so-
so" and the service "spotty" suggest "go for the beer" on
tap, a rotating selection of six proprietary creations by
brew-master Mike Engelke.

Gold Coast Dogs   19 | 8 | 13 | $9
159 N. Wabash Ave. (bet. Lake & Randolph Sts.),
312-917-1677 S
17 S. Wabash Ave. (Madison St.), 312-578-1133
2 N. Riverside Dr. (bet. Canal St. & Madison Ave.),
312-879-0447 ⌿
Union Station, 225 S. Canal St. (Jackson Blvd.),
312-258-8585 S ⌿
Midway Airport, food court, 773-735-6789 ◖ S
O'Hare Int'l Airport, Terminal 3, 773-462-9942 S
O'Hare Int'l Airport, Terminal 5, 773-462-0125 S ⌿
Old Orchard Shopping Ctr., 275 Old Orchard Arcade
(bet. Golf Rd. & Skokie Blvd.), Skokie, 847-674-4171 S ⌿
◪ Though it's "a travesty they closed the original location"
on State Street, dogged loyalists who "love that char-
broiled taste" still "go out of their way" for the "great
grease" at this "classic" city and North Suburban chain of
"hot doggers" that also serves chicken and "good burgers"

(including a "spicy veggie" version); true, there are "no frills", but then again "you're paying for none."

Goose Island Wrigleyville S   15 | 16 | 16 | $19
1800 N. Clybourn Ave. (Sheffield Ave.), 312-915-0071
3535 N. Clark St. (Addison St.), 773-832-9040
■ Microbrew mavens maintain there's "always a smile" at these "nothing-fancy" homegrown brewpubs serving Lincoln Park and Wrigleyville; though "both locations offer" "above-average pub grub" to go with their "awesome selection" of "fresh beer" made "on the premises", some warn "steer clear of anything but" the "good burgers" and "terrific chips."

Graziano's Brick Oven Pizza S   ▽ 22 | 21 | 21 | $22
5960 W. Touhy Ave. (Lehigh Ave.), Niles, 847-647-4096
■ Northwest Suburbanites credit this "delightful, if noisy, family Italian" for a "steady" kitchen that dishes up "huge portions" of "terrific food" like its signature bowtie pasta with vodka sauce, a "great bottomless salad bowl" and, as the name suggests, pizza; "good service", a "casual" vibe and "comfortable decor" with movie posters on the walls make it a popular "local place."

Greek Islands S   20 | 18 | 19 | $24
200 S. Halsted St. (Adams St.), 312-782-9855 ●
300 E. 22nd St. (Highland Ave.), Lombard, 630-932-4545
■ "One of the most consistent in Greektown", the "Halsted location" of this Hellenic pair has been "a favorite for 30 years", and its younger West Suburban sibling has fans too; regulars muse each is "a real value" for "well-executed standards" of "Greek comfort food", "efficiently served" by "sprinting waiters" in a "busy, noisy" "family" setting.

Green Dolphin Street S   20 | 21 | 18 | $43
2200 N. Ashland Ave. (Webster Ave.), 773-395-0066
◪ "What more do you need" for nights beyond forgetting ask aficionados of this Lincoln Park New American supper club that supplies the setting with "great food, service and ambiance", as well as "excellent" "live entertainment", "all under one roof"; even so, the jaded aren't jazzed by the "overpriced" and "small portions" or the sometimes "inattentive" staff (though diners do appreciate getting "free admission to the lounge").

Green Door Tavern S   15 | 18 | 17 | $19
678 N. Orleans St. (Huron St.), 312-664-5496
■ "Oozing atmosphere that can't be replicated", this "classic" American premiered as a 1921 Prohibition-era speakeasy in a River North structure built just after the Great Chicago Fire of 1871; folks "go to see" its "fun" "paraphernalia" – a "unique" assemblage of fire helmets,

political mementos, sports pennants, et al. – more than for its "huge burgers" and other "standard bar food."

Grill on the Alley, The 🆂 | 19 | 21 | 20 | $41 |
Westin Hotel, 909 N. Michigan Ave. (Delaware Pl.), 312-255-9009
☑ A two-year-old offshoot of the Beverly Hills original, this Streeterville steakhouse in the Westin strikes some as a "good place to relax after shopping" or to convene for a "power lunch", with "great American cuisine (for a hotel restaurant)" served amid dark oak furnishings and "loads of fun art on the walls"; critics caution, though, that it "has not lived up to expectations" yet.

Grillroom, The 🆂 | 19 | 16 | 18 | $34 |
33 W. Monroe St. (bet. Dearborn & State Sts.), 312-960-0000
☑ Loopsters like the "innovative preparations" of this "classy" "sleeper" of a steak-and-seafood house, especially for a "business lunch", "getting a drink and dinner after work" or "before going to the Shubert Theatre" directly across the street; still, the less impressed say simply that it's a "good" but "not-very-special" "standby."

Hackney's 🆂 | 18 | 14 | 17 | $18 |
733 S. Dearborn St. (Polk St.), 312-461-1116
1241 Harms Rd. (Lake Ave.), Glenview, 847-724-5577
1514 E. Lake Ave. (bet. Sunset Ridge & Waukegan Rds.),
Glenview, 847-724-7171
880 N. Old Rand Rd. (Main St.), Lake Zurich, 847-438-2103
12300 S. La Grange Rd. (123rd St.), Palos Park, 708-448-8300
241 S. Milwaukee Ave. (Dundee Rd.), Wheeling, 847-537-2100
■ "Big burgers are the big draw here" at these "suburban classics" and their newer Downtown sibling where "you always know what you're going to get" with your "thick" patty – their famous "heart-stopping onion loaf" and "average service"; the original Harms Road location has a "dark" "martini-on-the-rocks atmosphere", while the city branch is more "cheerful."

Hai Yen 🆂 | ▽ 19 | 11 | 14 | $18 |
1055 W. Argyle St. (Broadway), 773-561-4077
☑ While this "bright" and "lively" Edgewater eatery's "authentic" Vietnamese cuisine (with some Chinese dishes) is "very good" and the signature Seven Courses of "Beef dinner is wonderful", protestors propose that the "nothing-fancy" decor and "noisy" atmosphere make for an "unappealing room" and say that the "eager-to-please" staff provides somewhat "disorganized service."

Half Shell ◗🆂⊅ | 21 | 10 | 14 | $26 |
676 W. Diversey Pkwy. (Orchard St.), 773-549-1773
■ "Awesome-shellfish" seekers dig this "delightfully dingy" and "dumpy" "underground dive", a Lakeview "hole in the wall" (or should we say floor?) that's been "going for years"

on the strength of some of "the best crab legs in town"; with such "great seafood" "at reasonable prices", "love"-blinded lauders swear that the "service is good – even when they yell at you!"

Happy Chef Dim Sum House 🌙 [S] ▽ 21 | 6 | 12 | $15

2164 S. Archer Ave. (Cermak Rd.), 312-808-3689

◪ "Even if they don't have carts", this "inexpensive" spot in the Chinatown Square Mall is an "always-busy" "standout" thanks to "always-good" "Hong Kong–style dim sum"; still, the "crowd"-conscious complain it's a "madhouse on weekends", and the style-savvy say that using the plastic tablecloths as "garbage bags is just a bit too pragmatic."

Hard Rock Cafe [S] 12 | 20 | 15 | $21

63 W. Ontario St. (Clark St.), 312-943-2252

◪ Starstruck surveyors say the chance to "eat in a rock museum" makes this "trendy" River North headbanger "a fun place for all ages" and report that the American eats are "surprisingly good for such a touristy spot"; however, cons criticize the "mediocre food and service" (not to mention all that "noise"), and simply advise "get your T-shirt and go."

Harry Caray's Rosemont [S] 20 | 19 | 19 | $32

33 W. Kinzie St. (Dearborn St.), 312-828-0966

Holiday Inn, 10233 W. Higgins Rd. (Mannheim St.), Rosemont, 847-699-1200

Harry Caray's Seventh Inning Stretch [S]

Midway Airport, 5757 S. Cicero Ave. (55th St.), 773-948-6300

◪ A triple-header of tributes to their late namesake, these Downtown and airport area Italian steakhouses offer "casual dining" "for baseball and steak fans" within "friendly" confines full of "Cubs kitsch" and other "sports memorabilia"; the opposing team, though, curtly counters they're "below par."

Harry's Velvet Room 🌙 [S] ▽ 15 | 21 | 15 | $31

56 W. Illinois St. (bet. Clark & Dearborn Sts.), 312-527-5600

◪ "Funky, cool and velvety", this "stylin'", "smoky" River North American "joint just oozes sex", earning it the lounge-lizard vote as the "best late-night fun" "spot for after-dinner drinks and people-watching"; those who "have never understood why it offers meals" say stick to the "good appetizers" or "just have the martinis."

Harvest on Huron 22 | 20 | 20 | $42

217 W. Huron St. (bet. Franklin & Wells Sts.), 312-587-9600

◪ "Hip, fun", "sophisticated dining" is on the menu at this River Norther where Allen Sternweiler's "dazzling" globally influenced New American cuisine, including "spectacular wild game dishes", meets "a wine list of considerable depth"; detractors deem the "handsome room" "uninviting" due to "noise" and say the "unpredictable service" "is a gamble" – sometimes "fantastic", sometimes "spotty."

Hashalom ⊄ ▽ 23 | 10 | 16 | $14

2905 W. Devon Ave. (Francisco Ave.), 773-465-5675

■ For "a real change of pace", Chicagoans visit this "favorite kid-friendly dive" in Rogers Park, a "standby for Middle Eastern food" "at fair prices"; its "innovative menu" of "authentic and well-prepared" "Israeli and Moroccan" dishes – including "special soups", "unusual salads" and "good combo plates" – has some sighing "too bad it's not open on weekends."

Hatsuhana 22 | 16 | 19 | $32

160 E. Ontario St. (bet. Michigan Ave. & St. Clair St.), 312-280-8808

◪ "Bring on the raw fish" cry fans of the "excellent" and "very fresh sushi" at this "small" Streeterville Japanese that's also a "favorite" for "out-of-this-world tempura", despite some protests that it's "pricey" ("you pay for its location" near the Magnificent Mile); also, the "efficient" service strikes some as "surly", and the "modern decor" and "cramped tables" leave others cold.

Heartland Cafe [S] 16 | 15 | 16 | $16

7000 N. Glenwood Ave. (Lunt Ave.), 773-465-8005

◪ "Like going back to Woodstock", this Rogers Park "blast from the past" is still golden with groupies for its "good (not great)" "mélange of cooking" – from "healthy, tasty" vegetarian fare to "yummy buffalo"; its "comfortable" digs host "great live music" acts and poetry readings for "bohemian people" trying to get their souls free.

Heat ▽ 22 | 21 | 22 | $60

1507 N. Sedgwick St. (North Ave.), 312-397-9818

◪ Raters blow hot and cold over this "trendy" Old Town Japanese whose "gimmick" is tremendous tanks teeming with a quarter ton of swimming soon-to-be-sushi; pros call it "truly innovative" and "ahead of its time", with "exquisite menu selections", "creative maki" and an "excellent sake collection" in a "stark", "elegant" space; detractors who disapprove of "floppy fish on the plate" dismiss it as an "overpriced novelty."

Heaven on Seven 20 | 17 | 18 | $23

600 N. Michigan Ave., 2nd fl. (bet. Ohio & Ontario Sts.), 312-280-7774 [S]

3478 N. Clark St. (Cornelia Ave.), 773-477-7818 [S]

111 N. Wabash Ave., 7th fl. (Washington Blvd.), 312-263-6443 ⊄

■ Heaven has been easier to get into since this "bustling, harried" original Loop location spun off its Cajun-Creole cousins; though the "good, authentic food" is "spicy", hotheads can "add heat as needed" with a "great collection of sauces", and it's "always Mardi Gras" within the "casual New Orleans"–inspired settings; N.B. menus and hours vary by location.

Hilary's Urban Eatery S   18 | 14 | 18 | $16

1500 W. Division St. (Greenview St.), 773-235-4327
■ Urbanites are utterly "glad" this "whimsical" Wicker Park Eclectic eatery is "in the neighborhood"; "unpretentious and relaxing", it's a "colorful" "hangout" where "Gen-Xers" "huddle cozily" over a "good menu" offering "creative and tasty" "twists on normal dishes" (and a "great Sunday brunch"); P.S. folks "love the jelly beans" "on the table."

Hi Ricky S   17 | 13 | 16 | $17

941 W. Randolph St. (bet. Morgan & Sangamon Sts.), 312-491-9100
1852 W. North Ave. (Wolcott Ave.), 773-276-8300
3730 N. Southport Ave. (north of Addison St.), 773-388-0000
833 Deerfield Rd. (Robert York Ave.), Deerfield, 847-948-0400
◪ Ricky's friends say "it's fun to work your way down the menu" of "interesting concoctions" at this "loud, crowded and entertaining" city and suburban chain, where the "cheap, tasty and plentiful" Asian and noodle dishes are a "cut above fast food"; foes say even if you like the "generally bland", "Americanized fare", "inconsistent" service can "ruin" the experience.

Hong Min S   23 | 6 | 15 | $17

221 W. Cermak Rd. (bet. Archer & Wentworth Aves.), 312-842-5026 ◐
8048 W. 111th St. (Roberts Rd.), Palos Hills, 708-599-8488
◪ This "favorite" Chinatown "diamond in the rough" and its Southwest Suburban satellite are ranked "best Chinese" in our *Survey*; clearly, however, the "huge menu" of "inexpensive", "excellent and authentic" dishes outclasses the housekeeping-challenged, "old and run-down" settings, so "just close your eyes while you're eating"; N.B. the city location is BYO.

Hot Doug's ⊟   ▽ 24 | 16 | 24 | $7

2314 W. Roscoe St. (bet. Clairmont & Oakley Sts.), 773-348-0326
■ "Not your typical hot dog joint", this Roscoe Village wiener wonderland is "a place for sausage lovers to call home"; surveyors crown "creative" chef-owner Doug Sohn "the king of encased meats", giving him an "A for ingenuity" in creating an "awesome variety" of "tasty and cheap" bun embellishers, including a different game version weekly, and for "cooking French fries in duck fat on [Fridays and] Saturdays."

Hot Tamales [S] ▽ 22 | 15 | 17 | $18

493 Central Ave. (St. John Ave.), Highland Park, 847-433-4070
Butterfield Plaza Shopping Ctr., 700 S. Butterfield Rd. (Rte. 60), Mundelein, 847-247-8511

■ Sombreros off to these "crowded" "neighborhood Mexican" spots in the North Suburbs that may "look ordinary, but are much, much more"; both the original near Port Clinton Square and its spin-off in the Butterfield Plaza shopping center offer "good service" and "unusual, creative and delicious fare" including "wonderful duck tacos", "great tamales" (natch) and "veg options galore", all washed down with "fab margaritas."

House of Blues [S] 15 | 21 | 15 | $27

329 N. Dearborn St. (Kinzie St.), 312-923-2007

◩ With "some of the best music in the city" and "great outsider and folk art", this "fun-and-funky" River North venue (part of a national chain) serving Cajun-Creole and Southern fare has its followers, especially for the "engaging gospel brunch" on Sundays; still, some sigh "if only the food and service were as good as" the "live bands."

HUGO'S FROG BAR 🌙 [S] 24 | 20 | 23 | $42

1024 N. Rush St. (bet. Bellevue Pl. & Oak St.), 312-640-0999

■ "Always hopping", this Gold Coaster is a "saner", "not-as-noisy", "easier-to-get-into" but still "clublike" seafood "version of Gibsons" Steakhouse, its beefy, abutting big brother; in addition to the signature frogs' legs and "great" *mer* fare like "crab cakes par excellence" and "fresh", "well-prepared fish", you can also "have them bring you a steak from" next door (they "share a kitchen") – "who could ask for more?"

Iggy's 🌙 [S] 18 | 18 | 15 | $24

700 N. Milwaukee Ave. (Huron St.), 312-829-4449

■ Night-owls hoot for this "hip" Near West hangout, a "low-key" lounge-restaurant favored for "really late dining" (the kitchen closes at 3:15 AM most mornings) from an Eclectic menu of "Iggy's eggs", "quality" pastas and "great snacks"; with its "funky" velvet-curtained decor, it's a "dark and mysterious" place where "bikers meets yuppies and they all get along", thanks in part to "killer martinis."

Ina's [S] 21 | 17 | 20 | $22

1235 W. Randolph St. (Elizabeth St.), 312-226-8227

■ With two defunct morning-themed spots under her belt, Chicago's self- and surveyor-proclaimed "breakfast queen" "has done it again" with this "cheery", "warm" Market District yearling whose "kitschy decor" features a "cute" "salt-and-pepper-shaker collection"; though her "upscale food with homemade flavor" includes lunch and dinner fare, early-birds crow that "nothing could be finer than the pancakes served by Ina."

Indian Garden 🇸   20 | 14 | 17 | $22

2548 W. Devon Ave. (Rockwell St.), 773-338-2929
247 E. Ontario St., 2nd fl. (bet. Fairbanks Ct. & Michigan Ave.),
312-280-4910
855 E. Schaumburg Rd. (Barrington Rd.), Schaumburg,
847-524-3007

☑ "Wonderfully flavored" "fiery food" and "plenty of it", as
well as some "not-too-spicy" selections, have compatriots
crooning kudos to this Indian trio; "bring friends", as they're
"great for vegetarians" and their "buffets are excellent
for those interested in trying new food"; service is either
"attentive" or "slow", depending on whom you ask, but all
agree the "moderate prices" are "bliss."

Irish Oak Restaurant & Pub 🇸   ▽ 18 | 20 | 20 | $18

3511 N. Clark St. (Addison St.), 773-935-6669

■ "A super stop" in Wrigleyville for Emerald Islers ("or
those wanting to be"), this "real Irish pub" run by a family
of Galway natives serves "fresh fish 'n' chips" and "great
shepherd's pie" that are washed down with a "wide
and lovingly poured selection of draughts"; expats say
"the imported bar and other woodwork add a sense of
authenticity" to the "pleasant" proceedings.

Isaac Hayes   – | – | – | M
Music·Food·Passion 🇸

739 N. Clark St. (bet. Chicago Ave. & Superior St.), 312-266-2400
Isaac Hayes of *Shaft* and *South Park*'s 'Chef' fame (who is
also a cookbook author) wants you to dig him at this new
branch of his Memphis joint, situated in the former Famous
Dave's site in River North; the Soul Food and BBQ fare runs
from ribs and brisket sandwiches to turkey meatloaf,
and the nightly entertainment is predominantly R&B, with
comedy on Wednesdays.

Itto Sushi ●   22 | 14 | 18 | $26

2616 N. Halsted St. (Wrightwood Ave.), 773-871-1800

☑ "Grab a quick bite of dependable" and "affordable" "high-
quality sushi" at this long-standing "Lincoln Parker", a
"casual alternative to the more swanky [Japanese]
establishments in town"; though the "friendly", "eager-
to-please" staffers "make you feel welcome", detractors
declare the "food is good" but "not exceptionally good"
and decry the setting as "nothing fancy."

Ixcapuzalco 🇸   23 | 19 | 19 | $34

2919 N. Milwaukee Ave. (Diversey Pkwy.), 773-486-7340

■ Even those who "can't say" its "hard-to-pronounce
name" ('eeks-ka-poo-sal-ko') love to twist their tongues
around this Logan Square Mexican's "absolutely exciting
moles", the highpoints of an "imaginative menu" of "regional
cuisine" "expertly executed" by "creative" chef-owner
Geno Bahena (a Frontera Grill veteran who also helms

Chilpancingo and the new Mi Sueño, Su Realidad) and "nicely presented" by a "helpful staff" "in a surprisingly elegant yet comfortable atmosphere."

Izalco S | – | – | – | I |
1511 W. Lawrence Ave. (bet. Ashland Ave. & Clark St.), 773-769-1225
El Salvadoran cuisine takes center stage at this low-key, Near North triple-storefront BYO, distinguishing it from other ethnic spots lining Lawrence Avenue; don't miss the huge tortilla-like *pupusas* stuffed with beans, cheese or *loroco* (a cactus-like plant), the fried yuca topped with pork and pickled cabbage or the roasted or fried green plantains – all at prices that can't be beat; N.B. there's also a lunch buffet.

Jack's on Halsted S | 22 | 19 | 22 | $34 |
3201 N. Halsted St. (Belmont Ave.), 773-244-9191
■ This "stylish" Boys Towner showcases an "inspired menu" by chef-owner Jack Jones (proprietor of Atlantique and Bistro Marbuzet, as well) featuring "innovative takes on American classics" and "fabulous fish" dishes such as the signature ahi tuna; its "wild, contemporary decor" is "comfortably upscale", and its "great location" "on the corner" of Belmont and Halsted makes it a "nice spot" "to watch the area's colorful crowd."

Jackson Harbor Grill S | ▽ 18 | 22 | 15 | $24 |
6401 S. Lake Shore Dr. (64th St.), 773-288-4442
⊠ Those who visit this South Shore summer-season spot from May through October swear the "beautiful views" afforded by its "unique setting" in a "charming waterfront cottage" ("an old Coast Guard station") "overlooking the harbor" will "make you think you're away on an island vacation"; most concur its "ambiance makes it", though, saying the "good" Cajun-Creole fare "could be improved" and the "service still needs work."

Jacky's Bistro S | 24 | 21 | 21 | $40 |
2545 Prairie Ave. (Central St.), Evanston, 847-733-0899
⊠ Prizers of "great chef Jacky Pluton's" "sophisticated" North Suburban bistro (a two-year-old reincarnation of the Winnetka original destroyed by fire in 1999) praise its "terrific" menu of "highly flavored" Regional American and New French "classic dishes" reinterpreted "with modern concepts", as well as its "intimate, inviting surroundings"; the resistance reports "downtown prices" and "some attitude" from a few "inflexible" staffers.

Jaipur Palace S | 19 | 17 | 18 | $25 |
22 E. Hubbard St. (State St.), 312-595-0911
■ Aficionados of this "above-average" River North Indian say its "authentic" and "tasty food" – from "good basics"

to "amazing desserts" – is "always a treat", as is the "caring service"; its colorful, "upbeat" interior features "culturally influenced decor", with walls and alcoves lined with artwork and images of India.

Jane's S   21 | 19 | 19 | $28
1655 W. Cortland St. (Paulina St.), 773-862-5263

◪ The "healthy", "fabulous tasting" and "reasonable" Eclectic–New American fare and "cool-but-comfy" "exposed-brick" surroundings of this "funky" "Bucktown hangout" and "date place" have caused cases of Jane's addiction; still, claustrophobes quarrel with "cramped quarters" "too small to handle the weekend crowds", and PETA people are peeved that the "vegetarian choices are becoming fewer" on its "limited menu."

Jang Mo Nim   – | – | – | I
6320 N. Lincoln Ave. (Devon Ave.), 773-509-0211

Middle-of-the-night Korean cravers covet this Northsider that offers a broad menu of specialties – fried oysters in pepper sauce, spicy octopus and stewed goat served with beer or sake – until 6 AM; adventurous do-it-yourselfers opt for a table on the perimeter of the room and cook their own *bulgoki* (beef) or *kalbi* (short ribs).

Jia's S   19 | 15 | 16 | $22
2545 N. Halsted St. (bet. Fullerton Pkwy. & Wrightwood Ave.), 773-477-6256
2 E. Delaware Pl. (State St.), 312-642-0626

◪ Though no longer affiliated, this "consistent" Lincoln Park original and its Gold Coast spin-off both serve a "nice selection of Asian" dishes from expansive Chinese-Japanese menus ("allow 30 minutes to read" them) and "fresh sushi" bars featuring "some interesting rolls"; though some say their "bland" "atmospheres could use some help", most maintain they offer "excellent food considering the price."

Jilly's Cafe S   21 | 19 | 21 | $34
2614 Green Bay Rd. (Central St.), Evanston, 847-869-7636

■ "Fine fare is served with grace" at this "dignified" and "darling" New French–New American cafe, a "romantic place to take your sweetheart" in the North Suburbs; "the jury is still out" on whether "new chef-owner" Brian Newkirk will "keep up" its "reputation" for "terrific food", but co-toque Miguel Sanchez remaining from the last regime bodes well for continuity; P.S. it's not affiliated with the similarly named "supper club" Downtown.

Jin Ju S   – | – | – | M
5203 N. Clark St. (Foster Ave.), 773-334-6377

A stylish Andersonville newcomer with a serene, minimalist atmosphere, this Korean offers contemporary, visually appealing versions of authentic dishes – toned down, spice-wise, but still allowing the flavors of the chiles, black beans and kimchi to shine through; alcohol is also served, including martinis made with *soju*, a sweet-potato liquor.

Joe's Be-Bop Cafe S   14 │ 16 │ 15 │ $22 │
Navy Pier, 600 E. Grand Ave. (bet. Lake Shore Dr. & McClurg Ct.), 312-595-5299

▰ "If you're at Navy Pier" and feeling hungry, this "popular jazz joint" with "pictures of musicians on the walls" and an "outside area for people-watching" is an "adequate" spot for a meal of "good", if somewhat "routine, BBQ" and Southern fare; "the music's the reason to go", though, and foes tune it out altogether as "too touristy" and "noisy."

JOE'S SEAFOOD,   25 │ 22 │ 24 │ $47 │
PRIME STEAK & STONE CRAB S
60 E. Grand Ave. (Rush St.), 312-379-5637

■ "Are we in Florida?" ask claw-crackers complimenting this "retro-stylish" sophomore Near North "extension of the great Miami flagship", Joe's Stone Crab, which has been serving it up in season since 1913; a "successful Lettuce Entertain You partnership", it brings "big flavors" to Chi-town in "big portions" ("at big prices") of "hands-on seafood grub", as well as steaks "so good" that some can find "no words" to express their feelings.

John Barleycorn ◗S   14 │ 15 │ 14 │ $18 │
658 W. Belden Ave. (Lincoln Ave.), 773-348-8899
3524 N. Clark St. (bet. Sheffield Ave. & Addison St.), 773-549-6000

■ These "casual" brothers are American pubs known for "tasty burgers" buoyed by "beer and atmosphere" (the Lincoln Park original has been a tavern since 1890); most say, though, that the "good wings" and other "regular bar food" are "secondary", since "these are drinking joints" first and foremost; P.S. the Belden Barleycorn also has a "great outdoor garden."

Johnny Rockets S   16 │ 15 │ 15 │ $13 │
901 N. Rush St. (Delaware Pl.), 312-337-3900

▰ Grab a "greasy, guilty pleasure" at this Gold Coast slinging American diner eats while spinning "thick", "old-fashioned milkshakes" in the blender and "non-stop golden oldies" on the jukebox; what's a "retro junk-food heaven" to some, though, strikes others as a "hokey" attempt at "'50s atmosphere without the great '50s food."

John's Place S   20 │ 16 │ 19 │ $19 │
1200 W. Webster Ave. (Racine Ave.), 773-525-6670

■ John Manilow's Lincoln Parker "pleases everyone from vegetarians to the meat-and-potatoes crowd" with its "consistently good" Eclectic homestyle menu; a "neighborhood brunch favorite", it offers "the best pumpkin pancakes" and "oatmeal better than mom's" – just ask the "mothers with babies", "kids" and "toddlers everywhere" in this "bright, airy", "family-friendly" place.

Joy Yee's Noodle Shop [S] ▽ 24 | 17 | 22 | $13

2159 Chinatown Sq. (Archer Ave.), 312-328-0001
521 Davis St. (Chicago Ave.), Evanston, 847-733-1900

■ A "huge selection (and huge portions)" of "great noodles" and other "tasty Thai", Chinese, Korean and Vietnamese dishes keep these "popular" Pan-Asians positively "packed"; though some say the "friendly wait staff" is "fast", a few Siamese cats growl "don't let the secret out – the wait is long enough already"; P.S. the North Suburban is BYO, the Chinatown is alcohol-free.

Julio's Cocina Latina ▽ 24 | 21 | 20 | $31

(fka Julio's Latin Cafe)
Lakeview Plaza, 95 S. Rand Rd. (Whitney Rd.), Lake Zurich, 847-438-3484

■ It may be "a surprise to find delicious Latin fare in a strip mall", but that's what surveyors say to expect at this Northwest Suburban cantina that's generating heat with its "well-prepared", "nontraditional" food – a "creative" mix of South American, Caribbean and Mexican cuisines – and "delightful service"; P.S. live jazz and Brazilian music on weekends provides "great entertainment."

Kabul House [S] – | – | – | I

3320 Dempster St. (McCormick Blvd.), Skokie, 847-763-9930

"Authentic Afghan food" comes to the Northern Suburbs courtesy of this "nicer-than-casual" BYO where jaded palates can indulge in "simple, inexpensive fare" that's both "tasty and unusual"; gregarious Abdul Qazi, "the owner, exemplifies the warm hospitality" of his native country and has transformed his "small" mini-mall space with photos, posters, costumes, textiles and traditional music from his homeland.

Kamehachi [S] 23 | 19 | 19 | $28

1400 N. Wells St. (Schiller St.), 312-664-3663 ◐
240 E. Ontario St. (Fairbanks St.), 312-587-0600
Village Green Shopping Ctr., 1320 Shermer Rd. (Waukegan Rd.), Northbrook, 847-562-0064

■ "Always bustling", this Old Town Japanese can be "tough to get into", but "fresh sushi" from a "diverse menu" of "unique options" makes it worth the effort; the "young, hip crowd" likes its "late hours" and "cool bar upstairs", while purists prefer the more "rigid environment downstairs"; its North Shore sibling also offers "great food" at a "reasonable cost"; N.B. the new Ontario Street location is unrated.

Karizma 🖪
20 | 17 | 19 | $32

4741 Main St. (Skokie Blvd.), Skokie, 847-674-6163

☑ "Fine dining in Skokie? – yes!" kvell kindred spirits keen on this North Suburban "Chi-style grown-up place" with the "silly spelling" that "caters to customers" clamoring for a "creative menu" of "modern American cuisine"; killjoys, though, put the kibosh on the kudos, clobbering the "slow service" and claiming the "prices are high" relative to the "small portions."

Karma 🖪
– | – | – | E

Crowne Plaza Hotel, 510 E. Rte. 83 (Rte. 45), Mundelein, 847-970-6900

North Suburban Mundelein's Crowne Plaza Hotel is home to this haute Pan-Asian where an imaginative multi-ethnic menu is paired with a limited wine list and several sake options; the chic, serene decor includes glowing blown-glass bamboo and hydrotherapy in the form of a waterfall and rice paddy–inspired pond; N.B. breakfast, lunch and dinner are served.

Keefer's
22 | 22 | 22 | $44

20 W. Kinzie St. (Dearborn St.), 312-467-9525

■ "Another good" "steak-and-seafood" "joint" (just "how many does Chicago deserve?"), this River North "noteworthy newcomer" serves up "classy comfort food" "with winning service" in an "attractive room"; supporters claim owner "Glen Keefer is a pro" and say chef John "Hogan's a hero", crediting the duo for making it not only a "bright new star on the scene" but an "'in'-spot for TV and radio personalities" as well.

Kevin 🖪
∇ 28 | 27 | 26 | $48

9 W. Hubbard St. (State St.), 312-595-0055

■ When "one of Chicago's most creative chefs", Kevin Shikami (ex Jimmy's Place and The Outpost), launched his namesake this year in River North, he quickly generated interest in his "excellent and adventurous" New American fare (such as wasabi-spiked tuna tartare), which employs "the highest-quality ingredients" and "delivers pure pleasure"; the "stunning" yet "comfortable" storefront echoes the cuisine's Asian accents.

KIKI'S BISTRO
24 | 22 | 22 | $40

900 N. Franklin St. (Locust St.), 312-335-5454

☑ Tucked into an "out-of-the-way" section of River North, this "congenial" and "consistently solid" "old favorite" with an "authentic Gallic presence" is prized by a "mature crowd" for "well-prepared, quality bistro food" within a "charming Country French" setting; though generally "professional", the service can "falter when the dining room is too busy"; P.S. there's "nice, free valet parking" (lunch and dinner).

King Crab S
17 | 13 | 16 | $29

1816 N. Halsted St. (Willow St.), 312-280-8990

☑ The "good seafood and specials" at this "casual", "low-key" Lincoln Park place make many "glad it's there", such as drama divas who drop by "before the Steppenwolf" or "after the Royal George Theater"; crabs claim its "location brings locals back", not its "ok food", adding that it's "not too busy" for a reason.

Kinzie Chophouse
20 | 18 | 19 | $37

400 N. Wells St. (Kinzie St.), 312-822-0191

☑ "Mouthwatering steaks" that are "worth the money" draw diners to this "quaint and cozy" River North chophouse, also popular with those "shopping at the Merchandise Mart" for "good salads and pastas at lunch" and for "happy-hour" hanging-out; despite this, a few doubters declare it's "nothing really special", deeming it "disappointing, especially for the price."

Kismet ⊉
∇ 25 | 14 | 20 | $25

1466 N. Ashland Ave. (North Ave.), 773-772-7538

■ "A little quirky" is one way to describe this "refreshingly unpretentious" and "cozy" Lincoln Park lair, "a wonderful find" where "clever and creative" chef-owner Wendy Gilbert (of the relocated Savoy Truffle) creates "innovative and delicious" North African kebabs and couscous dishes that are "interestingly spiced" and at "the right price"; N.B. BYO, cash only and no children.

Kit Kat Lounge &
Supper Club ◐ S
18 | 21 | 19 | $32

3700 N. Halsted St. (Waveland Ave.), 773-525-1111

☑ Gender-benders generate "amazing energy" at this "loud" Boys Town venue where "surprisingly good" New American fare is paired with "strong" martinis and a "must-see" revue of "fun female impersonators"; still, peeved patrons pen poisonous proclamations, purporting "they distract you with drag queens" so you won't notice the "unexceptional food" and "arrogant" staff.

Kitsch'n on Roscoe S
16 | 19 | 16 | $16

2005 W. Roscoe St. (Damen Ave.), 773-248-7372

☑ While this "fun retro diner" with "real" "comfort food" and a "good '70s-atmosphere gimmick" "reminds" some nostalgics of a Roscoe Village "*Leave It to Beaver* with Julia Child as the mom", others call it "one joke taken too far" and complain about "spotty food and service"; still, "where else can you get Tang?"

Klay Oven S
20 | 16 | 17 | $27

414 N. Orleans St. (Hubbard St.), 312-527-3999

■ "You'd have to go to Devon" Avenue in Chicago's Little India area, "to find dishes that compare" to the "high-quality food" served at this "cozy" yet "upscale" spot, the "place for Indian in River North"; there are "plenty of choices for the vegetarian and non-vegetarian alike", so many enjoy a "leisurely lunch" making multiple visits to its "great bargain buffet."

Kuni's S   23 | 17 | 19 | $28

511 Main St. (bet. Chicago & Hinman Aves.), Evanston, 847-328-2004

■ North Suburban natives say there's "no need to go into the city" in search of "authentic Japanese fare" such as "splendid tempura and great sushi" fashioned from "fish of pristine freshness", since chef-owner Yuji Kunii's creations are so much "the real thing" "you'll feel like you are in Tokyo"; aficionados call him "a prince" and "love" to watch him at work in the "clean but not spartan" surroundings.

Kyoto   ▽ 22 | 12 | 17 | $27

2534 N. Lincoln Ave. (bet. Altgeld St. & Lill Ave.), 773-477-2788 S
1408 Butterfield Rd. (bet. I-355 & Lloyd Ave.), Downers Grove, 630-627-8588

☑ Belly up to the bar (sushi, that is) for "tasty" Japanese food at these "super-understated" Lincoln Park and West Suburban siblings; they may "look like holes in the wall", but with "reasonable prices", friendly" staffers "without an attitude" and some of "the freshest [fish] in the city", determined diners don't mind that the "decor needs help."

La Bella Winnetka S   17 | 17 | 19 | $29

505 Chestnut St. (bet. Elm & Oak Sts.), Winnetka, 847-441-6002

☑ Italian fare that's "dependable if not exciting" can be found at this North Suburban stalwart, but it's equally known for its "must-see character" of an owner; though most say its "great outdoor tent" (illuminated by twinkling lights and heated on chilly nights) "makes for relaxing" and "fun" "outdoor dining worth waiting for", some judges still find this beauty "past its prime."

La Bocca della Verità S   21 | 14 | 19 | $30

4618 N. Lincoln Ave. (bet. Damen & Wilson Aves.), 773-784-6222

■ Proponents pronounce this "intimate" Lincoln Square Italian "a storefront treasure" for "always-authentic" and "great food" (like its signature "homemade" "duck ravioli to die for") that's "simply prepared", "outstandingly presented" and offered "at neighborhood prices" that make it a "good value"; the "warm, homey staff" helps compensate for the "unassuming", "dated decor."

La Borsa   ▽ 17 | 17 | 15 | $26

375 N. Morgan St. (bet. Carroll Ave. & Kinzie St.), 312-563-1414

☑ Though it's "certainly an odd place", this Near West Italian "well hidden" in an "out-of-the-way industrial district" offers "affordable", "large portions" of "hearty", if "not refined", fare; some quibble with its "offbeat decor", but train-spotters tout its "weird locale" (a converted railway station), saying the "commuter trains racing by the windows" and "spectacular" "skyline views "make up for what's missing with the food."

La Cantina Enoteca ▽ 20 20 22 $29
71 W. Monroe St. (bet. Clark & Dearborn Sts.), 312-332-7005
■ Though all three of the "Italian Village restaurants" under one Loop roof are convenient "before the theater or a concert", Cantina coveters claim this subterranean sibling is the most "cozy", with "attentive waiters" and "consistently good food"; as its moniker suggests, it also boasts a bevy of bottles, but you won't "find" the "great wine list" on the menu – "ask for" the big, bound book.

La Cazuela Mariscos S _ _ _ I
6922 N. Clark St. (bet. Farwell & Morse Aves.), 773-338-5425
An upbeat apricot-colored room sets the stage for a feast that's anything but your typical Mexican meal at this fresh-not-fancy Rogers Park seafooder where abundant fish stews, tacos and chilled cocktails of octopus, clams, oysters and shrimp are served alongside fried lime-drizzled snapper; with all that bounty from the sea, who needs nachos?; N.B. outdoor dining is also an option.

La Crêperie S 19 15 16 $19
2845 N. Clark St. (bet. Diversey Pkwy. & Surf St.), 773-528-9050
☑ Crêpe crusaders "want to do the cancan" over the "authentic" namesake noshes tucked with "different fillings" at this "unchanged classic" in Lakeview that's "still crêpe-ing [along] after all these years"; though some despair over the "cluttered", "dumpy decor" and service that's "typically French", others say you "can't beat the garden on a warm night."

La Donna S 20 15 19 $26
5146 N. Clark St. (bet. Foster Ave. & Winona St.), 773-561-9400
☑ "Big portions of authentic Italian" food ferried by "friendly" staffers make regulars "feel at home" in this "romantic" Andersonville "favorite"; still, holdouts who don't hanker for the "predictable" fare harrumph that what some call a "cozy" setting is just "cramped tables in close quarters" that get "too crowded on weekends", causing the otherwise "good service" to be "slow."

La Gondola S ▽ 22 13 21 $24
Wellington Plaza, 2914 N. Ashland Ave. (Wellington Ave.), 773-248-4433
☑ Gratified gondoliers gloat that "hospitality, warmth" and "wonderful Italian food" (including "great pizza" and

some of the "best eggplant parmesan in Chicago")
wait within this "affordable" Lincoln Parker despite its
"deceptively modest exterior"; still, the "spartan" "strip-
mall" setting and "small", "nothing-fancy" "dining room
with only a few tables" have some saying it's "best" to
either phone them up for "delicious" delivery or glide on
in for "high-quality carryout."

Lambay Island at the Abbey Pub $\boxed{S}$ — — — M

3420 W. Grace St. (Elston Ave.), 773-463-5808
Tucked away behind the green-and-white awning of a
somewhat divey Northwest Side pub, you'll find this
small but striking dining room appointed with evocative
photographs of the Gaelic countryside; the menu is
straight from the Old Sod, as well – Irish breakfast,
shepherd's pie and beer-battered fish and chips to be
enjoyed with a pint of stout or a Black & Tan; N.B. the
Abbey offers live music seven nights a week.

La Mora $\boxed{S}$ — — — M

2132 W. Roscoe St. (Hamilton Ave.), 773-404-4555
Roscoe Village is the suitable setting for this cozy Italian
combining eclectic and classic dishes – blue-cheese-
crusted fillet, calamari *griglia*, spaghetti carbonara – all
complemented by a short wine list and served by a friendly,
accommodating staff; the inviting ambiance is abetted by
velvet curtains, a fireplace in the center of the room and a
lounge in back with comfortable couches and armchairs.

L'anne — — — E

*221 W. Front St. (bet. Hale St. & Wheaton Ave.), Wheaton,
630-260-1234*
The Western Suburbs receive an infusion of fusion at
this stylish new contemporary French-Asian whose name
honors owner Lanny Nguyen's two favorite flowers – her
daughter, Lynnanne, and the orchid ('lan' in Vietnamese),
examples of which abound in the intimate and elegantly
exotic room of floor-to-ceiling windows, hand-painted walls,
bamboo floors and soft-silk-swathed ceilings.

Lao Sze Chuan Spicy City $\boxed{◑S}$ ∇ 19 8 13 $19

2172 S. Archer Ave. (Fuller St.), 312-326-5040
Lao Sze Chuan Express $\boxed{S}$⇗
1520 W. Taylor St. (Ashland Ave.), 312-455-0667
Lao Sze Chuan $\boxed{S}$
*Oak Court Shopping Ctr., 500 E. Ogden Ave. (bet. Cass Ave. &
Rte. 83), Westmont, 630-455-4488*
■ "Go with a group and feast" upon "gigantic portions"
from the enormous menus of these city-and-suburban
siblings; all serve "good" multiregional fare, but the
Chinatown branch specializes in "authentic Szechuan

cooking", including hard-to-find "Chinese hot pots" that may be a "bit too" much of "the real thing" for "the unadventurous eater"; N.B. owner Tony Hu hosts a Channel 13 cooking show.

La Peña [S] – – – M

4212 N. Milwaukee Ave. (Montrose Ave.), 773-545-7022

The Portage Park neighborhood of the Northwest Side is home to this lively, hospitable Ecuadoran eatery, brightly colored and festooned with tropical bird figurines, where a host of Latin dishes – ceviche, tostones, fried yuca, ropa viejo – is served along with freshly made plantain chips and drinks from the full bar; on weekends, its stage hops with live Andean music from a seemingly unending variety of instruments.

La Petite Folie [S] 24 19 21 $40

Hyde Park Shopping Ctr., 1504 E. 55th St. (Lake Park Ave.), 773-493-1394

■ "Yes, Virginia, there is fine dining on the South Side"; and it can be found in the form of this "little-known", "pleasant French cafe" serving a "well-balanced menu" of "simple" yet "consistently superior" cuisine that "selective Hyde Parkers" find both "elegant and satisfying" ("especially the prix fixe menu", "a bargain"); "perfect for conversations", its "peaceful", "attractive room" is a "lovely place for a quiet, romantic dinner", and "it's handy to the Court Theatre."

La Rosetta 19 15 17 $27

3 First National Plaza, 70 W. Madison St. (bet. Clark & Dearborn Sts.), 312-332-9500

◪ Show-goers know this "reliable" and "welcoming" Rosebud-group Italian "in the Loop" is a "great place before the theater", but it's also a triple threat for nose-to-the-grindstoners – it's "popular for business lunches", the "happy hour is worth going for" and stiffs "working late" are "glad it's in the building" for "excellent takeout"; still, what some call "always-tasty" food others opine is a bit "middle-of-the-road."

La Sardine 22 20 20 $37

111 N. Carpenter St. (bet. Randolph St. & Washington Blvd.), 312-421-2800

◪ Despite its name, this "trendy" Market District bistro by "masterful Jean-Claude" Poilevey is a bigger fish than its "tiny sister, Le Bouchon", but its "abundant portions" of "intensely flavored", "plate-licking-good" Gallic food similarly "warms the soul"; still, some panelists are put off by sometimes "indifferent service" and the occasionally "noisy" atmosphere of its formerly industrial space, a "mix of quaint French and hard-edged urban" influences; P.S. "the chocolate soufflé is worth the trip."

Las Bellas Artes [S] ▽ 25 21 23 $39

112 W. Park Ave. (York St.), Elmhurst, 630-530-7725

■ "What a delight" vouch vociferous voters vaunting the "excellent gourmet" fare at chef-owner Gloria Duarte's West Suburban specializing in the European-influenced cuisine of Mexico City ("not at all what most people think of as Mexican"); "go for the Sunday brunch" and its spiced "oatmeal to die for", the "wonderful" afternoon tea or "exciting" dinners, all "graciously served" in a "charming" fine-arts-filled setting.

La Scarola [S] 23 14 19 $30

721 W. Grand Ave. (Milwaukee Ave.), 312-243-1740

◪ With "massive portions" of "wonderful" "old-school" "homemade Italian food at reasonable prices", this "terrific [Near West] hideaway" makes "you feel like grandma is going to walk out of the kitchen and pinch your cheeks"; "now that lots of folks have discovered it", however, rueful regulars report that the "service falters when it gets busy" and claim it can get "close and noisy."

Las Tablas [S] 24 15 18 $20

2965 N. Lincoln Ave. (Wellington Ave.), 773-871-2414

■ "A real find", this "charming" and "fun" Lincoln Park churrascaria ("Colombian steakhouse") not only "feels authentic" but is, thanks to chef-owner Jorge Suarez, who hails from south of Bogota; along with its "excellent grilled meats" and "paella with South American flair", there are "yummy" sides like "delicious plantains with melted cheese" and "Latin root vegetables" like yuca; P.S. "BYO or try the juice drinks."

La Strada Ristorante 19 18 18 $37

155 N. Michigan Ave. (Randolph St.), 312-565-2200

■ This "venerable Italian spot" has surveyors standing on opposite sides of the street – some shout that it's an "underappreciated" Loop longtimer that "welcomes you like family", with "high-quality food" and "friendly" service, while others bellow back it's "nothing special", with a "tired menu and decor"; either way, its "location on Michigan Avenue" makes it "convenient to the Art Institute, Grant Park" and "the symphony."

Lawry's The Prime Rib [S] 23 22 22 $41

100 E. Ontario St. (Rush St.), 312-787-5000

■ "Don't change a thing" implore purists who prize this "wonderfully old-fashioned" Near North "classic" (based on the Beverly Hills original) that's been "keeping it simple and good" since 1974; expect "grand" "mansion decor" and "tableside service", including some of the "best prime rib" around "cut (in front of you)" from carts wheeled by staffers in "throwback" uniforms; P.S. "the Chocolate Bag dessert is reason enough to go."

LE BOUCHON

25 | 19 | 20 | $35

1958 N. Damen Ave. (Armitage Ave.), 773-862-6600

◪ It "feels like Paris" has been "teleported to Bucktown" within this diminutive "darling" that devotees declare is "exactly what a bistro should be"; Jean Claude Poilevey's "real home cooking" yields "unbelievably delicious French" fare such as "outstanding duck", but some say it's served up with a side of "authentic snobbery"; the "claustrophobic" complain, as well, of an "uncomfortably" "cramped" setting where "long waits" are de rigueur.

LE COLONIAL S

23 | 24 | 21 | $41

937 N. Rush St. (bet. Oak & Walton Sts.), 312-255-0088

■ "Flavors shine at this trendy" Gold Coaster – the Third Coast quarter of an otherwise bicoastal quartet – where the "refined haute Vietnamese cooking" is "delicate and well-seasoned" and the "stunning" French Colonial setting seems so "seductive" and "decadent" you'll "feel like becoming a spy", especially in the "swank" and "exotic upstairs bar"; P.S. "for special occasions", "ask for a balcony seat overlooking the street."

LE FRANÇAIS

28 | 26 | 27 | $75

269 S. Milwaukee Ave. (bet. Dundee Rd. & Strong St.), Wheeling, 847-541-7470

■ Chef Don Yamauchi is "keeping up the great tradition" of founding toque Jean Banchet – so judge jurists a year after a deed juggle jostled Northwest Suburban Wheeling's (once Classic, now New) French standard bearer known for "exceptional cuisine, wine and service"; "holding its own", the "beautifully prepared", "lighter" food remains "picture perfect" and "extremely pricey."

Lem's BBQ ◖S

-| -| -| I

5914 S. State St. (59th St.), 773-684-5007
311 E. 75th St. (bet. Calumet & Prairie Aves.), 773-994-2428

Keeping the campfires burning till the wee hours, these Southside BBQ basics bring in the urban midnight cowboys, ringing the dinner chime and rustlin' up Southern fried chicken and smoky, hickory-laced ribs and tips; they're perty much for carryout only, though, since there ain't a lot of room in the corral – ok, the State Street location, nearly 50 years old, has three coveted seats.

Leona's S

15 | 14 | 15 | $19

3215 N. Sheffield Ave. (Belmont Ave.), 773-327-8861 ◖
1419 W. Taylor St. (bet. Bishop & Loomis Sts.), 312-850-2222
1936 W. Augusta Blvd. (Damen Ave.), 773-292-4300
11060 S. Western Ave. (111th St.), 773-881-7700
1236 E. 53rd St. (Woodlawn Ave.), 773-363-2600
646 N. Franklin St. (bet. Erie & Ontario Sts.), 312-867-0101
3877 N. Elston Ave. (bet. Drake & St. Louis Aves.), 773-267-7287
6935 N. Sheridan Rd. (Morse Ave.), 773-764-5757

(continued)
Leona's
848 W. Madison St. (bet. Grove & Kenilworth Aves.), Oak Park,
708-445-0101
3517 W. Dempster St. (bet. Drake & St. Louis Aves.), Skokie,
847-982-0101
Additional locations throughout the Chicago area
▣ Rater responses to these "down-to-earth" Italian-and-pizza "family restaurants" are all over the map, just like the extensive chain itself; regulars report "you get a lot for your money", namely an "amazing selection" of "dependable and satisfying" chow, but upstarts unleash their umbrage on the "million-item menu of mediocre food", not to mention the "iffy service."

Leo's Lunchroom ⬛⌿   18 | 12 | 16 | $14 |
1809 W. Division St. (bet. Ashland & Damen Aves.), 773-276-6509
▣ "Creative, tasty", "cheap grub" makes for "unpretentious dining" at this "funky" Wicker Park "dive" where the "short menu" combines "good, greasy breakfasts", "well-executed diner standards" and "unusual [New American] entrees"; some say "the space is so shabby" "you're overdressed in jeans and a T-shirt", but "one man's dump is another man's treasure" ("stay away – we want it for ourselves").

Le Passage ●   16 | 23 | 18 | $42 |
1 E. Oak St. (Rush St.), 312-255-0022
▣ Though some say it's "nice for dinner and dancing", the upshot on this "dark", "hip, speakeasy-esque club" beneath the Gold Coast's Le Colonial is that it's "too bad" its "pricey", "ordinary [French] bistro food" "doesn't measure up to" its "beautiful" and "funky" decor or the "eye-candy" offered by the "younger crowd [it] appeals to"; N.B. a lighter menu is offered after 10 PM.

LES DEUX GROS ⬛   27 | 20 | 23 | $50 |
462 N. Park Blvd. (bet. Hill & Pennsylvania Aves.), Glen Ellyn,
630-469-4002
▣ Brothers Thomas and Michael Lachowicz, the self-proclaimed "two fat guys", "are not afraid of butter", and it shows at their West Suburban French, which is "formal" but "with a sense of humor"; the "thoughtful menu" of "excellent food" is "well-prepared" (some say "the degustation is the way to go"), making up for the "uninspiring" decor and "strip-mall" setting.

LES NOMADES   28 | 26 | 27 | VE |
222 E. Ontario St. (bet. Fairbanks Ct. & St. Clair St.), 312-649-9010
■ A showcase for "talented chef" Roland Liccioni's "exciting", "visually stimulating" and "sensational" New French prix fixe–only menus, this popular spot is revered by well-heeled wanderers as an "oasis of refinement"; though it's no longer a private "club", "you'll feel a little

privileged to be seated" within its "formal" yet "lovely Streeterville townhouse" setting where "needs are anticipated" by a "professional" staff; P.S. the wine collection is "stupendous."

LE TITI DE PARIS   28 | 25 | 27 | $55 |
1015 W. Dundee Rd. (Kennicott Ave.), Arlington Heights, 847-506-0222

■ "They get everything right" at "always-nice owner" Pierre Pollin's haute French – from "imaginative" chef Michael Maddox's "ever-evolving" menu of "excellent", "superbly presented" creations to the "outstanding service" "without snobbery" and the "lovely" surroundings; a bastion of "elegance and quality", it has smitten surveyors saying it's "worth the drive" to the Northwest Suburbs and "the place to go when you want to be spoiled."

LE VICHYSSOIS 🗒   25 | 21 | 23 | $47 |
220 W. Rte. 120 (bet. Hollywood Terrace & Willow Rd.), Lakemoor, 815-385-8221

■ "Marvelous" chef-owner Bernard Cretier "brings Vichy, France to the [Illinois] countryside", not to mention intrepid Chicagoans who've been braving the "long" journey to this "charming", "intimate" "diamond in an unlikely" Far Northwest Suburban setting for more than 25 years; the draws are "homey but proper French" cooking, "lovely rooms" that afford a "quiet, relaxed" experience and service that's "warm", if "not polished."

Lexi's 🗒   ▽ 19 | 19 | 20 | $36 |
1330 W. Madison St. (bet. Ashland & Racine Aves.), 312-829-4600

🗲 A conceptual shift by "gregarious owner Nick" Andrews has brought this former New American West Looper into the "Italian steak"-house family, serving "solid fare" that's "great for "meat-and-potatoes guys"; still, some call the food "unmemorable" and wish they'd "take some risks with the menu"; P.S. there's a "free shuttle to the United Center."

Lincoln Noodle House   – | – | – | I |
5862 N. Lincoln Ave. (Sacramento Ave.), 773-275-8847

Forerunner to some of the better-known noodle chains, this modest Northwest Side BYO has for years been quietly putting out miles of its namesake dish in various combos of hot and cold, mild and spicy – as well as soups, stews and dumplings stuffed with meat or vegetables – all with full flavors, huge portions and low prices.

Lindo Mexico 🗒   15 | 15 | 15 | $20 |
2642 N. Lincoln Ave. (bet. Diversey Pkwy. & Wrightwood Ave.), 773-871-4832
8990 N. Milwaukee Ave. (Ballard Rd.), Niles, 847-296-2540

🗲 "Tasty, basic Mexican" eats at "fair prices" are the reason to frequent this Lincoln Park and North Suburban duo, both "good places to grab" a "fix" of "margaritas and tacos" as long as you're prepared to overlook the "slow service"; amigos approve of the city spot's patio "that makes you feel like you're on vacation" but don't care for the "dumpy decor" at the Niles location.

Lino's Ristorante   20   19   21 $35
222 W. Ontario St. (bet. Franklin & Wells Sts.), 312-266-0616
■ "It's nice" for River North neighbors that this "friendly" Northern Italian veteran from Phil Stefani – owner of numerous area restaurants including Tuscany, Tavern on Rush and Riva – and his uncle, the eponymous Lino, continues to be a "reliable" spot for "good service", "delicious food" like "great chicken Vesuvio" and a "cozy and warm atmosphere."

Little Bucharest ●S   16   13   16 $23
3001 N. Ashland Ave. (Wellington Ave.), 773-929-8640
☑ "Hearty, tasty meals" of "Old European grub" are an "ethnic change of pace" at this rollicking Romanian, a 32-year-old Lakeview veteran now calling itself a 'Euro cafe'; the "fun, crazy owner" and strolling minstrels (on weekends) add to a "festive atmosphere" (Saturday night patrons are even permitted bar-top-dancing and dish-breaking), which helps the hungry ignore the "dated decor"; P.S. fans also favor the "free limo service."

Lobby, The S   –   –   –   E
Peninsula Hotel, 108 E. Superior St., 5th fl. (bet. Michigan Ave. & Rush St.), 312-573-6754
Despite its humble name, this posh Near Norther on the Peninsula Hotel's fifth floor is a dining destination in its own right, serving breakfast, lunch, dinner and formal tea; its Eclectic cuisine blends American and Asian influences with a seafood focus and is suitably sedate for its sophisticated environment of gilded ceilings and sweeping floor-to-ceiling windows overlooking tony Boul Mich.

L'Olive ●S   17   15   18 $30
1629 N. Halsted St. (bet. North Ave. & Willow St.), 312-573-1515
■ The "uniquely spiced food", such as "good couscous" dishes and "comforting tagines", is "exotic yet accessible" at this "unpretentious" but "alluring" Moroccan "tucked below street level" in Lincoln Park; it's a "good pre-theater choice", with a "friendly, knowledgeable" staff and an "interesting", if "limited", native wine selection.

Lou Malnati's Pizzeria S   21   12   16 $17
439 N. Wells St. (Hubbard St.), 312-828-9800
3859 W. Ogden Ave. (Cermak Rd.), 773-762-0800
958 W. Wrightwood Ave. (Lincoln Ave.), 773-832-4030
(continued)

(continued)
Lou Malnati's Pizzeria

85 S. Buffalo Grove Rd. (Lake Cook Rd.), Buffalo Grove,
847-215-7100
1050 E. Higgins Rd. (bet. Arlington Heights & Busse Rds.),
Elk Grove, 847-439-2000
6649 N. Lincoln Ave. (bet. Devon & Pratt Aves.),
Lincolnwood, 847-673-0800
131 W. Jefferson Ave. (Washington St.), Naperville,
630-717-0700
1 S. Roselle Rd. (Schaumburg Rd.), Schaumburg, 847-985-1525
Additional takeout-only locations throughout the Chicago area
■ The late Lou Malnati's "very name causes" fans of this "dependable" chain of "old-fashioned pizza parlors" "to start drooling" for his "best-ever" creations, which have earned his heirs bragging rights for the top-rated 'za in our *Survey*; pie-pipers report that "heavenly sauce" and "lots of cheese" and toppings add up to "deep dish that can't get any better", but "be sure to request the butter crust."

Lou Mitchell's S⊕   20 12 18 $14

O'Hare Int'l Airport, Terminal 5 (I-90), 773-601-8989
565 W. Jackson Blvd. (Jefferson St.), 312-939-3111
■ For a "lip-smacking good" "breakfast dream", wake up to this West Loop "institution", an "old-fashioned diner" where morns commence with "Milk Duds and doughnut holes" (while "waiting in line"), "double-yolk omelets" and "strong coffee", all served with "a blatant disregard for fat and cholesterol"; lament not, late-risers – this "sassy-waitress heaven" serves lunch too; N.B. the O'Hare take-out serves soups, salads and sandwiches.

Lovells of Lake Forest S   21 24 21 $46

915 S. Waukegan Rd. (Everett Rd.), Lake Forest, 847-234-8013
☑ "Dine with the blue bloods" at this "classy, pricey" Suburban North New American whose "country-club atmosphere" comes complete with "fireplace and cigar lounge"; "owned by [Apollo 13] Captain James Lovell" and toqued by the "astronaut's son Jay", its "flavorful", "creative food" sends many "to the moon", but the less enthusiastic assert the experience is "unremarkable except for the space memorabilia."

Lucca's S   22 21 21 $36

2834 N. Southport Ave. (Wolfram St.), 773-477-2565
■ Its name is Lucca's (a hybrid of owners Michael Laconte's and chef Thomas Talucci's appellations), and this "low-key" Mediterranean-American "treasure" lives on the first floor of a "romantic" restored building in Lakeview; with "terrific choices" on the "creative menu" (like "heavenly shiitake mushroom pancakes"), a "wonderful, intimate setting" and "warm service", a visit to this "charmer" is "like curling up with a good book."

Lucky Platter S   18 | 15 | 17 | $16
514 Main St. (bet. Chicago & Hinman Aves.), Evanston,
847-869-4064

■ "Healthy portions" of "down-to-earth" Eclectic "cheap eats" – from "tasty" tandoori salmon to "excellent pumpkin soup" to one of "the best tuna melts with sweet-potato fries in the city" (and "good vegetarian options" too) – make this "fun, funky", "folksy" and "kid-friendly" North Suburban a popular "hangout", even if it is "no-frills."

Lula Café S   ▽ 22 | 13 | 17 | $19
2537 N. Kedzie Blvd. (bet. Fullerton Ave. & Logan Blvd.),
773-489-9554

■ "Please stop telling everyone about" it beg boosters of this "affordable" Logan Square Eclectic-American eatery serving up a "creative" menu of "contagious comfort cuisine", including an "excellent brunch"; it's a "delicious dive" catering to a "cool, funky clientele" of "hepcats", "cute rock girls" (who sometimes perform) and "local artists" (whose work adorns the walls), so don't be surprised if you experience some "weird service."

LuLu's Dim Sum & Then Sum S   17 | 12 | 17 | $16
626 Davis St. (bet. Chicago & Sherman Aves.), Evanston,
847-869-4343

☑ LuLu-lovers laud this "funky" and "happening place", an Evanston "original" for "fast, healthy and delicious" Pan-Asian fare that's not only "great for the price" but offers "new tastes galore" to its young "college-student clientele"; still, the jaded judge it "generic food" served up in a "mediocre atmosphere"; N.B. at press time, Lulu's planned to move to 804 Davis Street in late September 2002.

Lupita's S   21 | 15 | 19 | $19
700 Main St. (Custer Ave.), Evanston, 847-328-2255

■ An "authentic" "favorite", this North Suburban spot overseen by "solicitous and always-present owner Lupita" Carson has "haute" Mexican fare (with a few American dishes as well), "cute decorations" and a "homey feel"; on "special occasions" such as Valentine's, Mexican Independence (September 16) and Thanksgiving Days, it offers a *"Like Water for Chocolate* menu" featuring "wonderful dishes" from Laura Esquivel's novel.

Lutnia S   ▽ 20 | 20 | 21 | $32
5532 W. Belmont Ave. (Central Ave.), 773-282-5335

☑ "Good" "traditional Polish food", dramatic "tableside cooking", glittering "candles and [live] piano" music make for "a little romance" at this Northwest Side Continental; though most say it's a "one-of-a-kind" "pleasure to visit", the supercilious scoff that "the overdone old-world formality is a hoot", and the "limited wine menu" has quaffers quipping "I guess you're expected to stick to vodka."

Lutz Continental Cafe & Pastry Shop [S] 19 | 18 | 18 | $20

2458 W. Montrose Ave. (bet. Rockwell St. & Western Ave.), 773-478-7785

■ A cross between a genuine "German *konditorei*" (confectionery) and an "authentic Viennese cafe", this "restful" Northwest Side Continental classic offers a "slice of Europe" "in Chicago" with "wonderful pastries" that are "just like in the Old Country" and so "delicious" some even "skip the main course"; traditionalists also savor the "enchanting garden" and "step-back-in-time" atmosphere ("my dad took my mom on dates here").

L. Woods Tap & Pine Lodge [S] 18 | 18 | 19 | $25

7110 N. Lincoln Ave. (Kostner Ave.), Lincolnwood, 847-677-3350

◪ Suitable "for all ages", this "casual, crowded" North Suburban "Lettuce Entertain You theme place" serves an "American menu for hungry meat-eaters", as well as a "good kids' menu", in a "folksy" atmosphere "that feels like a Wisconsin lodge"; snipers suggest it "tries to be what it is not" and wryly point out that "after the wait for a table you'll eat just about anything."

Mac's ◐ [S] – | – | – | M

1801 W. Division St. (Wood St.), 773-782-4400

Providing something for everyone in diverse Ukrainian Village is a tall order, but Mac's is trying to fill it, blending traditional examples of American comfort food with thoughtful updates on its menu (prepared by a former Rushmore sous-chef) and serving them with cool music in a tin-ceilinged vintage-pub atmosphere with a prominent bar and plenty of TVs showing sporting events.

MAGGIANO'S LITTLE ITALY [S] 20 | 18 | 19 | $27

516 N. Clark St. (Grand Ave.), 312-644-7700
Oakbrook Center Mall, 240 Oakbrook Ctr. (Rte. 83), Oak Brook, 630-368-0300
1901 E. Woodfield Rd. (Rte. 53), Schaumburg, 847-240-5600
175 Old Orchard Ctr. (bet. Golf & Old Orchard Rds.), Skokie, 847-933-9555

◪ Even if you "come hungry" to any link in this "popular" chain of "boisterous" family spots, "expect" to trundle home toting "big doggy bags" thanks to the "bathtubsful of pasta" and "tremendous portions" of other "tasty" "straight Italian" fare they'll set before you; detractors declare it "noisy" and "hectic", with "inconsistent service" and "long waits" for "Americanized", "cookie-cutter food."

Magnolia Café [S] – | – | – | M

1224 W. Wilson Ave. (Magnolia Ave.), 773-728-8785

Upscale for Uptown, this hip-yet-homey New American raises the bar a bit for its locale, but its fare is nonetheless hearty (the signature dish is braised beef short ribs, though some dishes are more daring) and its prices don't bruise the wallet (generous entrees are under $20); exposed brick, earth tones, candlelight and photographs of magnolia blossoms create a serene setting.

Magnum's Prime Steakhouse   22 | 20 | 20 | $44

225 W. Ontario St. (Franklin St.), 312-337-8080 S
777 E. Butterfield Rd. (bet. Highland Ave. & Meyers Rd.), Lombard, 630-573-1010 S
1701 W. Golf Rd. (New Wilke Rd.), Rolling Meadows, 847-952-8555
☑ Make your day with "great steaks and cocktails" at these "fancy spots" that a majority of meat-eaters maintain "hold their own with the big steakhouse boys"; the "gaudy atmosphere" makes some "miss Vegas", while others say the "spotty service" is a roll of the dice in its own right; P.S. the city location charges a cover to enter its weekends-only "disco ball and cigars" nightclub.

Maison S   – | – | – | E

30 S. La Grange Rd. (Harris Ave.), La Grange, 708-588-9890
"Those with discriminating palates" report that this still-not-widely-known Contemporary French–Traditional American sophomore "in the Western Suburbs" "seems up to the challenge"; the husband-and-wife team in the kitchen – private-chefs-gone-public Mary and Christopher Spagnola – offers "excellent seasonal food" from an "inspired" menu that changes every six to eight weeks within a "beautiful, roomy interior."

Mama Desta's Red Sea S   ▽ 18 | 11 | 13 | $18

3216 N. Clark St. (Belmont Ave.), 773-935-7561
☑ "There's not much to this [Lakeview] spot" in terms of decor – in fact, it's a bit of a "hole-in-the-wall" – but the point of this "unique experience" is "authentic and inexpensive Ethiopian" eats (including vegetarian choices) that are "fun to eat with your hands" and served by a "casual", "friendly staff"; still, a few find the food "bland."

Mama Thai S   ▽ 20 | 14 | 14 | $18

1112 W. Madison St. (Harlem Ave.), Oak Park, 708-386-0100
■ Oak Parkers say this "good Thai" storefront spot is "better than most local joints", and those from other areas report it's "worth the drive" thanks to "consistently fresh-tasting" Siamese fare including its signature spicy basil chicken stir-fried with garlic, peppers and mushrooms – not to mention some of the "best potstickers around" – all "at great prices"; N.B. beer and wine only.

Mambo Grill   18 | 16 | 17 | $25

412 N. Clark St. (bet. Hubbard & Kinzie Sts.), 312-467-9797
■ "Enjoy the spices" and "different flavors" of this "fun" River North Nuevo Latino's "inventive" and "flavorful dishes", a "surprising blend" of traditional South and

Central American cuisines that amounts to "much more than" standard "south-of-the-border" fare; with "mostly hits and infrequent misses" from the kitchen and "interesting drinks" and "great sangria" from the bar, you may find yourself "doing the mambo."

Manny's Coffee Shop ⊄
| 23 | 10 | 16 | $14 |

1141 S. Jefferson St. (Roosevelt Rd.), 312-939-2855

■ "Over 60 years old and going strong", this beloved South Loop coffee shop–cum–"museum of Jewish cooking" is such a "real Chicago" "institution" that some swear they "couldn't live without it"; "even a cardiologist would be tempted" by the "mile-high corned-beef sandwiches" and "old-fashioned fare", and besides, "you never know who you'll see" – "cops", "politicians", "maybe your lawyer."

Maple Tree Inn
| 19 | 16 | 16 | $26 |

13301 S. Old Western Ave. (Canal St.), Blue Island, 708-388-3461

☑ Crawfish-cravers clash over the Cajun-Creole cookery at this "friendly, hectic" South Suburban spot; some swear by its "good home cooking" like "to-die-for hickory-buttered BBQ shrimp" and "great crawfish pie", but others call the food "inconsistent" and only "fairly authentic", as well as "questioning" the "off-kilter service", saying this "potentially bright star" is performing "below its potential."

Marché 🆂
| 21 | 23 | 20 | $40 |

833 W. Randolph St. (Green St.), 312-226-8399

☑ "Take your friends from Kansas" for a "wild" ride at this "still-hip", "circus-like" "winner" in the Market District that lures "ultra-trendy" "pretty people" with "whimsical" decor and an "exciting" New French–American "menu of temptations"; some say, though, that the "attentive" staff can be as "wacky" as Emerald Cityites and warn that the "loud, loud, loud" scene might have "small-towners" tapping their ruby slippers and hankering for home.

Margie's Candies ◗🆂
| 23 | 18 | 18 | $10 |

1960 N. Western Ave. (Armitage Ave.), 773-384-1035

■ "Sentimental" sweet-toothers insist that this "kitschy" and "quirky" "must-try" Bucktown "blast from the past" "becomes a must-return" once you've tried its "homemade candy" and "old-fashioned ice-cream creations" with "butterfat galore" and "hot fudge so thick your spoon stays vertical"; there is an American menu, but most maintain the "great desserts" "are a meal" in themselves.

Marion Street Grille 🆂
| ▽ 20 | 18 | 21 | $35 |

189 N. Marion St. (bet. Lake & Ontario Sts.), Oak Park, 708-383-1551

☑ "Quaint, cozy and romantic", this Suburban West Regional American "find" draws the faithful for "fresh fish" and "worthwhile steak" specialties amid "unique decor" of exposed brick, tin ceilings and vintage advertising posters; the "nice atmosphere" seems especially "quiet" given that the "comfortable" storefront is just a block from bustling Lake Street, but still some scowl that it's "pricey for Oak Park."

Mario's Gold Coast Ristorante 16 | 15 | 20 | $25

21 W. Goethe St. (Dearborn St.), 312-944-0199

◪ "Raving" respondents who "love hanging out" at this "locals' secret" call it "the *Cheers* of the Gold Coast"; even if not "everybody knows your name", count on owner Mario Stefanini (he "truly loves people!") and manager "Mike [Cordis to] treat everyone like an old friend"; with such "warm service", most don't mind that the "inexpensive" Italian "food is only adequate."

Mars [S] 15 | 16 | 16 | $19

3124 N. Broadway (Belmont Ave.), 773-404-1600

◪ While some say the "interesting food" at this "upbeat" and "upscale" Lakeview Chinese – like orange beef and crispy sesame shrimp – is "proof that quality ingredients don't have to cost an arm and a leg", the less impressed claim the "competent" kitchen is "hit or miss" and the "service leaves something to be desired", adding that "better options abound."

Mas [S] 22 | 19 | 19 | $34

1670 W. Division St. (Paulina St.), 773-276-8700

■ "Reliably awesome", this "energetic" Wicker Park Nuevo Latino has *señoras y caballeros* "crowded" at the bar, consuming "outstanding" caipirinhas and mojitos while eagerly anticipating *más* of chef John Manion's "edgy Latin cuisine" and its "quixotic combos of savory, complex spices"; the "long waits" aren't so "terrible" "now that they take reservations" and there's another one, baby brother Otro Mas in Lakeview.

Masck [S] – | – | – | E

Deerfield Commons Shopping Ctr., 730 Waukegan Rd. (bet. Deerfield Rd. & Osterman Ave.), Deerfield, 847-236-1400

In late 2001, husband-and-wife team Kevin and Michelle Nierman opened this ambitious North Suburban New American in the Deerfield Commons Shopping Center; it features an eclectic seasonal menu ranging from 'floppy cheeseburgers' and thin-crust pizzas to twice-roasted crispy duckling and garlic jumbo prawns (and a fun finish of hot, made-to-order mini-doughnuts), and the stylish dining room is lively, colorful – and often crowded.

Matsuya ◐ [S] 22 | 13 | 18 | $22

3469 N. Clark St. (Sheffield Ave.), 773-248-2677

■ There's a reason this "solid" "sushi goldmine" in Wrigleyville is "always crowded" (and "deservedly so") "no matter when you go" – they've been serving "fresh, authentic", "consistently good" Japanese fare (including "interesting rolls", "tasty tempura" and "well-flavored teriyaki") "at a great price" "for decades", which packs 'em in despite a near-absence of ambiance.

Max's S — 14 | 9 | 13 | $15

Crossroads Shopping Ctr., 191 Skokie Valley Rd. (bet. Clavey & Lake Cook Rds.), Highland Park, 847-831-0600

◪ Fans of this North Suburban Jewish deli appreciate the "good smoked salmon" and "monster matzo balls", but contrarians claim it's "average", "inconsistent" and "not as good as" its competitors, with some bellicose Big Apple boosters braying that it "can't compare to NYC" and insisting "it's a Chicago deli – in other words, mediocre."

Maza S — ▽ 23 | 17 | 21 | $26

2748 N. Lincoln Ave. (Diversey Pkwy.), 773-929-9600

■ "You can taste the TLC" at this Lincoln Park "gem" specializing in the "Lebanese staple" known as, you guessed it, "maza – small portions" of "a zillion" (well, 20) "tasty" tapas-style treats served "for two"; though you "can definitely make it the main course", "excellent" entrees and "great desserts" are also offered, and a "helpful staff" that makes you "feel at home" warms the "spartan" but "elegant" environment.

McCormick & Schmick's S — 21 | 21 | 20 | $39

41 E. Chestnut St. (Rush St.), 312-397-9500

◪ It's "good to have a seafood place in the middle of beefdom" declare devotees of this Gold Coast national chain outpost's "excellent menu" starring "any fish you can think of" proffered with a plethora of "preparation options" in a "dark", clubby setting with "cozy, semi-private booths"; still, some label it "inconsistent" and a trifle "institutional"; P.S. "the bar hops" "at happy hour."

Meritage Cafe & Wine Bar S — 23 | 20 | 21 | $40

2118 N. Damen Ave. (bet. Armitage & Webster Aves.), 773-235-6434

■ "Sophisticated cuisine" with "superb seasonings" draws "drools" for this Bucktown New American that purveys provender of the Pacific Northwest; whether you take your meal within the "posh and stylish" interior or "dine under the twinkle lights" of its "romantic" "heated patio" ("you can imagine you're in Northern California"), the "warm" ambiance makes it a "mainstay for a night out with a significant other."

Merle's Smokehouse S — 20 | 17 | 18 | $22

1727 Benson Ave. (Church St.), Evanston, 847-475-7766

■ Set in a "historic old bar", this North Suburban BBQ bonanza offers outlaws "awesome pork chops", "yummy brisket" and "amazing ribs" done Memphis-, Texas- and North Carolina–style; it's a "great" place "for guys to pig out" (even if their "girls don't like it" as much) amid "humorous" decorations such as "the sign that says 'cowboys, scrape boots before entering.'"

Merlo Ristorante S
– – – E

2638 N. Lincoln Ave. (Wrightwood Ave.), 773-529-0747

Distinctive Northern Italian fare is fully complemented by tasteful decor and a well-selected wine list (with 20 by-the-glass pours) at this welcome Lincoln Park newcomer; try the artichoke tart, lasagna verde and creamy panna cotta with homemade caramel drizzle, but don't try coming for lunch – they only serve dinner, seven days a week.

Mesón Sabika S
23 22 21 $29

1025 Aurora Ave. (bet. Berry Dr. & River Rd.), Naperville, 630-983-3000

Northfield Village Ctr., 310 Happ Rd. (bet. Willow Rd. & Winnetka Ave.), Northfield, 847-784-9300

■ "Tip-top" for "tempting"-and-"tasty tapas treats" in our *Survey*, these North and West Suburban haciendas offer "a true taste of Spain", with a "wide variety" of "the best" small plates that are "sublime for sharing" and "beautiful settings", especially the Naperville original's "historic" "pillared mansion with veranda"; the "good sangria (in both red and white)" and "sherry flights" go down smoothly too.

Metro Club S
– – – M

3032 N. Lincoln Ave. (bet. Belmont & Wellington Aves.), 773-929-0622

It's easy to miss this tiny, country-style Austrian pub nestled on a commercial stretch in Lakeview, but for those who lament the diminishing ranks of Chicago's German spots, it's an absolute must-find for generously portioned plates of Wiener schnitzel, spaetzle and goulash – and, of course, the accompanying array of German beers and schnapps; N.B. dinner only, closed Mondays and Tuesdays.

Mia Cucina S
19 18 17 $29

56 W. Wilson St. (Brockway St.), Palatine, 847-358-4900

■ "City atmosphere in the suburbs" is among the attractions at this Northwest Suburban "trendy Italian with upscale food" such as "good pastas", "terrific breads" and "tasty, nicely presented specialties from the wood-burning oven"; raters rank it "reliably good, especially for Palatine", and say the "noisy, happening" atmosphere is enhanced by a "beautiful bar area with live music on weekends."

MIA FRANCESCA S
24 19 20 $31

3311 N. Clark St. (School St.), 773-281-3310

■ "A total favorite", this "buzzworthy" Lakeview original was the launching pad of Scott Harris' captivating coterie of contemporary "casual Italians" offering "affordable", regularly changing menus of "superbly done" dishes from Rome and the surrounding areas of Tuscany, Umbria and Lazio; you'll have to "enjoy drinks at the bar as you wait" for a seat in its "crowded" dining room, though, since "they don't take reservations."

Midori Japanese [S] ▽ 19 15 18 $22

3310 W. Bryn Mawr Ave. (bet. Kedzie & Kimball Aves.), 773-267-9733

◪ Below the radar of most, this Northwest Sider has a cult following for fish that's "always fresh", as well as "tasty and surprising Korean snacks that come with your dinner"; some "Japanese-Americans and their visitors go for sushi" in its cozy tatami rooms and for karaoke and "bizarre videos" in the bar, but probably not for the service, which is "sometimes lacking."

Mike Ditka's [S] 20 20 19 $37

Tremont Hotel, 100 E. Chestnut St. (Michigan Ave.), 312-587-8989

◪ "Cigar-smoking jocks" seeking "power pork chops" head to this "solid", "not-just-for-tourists" Near North steakhouse with a "heavy-on-meat" menu and a "hall of fame–like memorabilia" collection; some fans of "da Bears" who like "da food" but find da dining room "stuffy" call an audible and head instead for the bar, "where there's more action" and "more fun."

Millennium Steaks & Chops 19 19 20 $40

832 W. Randolph St. (Green St.), 312-455-1400

600 E. North Ave. (Schmale Rd.), Carol Stream, 630-665-4500 [S]

◪ "An oasis for meat-and-potatoes guys on [Randolph], an exciting culinary street", this Market District Italian steakhouse descendent of the venerable Gino's has "memorable" meals in store; some scowl that it's "standard" and "pricey", adding that the "steaks are good but other items need improvement", though at least "the 32-ounce [bone-in] prime rib feeds a whole pride"; P.S. the "new location in Carol Stream" is unrated.

Miller's Pub ◐ [S] 16 14 17 $24

134 S. Wabash Ave. (bet. Adams & Monroe Sts.), 312-263-4988

■ A "Loop standard", this "bastion of old Downtown Chicago" "maintains tradition" with "classic" American "grub" ("not haute cuisine"), "early saloon decor" and a staff that "remembers you"; "huge nostalgic value" and a "late-night" kitchen cooking till 3 AM have regulars reporting they "hope it never closes."

Mill Race Inn [S] 18 22 19 $29

4 E. State St. (Rte. 25), Geneva, 630-232-2030

◪ Five venues in one, this "relaxing" compound "in the Western Suburbs" comprises the Country Inn (a "cultured" dining space) and Mallard Room (for private functions), both with "views of a wooded island park", the Duck Inn (a sports bar), the Grill (a tavern) and the summer-only Gazebo "pleasantly" placed "on the Fox River"; still, most say its "lovely setting" outruns its "conservative" American menus by a mile.

Millrose Brewing Co. S　　　　18　20　18　$30
45 S. Barrington Rd. (Central Rd.), Barrington, 847-382-7673
☑ Built from six relocated antique barns, this Northwest Suburban "lodgelike" microbrewery/restaurant/store comes by its "rustic country" feel honestly, and "every" one of its "large rooms" is "a treat"; quaffers claim the "hearty, beef and pork"–heavy menu of "basic American food" that "supports its great beer" is "a cut above average", but critics caution "expect to wait" for "so-so food and service."

Mimosa S　　　　24　19　23　$34
1849 Second St. (bet. Central Ave. & Elm Pl.), Highland Park, 847-432-9770
■ "Constantly innovating chef"-owner Kevin Schrimmer "pleases customers" of this "well-run" North Suburban with an "appealing menu" of "creative" New French–Italian fare that fans feel is "just incredible" and a "good buy", to boot; the atmosphere is "calm" and "uncluttered", maitre d' "Dan [Tarver] and [toque's wife] Karen always make you feel welcome" and the "friendly staff" "gets an A for professional service."

Mirabell　　　　∇　19　17　18　$27
3454 W. Addison St. (bet. Kimball & St. Louis Aves.), 773-463-1962
■ A "wonderful" "neighborhood German", and "one of the few left", this Northwest Sider offers "a night in Bavaria – in a booth!"; "great schnitzel and leberknödel soup" are served in its "rustic" dining rooms and washed down with imported beers on tap from the "convivial bar" where, rumor has it, "chef Werner [Heil] will do shots of Jägermeister on request" (it can't hurt to ask).

Mirai Sushi S　　　　24　22　19　$38
2020 W. Division St. (Damen Ave.), 773-862-8500
■ Wicker Park's chart-topping Japanese "screams 'repeat visit'", earning earnest encomiums for the "perfect presentations" of "inventive chef Jun" Ichikawa's "bold" "couture sushi" ("not cheap in either price or quality", it "compares favorably to Tokyo" spots'); P.S. the "beautiful people" head upstairs to the "sleek, hip lounge" to partake of the "awesome adult beverages" and "great sake list."

Misto　　　　17　16　18　$30
1118 W. Grand Ave. (bet. Halsted St. & Racine Ave.), 312-226-5989
■ A "comfortable" combo of American and Italian cuisines at "reasonable prices" makes this "nice" Near West "find"

"a pleasant surprise" for those tired of "the trendy
[restaurant] craze", and a new sidewalk cafe and "nice
hospitality add to the atmosphere"; P.S. "it's worth it just to
see [chef] Donny Greco in action" – "go Saturday night
when he sings" at 10 PM.

Mi Sueño, Su Realidad S

– – – E

1250 N. Milwaukee Ave. (Ashland Ave.), 773-782-1500
No longer just a dream of Geno Bahena's, this convivial,
vibrant Wicker Parker set in the former Mareva's space is
a reality and a recent addition to his expanding family of
regional Mexican spots; fans of his dreamy *moles* (his
mother's recipes) will rejoice anew in those intense flavors
and recognize many dishes from sister spots Ixcapuzalco
and Chilpancingo on the menu, as well as the expectedly
epic tequila list.

Mity Nice Grill S

18 17 18 $25

*Water Tower Pl., 835 N. Michigan Ave., mezzanine level
(bet. Chestnut & Pearson Sts.), 312-335-4745*
■ A "quiet" and "classy yet casual" "oasis in a storm"
(namely, the "upscale mall" called Water Tower Place), this
Streeterville American "really is mity nice" for an "always-
satisfying" menu ranging from "down-home comfort-food"
"standards" to fancier fare like "great garlic-crusted
whitefish"; regulars report it's "the best place to recharge
after a heavy day of shopping."

MK S

26 24 25 $51

868 N. Franklin St. (bet. Chicago Ave. & Oak St.), 312-482-9179
■ "Terrific food", a "stylish setting" and "expert service"
are a "powerful combination" at this River North New
American, where "genius chef[-owner] Michael Kornick"
(the 'M.K.' of mk) is "at the top of his game"; his "innovative
but approachable" food is paired with a "well-crafted and
complementary wine list" and followed by "divine desserts",
making this "a place to go back to as often as possible."

mk North S

23 20 21 $42

305 Happ Rd. (Willow Rd.), Northfield, 847-716-6500
☑ "Fresh, understandable Contemporary American fare"
that "fits right in" in its affluent North Shore neighborhood
makes this "happening" and "family-friendly" "cousin" of
Michael Kornick's Downtowner "a welcome newcomer" in
town; though doubters don't like the "noise", "high prices"
and service that's "not quite there yet", folks report
it's "becoming increasingly difficult to get reservations",
so plan accordingly.

MOD. S

23 22 20 $42

1520 N. Damen Ave. (North Ave.), 773-252-1500
☑ A mod nod to New American fare, this "hip" Wicker
Parker is "an eye-opener in every sense"; "don't be put

off" by the "funky" "*Jetson's* decor" – "the room may be
hard"-edged, but the "innovative and electrifying" cuisine is
paradoxically "real comfy"; P.S. though the menu remained
unchanged at press time, the Food rating may not reflect
the post-*Survey* departure of chef Kelly Courtney.

Molive S · 20 20 21 $44
Whitehall Hotel, 107 E. Delaware Pl. (Michigan Ave.),
312-573-6300
■ "Hidden" "in the Whitehall Hotel", in "an out-of-the-
way" Near North location "off Michigan Avenue", this
"under-attended treasure" is "sophisticated without
snobby excess", pairing "imaginative" New American–
Mediterranean cuisine such as "great fish" dishes with
"exceptional wine offerings" (including 40 by the glass)
in a "stylish", "intimate room" with a "friendly, casual
and uplifting atmosphere."

MON AMI GABI S · 23 22 22 $38
2300 N. Lincoln Park W. (Belden Ave.), 773-348-8886
Oakbrook Center Mall, 260 Oakbrook Ctr. (Rte. 83),
Oak Brook, 630-472-1900
■ Friends of Gabi (chef-partner Gabino Sotelino) consider
"both locations" of this "comfy", "bustling" city-and-
suburban bistro brotherhood – "another interesting Lettuce
Entertain You" enterprise – to be "spot-on" for "good French
favorites" (including "great steak frites") offered by servers
with "no affectations"; oenophiles effuse over the "rolling
wine cart", and expatriates appreciate the "European feel."

Moody's Pub ◐S⌐ · 19 15 16 $15
5910 N. Broadway (Thorndale St.), 773-275-2696
◪ "A real Chicago joint with all the greasy food you love",
this place has been serving "cheap eats" in Edgewater
since 1959; pleased pub-licans praise the "laid-back"
ambiance and "fireplaces that make it a favorite winter-
afternoon spot", as well as the "lovely beer garden under
the trees" in summer; perturbed ones dub it "dark, dingy
and smoky – and that's during the day."

MORTON'S OF CHICAGO S · 26 21 24 $53
Newberry Plaza, 1050 N. State St., lower level (Maple St.),
312-266-4820
9525 W. Bryn Mawr Ave. (River Rd.), Rosemont, 847-678-5155
1470 McConnor Pkwy. (Meacham Rd.), Schaumburg,
847-413-8771
1 Westbrook Corporate Ctr. (bet. 22nd St. & Wolf Rd.),
Westchester, 708-562-7000
■ "In the face of tremendous competition", these "clubby"
cum lauders continue to claim the coveted steakhouse
crown in our *Survey* and have since its inception; the city
original and its suburban spin-offs (part of a national chain)
each get the meat-eaters seal of approval as a "primo"

"red-meat heaven with attentive service" where "the bang lives up to the buck" – though many "thank goodness for expense accounts."

Mosaic S – | – | – | E
1204 W. Rand Rd. (Hintz Rd.), Arlington Heights, 847-670-1212
Set in an old schoolhouse with numerous intimate rooms, this Northwest Suburban newcomer cobbles together an Eclectic composite of cuisines – Cajun-spiced shrimp-scallop kebabs, grilled swordfish with pineapple salsa and lamb stew in Guinness Stout sauce, followed by baked-to-order hot apple pie or chocolate cake; they also offer brunch and patio dining.

Mossant Bistro 19 | 20 | 19 | $37
Hotel Monaco, 225 N. Wabash Ave. (bet. Lake St. & Wacker Dr.), 312-236-9300
☑ Respondents report that this "classy bistro" in the Loop's Hotel Monaco is "better than the usual" hostelry eatery, with a "comfortable, clubby" space that's a "good business lunch" or "date destination"; though the "interesting menu" (American-influenced New French) provides "well-prepared meals", the laissez-faire label it "undistinguished."

Moti Mahal S ∇ 19 | 9 | 14 | $17
1031-35 W. Belmont Ave. (Kenmore Ave.), 773-348-4392
☑ "Authentic", "inexpensive" and "tasty Indian food" from a "great variety of platters" and a "good buffet" draw bargain-hunters to this "great BYO" in Lakeview, the survivor of an erstwhile duo (the Rogers Park branch has closed), where devoted diners are undaunted by what some call "quaint" – others "sparse" and "tacky" – surroundings and "questionable service."

Mrs. Levy's Delicatessen 15 | 12 | 15 | $15
Sears Tower, 233 S. Wacker Dr., 2nd level (bet. Adams St. & Jackson Blvd.), 312-993-0530
☑ To some matzo mavens, this "reliable" "standard" in the Sears Tower is "the only place to get good deli in the Loop", delivering "quick service" and an "extensive menu" of "NY-style" favorites that are "great for the price"; critics contend the "corporate" concept is "getting stale", though, and outsiders opine that the building's "tough to get into with all the [post-9/11] security."

Mrs. Park's Tavern ◐ S 18 | 17 | 18 | $33
Doubletree Guest Suites Hotel, 198 E. Delaware Pl. (Michigan Ave.), 312-280-8882
☑ Run by the Smith & Wollensky Restaurant Group, this Traditional American in the Doubletree Guest Suites Hotel (the "casual" counterpart to its Park Avenue Cafe) has "offbeat, creative" dishes that are reliably "good" (the "mini-cheeseburgers are a must"); coming here may be

"like visiting mom at home" – but without having to listen to mom's advice.

Mt. Everest Restaurant S　　　– | – | – | M |
618 Church St. (bet. Chicago & Orrington Sts.), Evanston, 847-491-1069
"Besides standard Indian fare" and a "great lunch buffet", adventurous diners will find "good" "Nepalese dishes" to pique their interest at this "interesting" North Suburban where the signature goat dish is "great (for meat eaters)"; the "wonderful cuisine and service" are enjoyed in an "attractive" and colorful dining room dotted with Himalayan paintings and augmented by authentic music.

My Pie Pizza S　　　20 | 12 | 16 | $15 |
2010 N. Damen Ave. (Armitage Ave.), 773-394-6900
2417 N. Clark St. (Fullerton Pkwy.), 773-929-3380
■ For "great, fresh-tasting deep dish", the "campus crowd" and those looking for "cheap food" head to this duo of "neighborhood" pie peddlers that sport "wonderful salad bars"; loyalists of the Lincoln Park "1970s relic" say "bring a flashlight" to navigate the "dark", "weird, midnight picnic decor" then "snare a seat by the fireplace"; Bucktowners boast their branch's 'za is "just as good."

Myron & Phil's Steakhouse S　　　22 | 16 | 21 | $35 |
3900 W. Devon Ave. (bet. Crawford & Lincoln Aves.), Lincolnwood, 847-677-6663
■ "Always a top performer in steaks, chops, seafood and ribs", this "reliable" thirtysomething North Suburban "throwback" meat mecca also satisfies with a "wonderful [complimentary] appetizer tray" (including "cholesterol-bomb chopped liver") and "great green goddess dressing"; it may be "nothing fancy", but it's "pretty darn good", and even detractors who describe it as an "old-school Cadillac" admit the staffers are "reliable pros."

Mysore Woodland S　　　– | – | – | M |
2548 W. Devon Ave. (Rockwell St.), 773-338-8166
Locals line up at this Northwest Side meat-free Southern Indian BYO on the bustling ethnic stretch of Devon Avenue – home to a vast array of subcontinental markets, boutiques and restaurants – and its banquet-size dining room is frequently full of large families enjoying fare including fried lentil doughnuts, samosas and dosai.

Nacional 27　　　22 | 23 | 21 | $37 |
325 W. Huron St. (Orleans St.), 312-664-2727
■ "Order a mojito and enjoy" the "high-energy fusion" of this "hip Nuevo Latino", a "lively" Lettuce Entertain You River North hot spot where chef Randy Zweiban showcases the "wonderful, bold flavors" of 27 Latin American nations on his "imaginative" menu; "fantastic cocktails" enhance

the "glamorous" setting, which is even more "fun when the music starts" and the salsa dancing begins (on weekends).

NAHA   25   24   23 $54
500 N. Clark St. (Illinois St.), 312-321-6242
■ A "great addition to the fine-dining scene", this River North two-year-old "works" thanks to "chef Carrie Nahabedian's New American–Mediterranean fusion" featuring "seemingly simple dishes that uncover complex and fresh flavors"; the "polished", "passionate staff" "makes each diner feel special", and the "crisp, clean setting" "feels like a spa"; P.S. since you'll "eat like a king", loyalists laugh you'd better "bring the royal treasury."

Nancy's Original Stuffed Pizza S   17   10   14 $17
2930 N. Broadway (Wellington Ave.), 773-883-1977
3970 N. Elston Ave. (Irving Park Rd.), 773-267-8182
■ "Artistry with a crust" awaits at these deep-dish doppelgängers on the Northwest Side and in Lakeview, where the "stuffed giant pizza answers all prayers" and the "chicken cacciatore pie is a can't-miss"; they're "not much to look at" pout pie-philes who propose that they "need to renovate", but plenty are pleased with the takeout and "prompt delivery."

Napa Valley Grille S   21   21   20 $39
626 N. State St. (Ontario St.), 312-587-1166
☑ "Three cheers" for this "great new player" in River North, a link in a vino-centric national chain that features "delicious" New American–French offerings, "great wines by the glass" and "cozy surroundings" ("there's not a bad table in the house"); a cluster of grumpier grape-lovers grumbles it's a "long, long way from California" and gripes that the service is "still a little rough around the edges."

Narcisse ●S   ▽ 19   23   19 $37
710 N. Clark St. (bet. Huron & Superior Sts.), 312-787-2675
☑ River North locals "love the interior" of this "cozy" lair that's a "great after-dinner spot" and a "nice place for drinks", with "expensive wines" and "cocktails so strong no person could drink one and stay sober"; the "winning staff" and "way-upscale bar food" are a welcome treat to some, though the more down-to-earth deem it a bit self-absorbed and "pretentious."

New Japan S   21   17   20 $26
1322 Chicago Ave. (Dempster St.), Evanston, 847-475-5980
■ While this twentysomething "Evanston mainstay" isn't so new anymore, it continues to boast "superior presentations" of both "inventive" and "traditional Japanese" dishes, including sushi, on its "excellent and varied menu"; though some sigh it's a "jewel with no atmosphere", others say its "setting is serene and peaceful"; P.S. a recent change

in ownership has fans hoping its long tradition of "personal service" survives intact.

New Three Happiness 🅂　　　–|–|–|M
(fka Three Happiness)

2130 S. Wentworth Ave. (Cermak Rd.), 312-791-1228
Dim sum seven days a week keeps this sizable Szechuan-Mongolian "classic" in Chinatown busy, if not "frenetic", aided by a prominent corner location near the El stop; "fast service" and "fun people-watching" are additional bonuses, but hecklers hint at "slipping quality" in the kitchen and housekeeping issues; N.B. no longer affiliated with Three Happiness on West Cermak Road.

Next Door Bistro 🅂⊄　　　23 | 17 | 22 | $31
250 Skokie Blvd. (bet. I-94 & Lake Cook Rd.), Northbrook, 847-272-1491
■ You "can't go wrong with any special or menu item" at this "wonderful", "warm" North Suburban Italian-American bistro, kissing cousin to Francesco's Hole in the Wall, where coin counters compliment the "great value" as much as the "excellent" roast chicken; the "funky interior never changes" and neither do the "long waits" (some swear "they seat regulars first"), so "arrive early" and "bring cash."

Nick & Tony's 🅂　　　17 | 17 | 18 | $30
1 E. Wacker Dr. (bet. State St. & Wabash Ave.), 312-467-9449
601 Skokie Blvd. (bet. Dundee Rd. & I-94), Northbrook, 847-480-2200
☑ Though some find this Italian duo's "convenient location" in the Loop to be "great for a business lunch" or "pre-theater" dinner of "large, decently priced portions" (especially "outdoors in summer"), others say, quantity aside, both the city and the Suburban North nooks are still just "so-so" "joints" with "nothing special" going on.

Nick's Fishmarket　　　24 | 22 | 23 | $49
Bank One Plaza, 51 S. Clark St. (Monroe St.), 312-621-0200
O'Hare Int'l Ctr., 10275 W. Higgins Rd. (Mannheim Rd.), Rosemont, 847-298-8200 🅂
■ "A sure catch every time", these "classy", "awesome" Loop and O'Hare seafooders "consistently" net a huge school of fin fans – "even though they hook your wallet along with your palate" – thanks to their "elegantly presented" "fine-dining creations" (especially the signature Dover sole and "great lobster bisque") and "dynamite service teams" who "wait on you hand and foot."

Nicolinas Cucina 🅂　　　▽ 19 | 18 | 18 | $33
NBC Tower, 455 Cityfront Plaza Dr. (bet. Columbus Dr. & Michigan Ave.), 312-832-2600
■ "Tucked in an out-of-the-way" spot (in the NBC Tower), this Streeterville Italian seafooder is "worth hunting" for

according to satisfied seekers who report a "creative menu", "exciting surroundings" and an "attentive, friendly service" staff; while a few fret over what they call a "somewhat limited" selection, most acknowledge it has "lots of potential."

Nine 23 | 25 | 20 | $48

440 W. Randolph St. (bet. Canal St. & Wacker Dr.), 312-575-9900

◪ "If you have something to show, this is the place to go" – so say the "hip and trendy" about this "big, bold", "see-and-be-seen hot spot" in the West Loop where the "great" American steakhouse fare and "champagne-and-caviar bar" "match the dazzling ambiance"; though scenesters say the chance to "see someone famous" helps make for "a great evening out", the jaded just don't get the "pretension" and "high prices."

NOMI [S] 23 | 26 | 23 | $61

Park Hyatt Chicago, 800 N. Michigan Ave. (Chicago Ave.), 312-239-4030

◪ "You can't beat" the "stunning", "romantic view" at this "elegant", "sleek" New French-Asian fusion fantasy set in a "dazzling" room above the city lights that has the smitten sighing "can I live here? please?"; while foodies fawn over chef Sandro Gamba's "adventurous" and "artful" fare, a few frowners fuss over the "diminutive portions" and "high prices", adding it's time for the "arrogant staff" to "lose the attitude."

Nookies [S] ⊄ 17 | 12 | 17 | $14

1746 N. Wells St. (bet. Lincoln & North Aves.), 312-337-2454

Nookies, Too [S] ⊄

2114 N. Halsted St. (bet. Dickens & Webster Aves.), 773-327-1400

Nookies Tree ◐ [S] ⊄

3334 N. Halsted St. (Buckingham Pl.), 773-248-9888

■ Native Chicagoans of all persuasions head to this "fun, fast, cheap" trio of coffee shops for "consistent" American diner fare and "reliable" breakfasts served "any time of day"; red-eyed partiers hail it for the "best hangover meal around", but "get there early or you'll wait in line", especially on weekends; P.S. the Lakeview location is also a great "boy-watching cafe."

Noon-O-Kabab [S] – | – | – | I

4661 N. Kedzie Ave. (Leland Ave.), 773-279-8899

The main attractions at this tiny, impeccably clean family-run Persian BYO on the Northwest Side are its kebabs of marinated chicken, filet, salmon or spiced ground beef served atop mounds of fluffy, saffron-flecked basmati rice in portions so large you don't mind sharing; conveniently located right off the brown-line train, it's great for dining in or taking out.

NORTH POND S
24 25 22 $43

(fka North Pond Café)

2610 N. Cannon Dr. (bet. Diversey & Fullerton Pkwys.),
773-477-5845

■ You'll feel like you're "dining at Frank Lloyd Wright's home" at this "wonderfully restored" "gem" of an "Arts and Crafts building" "hidden" in Lincoln Park, but the real architect here is "inventive" chef Bruce Sherman, who builds "delicious" New American dishes "using fresh ingredients" from "local organic farms"; P.S. though the "spectacular" "lagoon and skyline view" remain, a recent remodeling is not reflected in the Decor score.

Northside Cafe ●S
14 14 14 $19

1635 N. Damen Ave. (Milwaukee & North Aves.),
773-384-3555

◪ Biased Bucktowners bill this Traditional American as a "fun burger joint" turning out "reasonably priced", "better-than-average pub grub"; nevertheless, non-locals lambaste its "hit-or-miss entrees" and "surly service", saying they'd sooner set their compasses southward instead.

Noyes Street Café S
– – – M

828 Noyes St. (Sherman St.), Evanston, 847-475-8683

A "dependable" "hidden treasure", this casual and family-friendly North Suburban cafe is "popular" for "large portions" from a varied menu of "good food at fair prices"; not only is it a "neighborhood pasta place" serving Italian classics, but it also proffers "Greek specialties" as well as salads and sandwiches within its cafe setting of booths and original works by local artists; N.B. beer and wine only.

Nuevo Leon S
22 13 17 $15

1515 W. 18th St. (bet. Ashland & Blue Island Aves.),
312-421-1517 ●⊅

3657 W. 26th St. (bet. Central Park & Lawndale Aves.),
773-522-1515

■ "An anchor of the neighborhood", Pilsen's popular 40-year-old BYO "Mexican diner" on 18th Street offers "dirt-cheap", "delicious, down-home fare" including "classic Mex breakfasts" in a "plain", "homey" space with "no-frills service"; needless to say, night-crawlers think it nice that it's open till 5 AM on weekends; N.B. the independently operated 26th Street location has a similar menu but serves beer.

Oak Terrace S
▽ 21 21 21 $32

Drake Hotel, 140 E. Walton St. (Michigan Ave.),
312-787-2200

■ "A favorite for lunch", this "very friendly" Traditional American in the Drake Hotel delivers "delicious food" – including "really good salads", sandwiches and fresh-baked breads – in a "warm, wonderful room" known

for beautiful views of Lake Michigan and its annual Dickens
Buffet, a holiday-season highlight; N.B. dinner is not served.

Oak Tree S　　　　　16　16　16　$19
Bloomingdale's Bldg., 900 N. Michigan Ave., 6th fl.
(bet. Delaware Pl. & Walton St.), 312-751-1988
▨ "On shopping days", Michigan Avenue marauders dodge
the "bustling crowds" and drop in to this Traditional
American in the Bloomingdale's building "where the
Near North crowd meets" for "breakfast or a midday
meal"; some browsers beef about "slow service" and
claim "it's really a coffee shop", but teetotaling "ladies
who lunch" ("no liquor" is served) say it's "ok" by them.

Oceanique　　　　　24　20　22　$45
505 Main St. (bet. Chicago & Hinman Aves.), Evanston,
847-864-3435
■ An "outstanding selection" of "exquisite" contemporary
French–New American "seafood creations" made with
"fresh, high-quality ingredients" is paired with the fruits of a
"top-notch wine cellar" at this "romantic, comfortable"
and "civilized" Evanston eatery; the kitchen's "precise
preparation and presentation", as well as the staff's
"polished service", make wallet-watchers wistfully "wish
they could afford to eat here more often."

O'Fame S　　　　▽　25　15　24　$20
750 W. Webster Ave. (Halsted St.), 773-929-5111
■ Famed for its "good food and family atmosphere" for
nearly 20 years, this "neighborhood spot" in the heart of
Lincoln Park prevails with a "great menu" of "inexpensive,
basic Italian" including "excellent thin-crust pizza",
"consistently fresh pasta" and "delicious salads" as
well as "terrific special steak" dishes; P.S. it's good "for
quick takeout" too.

Ofie　　　　　　▽　20　17　18　$22
3911 N. Sheridan Rd. (Irving Park Rd.), 773-248-6490
■ Tantalized taste-testers tout the "adventurous African
cuisine" at this Wrigleyville spot whose dishes from Ghana
and Nigeria represent a "delicious, different" and, in
some cases, "hot" alternative to the same-old, same-old;
"attentive" service as well as batik paintings and wood
carvings on the walls makes for a "cozy atmosphere" –
after all, the name means 'home'; N.B. wine and beer only.

Old Jerusalem S　　　17　8　13　$16
1411 N. Wells St. (bet. North Ave. & Schiller St.), 312-944-0459
▨ A Old Town "standby", this "bare-bones" Middle Eastern
"takes you back to the Old Country" with "authentic",
"interesting" and "cheap" fare ("ask for their homemade
hot sauce"); regulars recommend that you "don't look"
at the "grungy" dining space or focus on the "staff that

seems put out by your presence" – go for a "good, quick bite" and "just eat."

O'Neil's S

20 | 17 | 20 | $28

1003 Green Bay Rd. (Scott Ave.), Winnetka, 847-446-7100

☒ Kick back at this "easygoing" and "reliable" Northern Italian seafooder run by a "customer-conscious owner" who offers "upscale fare without breaking the bank" – "a rarity on the North Shore"; although its "no-frills" setting has some patrons perturbed, others call it "comfy" enough "for lunch or a romantic dinner"; besides, "in summer it's nice to sit outside" on the front patio.

ONE SIXTYBLUE

24 | 24 | 22 | $55

1400 W. Randolph St. (Ogden St.), 312-850-0303

■ "This could be the Michael Jordan of restaurants" fawn fans of this "airy" Market District New American, "a class act from start to finish" where "daring" chef Martial Noguier's "stellar", "stylish food" is complemented by "delicate wines and unobtrusive service" and set against Adam Tihany's "sleek", "chic" backdrop; it's "expensive", but most are happy to "pay for the hipness" and "the hope of seeing [silent partner] MJ."

120 Ocean Place S

23 | 25 | 23 | $43

120 N. Hale St. (bet. Front & Wesley Sts.), Wheaton, 630-690-2100

■ The "elegant" and "fabulous" environs of this New American in a "beautifully renovated" "former funeral home" may "take your breath away", but it's the "friendly staff" and some of the "freshest seafood in the Western Suburbs" (including the "best calamari and soft-shell crabs") that keep patrons rematerializing; penny-pinchers who consider it "pricey" "go for lunch, when almost the same menu" is available for less.

Orange S

21 | 16 | 18 | $15

3231 N. Clark St. (Belmont Ave.), 773-549-4400

■ "Too bad everyone knows about it" gripe the Lakeview lunch-and-brunch bunch about this one-year-old Eclectic BYO they predict "will become a Northside institution" for its "quirky", "inventive" menu including "to-die-for French toast kebabs" and the "must-try 'frushi'" (fruit sushi); "if you don't mind the wait", most say you'll find it "delightful."

Original Gino's East S

20 | 12 | 15 | $18

633 N. Wells St. (Ontario St.), 312-943-1124
2801 N. Lincoln Ave. (Diversey Pkwy.), 773-327-3737
1807 S. Washington St. (Bailey St.), Naperville, 630-548-9555
6156 W. 95th St. (Melvina Ave.), Oak Lawn, 708-598-5600
15840 S. Harlem Ave. (159th St.), Orland Park, 708-633-1300
1321 W. Golf Rd. (Algonquin Rd.), Rolling Meadows, 847-364-6644

(continued)

(continued)
Original Gino's East
9751 W. Higgins Rd. (bet. Mannheim & River Rds.), Rosemont, 847-698-4949
Tin Cup Pass Shopping Ctr., 1590 E. Main St. (Tyler Rd.), St. Charles, 630-513-1311
Additional locations throughout the Chicago area
◪ "A Chicago tradition", this veteran pie chain draws droves of deep-dish devotees who line up to devour their "favorite pizza in the whole universe" (it's the "cornmeal crust that makes the difference"); though "graffiti" gurus gleefully "write on the walls and booths to leave their mark" at the Wells Street spot (home of the relocated original Original), others say the sibling sites "miss the boat on atmosphere."

Original Pancake House S　　22 | 13 | 18 | $14
Village Ctr., 1517 E. Hyde Park Blvd. (bet. 51st St. & Lake Park Blvd.), 773-288-2323 ⊟
22 E. Bellevue Pl. (bet. Michigan Ave. & Rush St.), 312-642-7917 ⊟
2020 N. Lincoln Park W. (Clark St.), 773-929-8130 ⊟
10437 S. Western Ave. (104th St.), 773-445-6100
825 Dundee Rd. (Arlington Heights Rd.), Arlington Heights, 847-392-6600
1615 Waukegan Rd. (Willow Ave.), Glenview, 847-724-0220
200 Marriott Dr. (Milwaukee Ave.), Lincolnshire, 847-634-2220
5140 W. 159th St. (52nd Ave.), Oak Forest, 708-687-8282 ⊟
954 Lake St. (Forrest St.), Oak Park, 708-524-0955
106 S. Northwest Hwy. (Touhy Ave.), Park Ridge, 847-696-1381 ●
Additional locations throughout the Chicago area
■ With "famous eggs" and "killer apple pancakes" "served by happy people", this bevy of breakfast specialists with a flapjack focus is "a great way to start any day" – and "good on the wallet" too; "weekend waits" are the norm ("brutal" ones at the Lincoln Park locale) and it can be "chaos in the dining room", but "you don't go there for atmosphere."

Otro Mas S　　21 | 17 | 18 | $32
3651 N. Southport Ave. (bet. Addison St. & Waveland Ave.), 773-348-3200
◪ Surveyors are split on this "cozy" Nuevo Latino Lakeview follow-up that's "a lot like its parent" (Mas, in Wicker Park), reprising John Manion's "*muy bueno*" multi-national cuisine, including "amazing fish tacos" and "wonderful appetizers" (plus the "best caipirinhas in town"); the approving assert it's a "worthy sequel" that's "more intimate", while faultfinders feel that it's "stuffier", the service is spotty and it has the "same noise level" as its progenitor.

Outpost, The S　　20 | 16 | 19 | $32
3438 N. Clark St. (Sheffield Ave.), 773-244-1166
◪ "Not your typical Wrigleyville restaurant", this "casual", "low-key" New American anomaly is known as an incubator

for interesting chefs (e.g. Kevin Shikami of Kevin, Ted Cizma of Elaine); some say the "constant kitchen changes make it hard to define", but most agree the "creative", "cutting-edge cuisine" makes for "fine dining" even if "the decor could use some sprucing up" and service ranges from "attentive" to "slow."

Palaggi's ◐
▽ 16 | 18 | 19 | $32
10 W. Hubbard St. (bet. Dearborn & State Sts.), 312-527-1010
◪ Proponents praise this "friendly", "family-oriented" River North newcomer for its "tasty Italian comfort food" and "romantic" atmosphere created by "candles and draping"; malcontents moan, though, that the "uninspired" fare lacks "brio" and there's "too much confusion" in the service; N.B. live jazz perks things up on weekends.

Palm, The S
22 | 19 | 20 | $48
Swissôtel, 323 E. Wacker Dr. (bet. Lake Shore Dr. & Michigan Ave.), 312-616-1000
◪ The Loop's Swissôtel is home to Chicago's outpost of this "long-standing" national chain, a "clubby", "old-fashioned" "businessman's place" for "huge" steaks ("don't overlook" the "great big lobsters", though) with "straight-from-the-hip service" and "great caricatures on the walls"; yet some carnivores chew it out as "pricey" and say it's "not as good as" some of the company's other locations.

Pane Caldo S
20 | 18 | 19 | $44
72 E. Walton St. (bet. Michigan Ave. & Rush St.), 312-649-0055
◪ "Authentic Northern Italian food" (such as "fine risottos"), a "friendly, caring staff" and "intimate ambiance" put this "upscale, understated" Near Norther in the pantheon of "Chicago hidden treasures" for many; still, others aren't so warm toward it, painting the kitchen as "inconsistent", the meals as "pricey" (the "bill quickly adds up" to a lot of bread) and the "cramped" digs as in need of "expanding."

Panera Bread S
– | – | – | I
616 W. Diversey Pkwy. (Clark St.), 773-528-4556
Plaza del Grato, 1736 Algonquin Rd. (Wilke Rd.), Arlington Heights, 847-577-8793
190 Waukegan Rd. (bet. Central Ave. & Kales Rd.), Deerfield, 847-236-1123
7330 W. North Ave. (Fair Oaks Ave.), Elmwood Park, 708-452-2562
1700 Sherman Ave. (bet. Church & Clark Sts.), Evanston, 847-733-8356
7023 W. Dempster St. (bet. National & Sayre Aves.), Niles, 847-663-1640
39-41 S. Northwest Hwy. (Touhy Ave.), Park Ridge, 847-696-1880
1140 N. Plaza Dr. (Golf Rd.), Schaumburg, 847-969-9110
(continued)

(continued)
Panera's Bread
*2415 W. Schaumburg Rd. (Pembroke Dr.), Schaumburg,
847-895-0760*
Additional locations throughout the Chicago area
With outposts dotting the landscape, this popular deli/cafe/
bakery chain is considered by some the "best quick stop"
"for good food", including "an unusual variety" of "fresh
breads", "delectable sandwiches" and "delicious soups and
salads", all at a "good value" and served in "cozy" settings.

Pangea S　　　　　　　　–　–　–　M
*1935 W. Irving Park Rd. (Damen & Lincoln Aves.),
773-665-1340*
On the off-the-beaten-path Lakeview site of the former
Blue Stem has sprouted this New American, serving
eclectic homestyle dinners spiked with global accents
supported by a limited wine list and followed by simple,
satisfying desserts; the dimly lit, intimate contemporary
dining room of rich jewel tones is decorated with black-
and-white photography, and service is hospitable.

Papagus Greek Taverna S　　20　19　19　$28
*Embassy Suites Hotel, 620 N. State St. (Ontario St.),
312-642-8450*
*Oakbrook Center Mall, 272 Oakbrook Ctr. (Rte. 83), Oak Brook,
630-472-9800*
☑ "Lettuce Entertain You does it again" with this successful
Grecian formula, "charming and fun" River North and Oak
Brook sisters that are both "good at what they're supposed
to be"; while some Hellenes hint the food is "hardly
authentic" (i.e. "too American"), the majority is happy
with the "consistent", "delicious homestyle meals" and
"service with a smile" – all "without the trip to Greektown."

Papajin S　　　　　　　▽　17　14　17　$19
*1551 N. Milwaukee Ave. (Damen & North Aves.),
773-384-9600*
■ Chalk this laid-back Bucktown Chinese up as a "pleasant"
experience thanks to the clean tastes and light sauces of
its "nice-looking", "always-good food" (with many choices
for vegetarians and vegans) at "great prices" presented
within a "quiet atmosphere" of dimly lit "cool decor"
featuring a black-tiled bar illuminated by blue neon.

Papa Milano S　　　　　18　12　18　$23
951 N. State St. (Oak St.), 312-787-3710
☑ Die-hard "red-sauce" fans "haunt" this "classic" "hole-
in-the-wall" that's hitting the half-century mark this year,
hailing its "good basic Italian" – including "great pizza and
pasta for pennies" – and "friendly service"; modernists may
say it's "so-so", but the nostalgic "hope the wrecking ball
never takes it out" of its trendy Gold Coast neighborhood.

Pappadeaux Seafood Kitchen S | 19 | 18 | 19 | $30 |

798 W. Algonquin Rd. (Golf Rd.), Arlington Heights, 847-228-9551
921 Pasquinelli Dr. (Oakmont Ln.), Westmont, 630-455-9846

◪ Those who find this "big, busy" Cajun-Creole seafood duo in the West and Northwest Suburbs "a nice change from the usual chains" say its "great Louisiana cooking" "wakes up the buds"; not all are "won over" by this "taste of the bayou", though – some say it's "not so hot", seeing the same scene as "too frenetic, noisy" and "impersonal."

Park Avenue Cafe S | 24 | 21 | 22 | $46 |

Doubletree Guest Suites Hotel, 199 E. Walton Pl. (Mies van der Rohe Way), 312-944-4414

■ Patriots of this "creative" New American ("cousin of the New York" original) in Streeterville's Doubletree Guest Suites Hotel praise the "outstanding, innovative dishes" from its "open kitchen" (now in the capable hands of chef Todd Downs), such as its trademarked pastrami salmon, "unusual and delicious" dim sum–esque Sunday brunch and "awesome wine-tasting dinners", all served within a "comfortable" folk art–filled setting.

Parker's Ocean Grill S | 24 | 23 | 21 | $38 |

1000 31st St. (Highland Ave.), Downers Grove, 630-960-5701

◪ Some "serious" seafood lovers laud this West Suburban, saying the "delicious" "fine food" (as well as what "may be the best desserts in" Downers Grove), "great presentation", "knowledgeable staff" and "soothing", "quiet" atmosphere "never disappoint"; still, some express concern that it's "a bit expensive for the area" and say that the "room is cold" and a bit "sterile."

Parthenon ●S | 20 | 16 | 19 | $25 |

314 S. Halsted St. (bet. Jackson Blvd. & Van Buren St.), 312-726-2407

■ "A genuine Greektown" "rocking good time", this "noisy, bustling" and "family-friendly" "Chicago landmark" circa 1968 is "consistently solid, year in and year out", and "still among the best" for "good portions" of "real food" at "reasonable prices"; the *saganaki* [flaming *kefalotiri* cheese] is a must", and some say the "wonderful lamb chops" are "the best in the universe" (you'll have to ask the gods on that one).

Pasha ●S | 18 | 21 | 16 | $35 |

642 N. Clark St. (bet. Erie & Ontario Sts.), 312-397-0100

◪ Pasha partisans purport that the "atmosphere and ambiance surpass all others" at this "lively" River North refuge for "nightclub dining" where "the real draw is the deafening but fun music" (live some nights), despite a "good" assortment of New French and Italian dishes from the late-cooking kitchen; bickering buzzkills bemoan that it "doesn't live up to the hype" and whine about "weird service" from "snobby staffers."

Pasta Palazzo 🄢⌀   ▽ 18 | 14 | 18 | $17

1966 N. Halsted St. (Armitage Ave.), 773-248-1400

■ A "friendly, fast, low-budget" option in Lincoln Park, this "quaint Italian" is "reliably good" for "great pasta" and "daily specials", supplemented by a "reasonably priced wine list" and "unpretentious service"; its intimate interior with a colorful mosaic may not be palatial (perhaps contributing to its popularity as a take-out spot), but it's "one of the best values on North Halsted."

Pasteur 🄢   23 | 23 | 20 | $34

5525 N. Broadway (bet. Bryn Mawr & Catalpa Aves.), 773-878-1061

☑ A "pleasant" meal is in store at this "elegant, seductive" "oasis in Edgewater" where the "exciting taste treats" – "refined Vietnamese with French influences" – showcase "extremely fresh ingredients"; some surveyors say the staff is "unobtrusive" and the environment "relaxing", while others "would go more often if the service were as good as the food" and it weren't so "noisy."

Pauline's 🄢⌀   _ | _ | _ | I

1754 W. Balmoral Ave. (Ravenswood Ave.), 773-561-8573

A "kitschy" and "eclectic" "favorite" for all-American "omelets and burgers in Andersonville", this "nice place for a casual meal" (breakfast and lunch only) has "all sorts of retro things on the walls to look at"; even though food-wise, some say, "you could do as well at home, it's the place and the people" that keep regulars returning.

Pegasus ◑🄢   20 | 19 | 20 | $27

130 S. Halsted St. (bet. Adams & Monroe Sts.), 312-226-4666

■ "Great Greek grub" is the continuing tradition at this "solid Greektown establishment", a "classic" with a "good menu", a "friendly" and "courteous" staff that "makes you feel like part of the family" and an "amazing rooftop deck" that's the "perfect" place "for nibbling and drinking" – "there's no place like it with its views of the city and live" "band on summer" weeknights.

Penang ◑🄢   19 | 14 | 15 | $20

2201 S. Wentworth Ave. (Cermak Rd.), 312-326-6888

☑ You don't hear someone say "great Malaysian" every day, but you might if you frequented this "cheap and effective" Chinatown nonconformist known for an "interesting, eclectic" and "broad menu" with "a little of everything" Asian ("they even have a sushi bar" and "well-done Thai" dishes); unfortunately, you might also hear someone say it's "not much to look at" and the "service declines when it's crowded."

Penny's Noodle Shop [S]⊭ 21 13 17 $14

1542 N. Damen Ave. (North Ave.), 773-394-0100
3400 N. Sheffield Ave. (Roscoe St.), 773-281-8222
950 W. Diversey Pkwy. (Sheffield Ave.), 773-281-8448

■ "Fast and filling", these "reliable" and "affordable Asian" "staples" (including the "newest location in Wicker Park") have become "city favorites" for "oodles of noodles", "great gyoza", "flavorful" "Vietnamese spring rolls, "tasty" "Thai ravioli" and "to-die-for Tom Yum soup" that "helps you through the Chicago winter", all dished up "for just pennies" in "spartan but clean" spaces.

Pepper Lounge ◐[S] ▽ 20 20 18 $28

3441 N. Sheffield Ave. (Clark St.), 773-665-7377

■ "An outpost of good food in the Wrigleyville wasteland", this "loungey" New American draws an "eclectic crowd" lured by a kitchen that turns out an "inventive menu" until 1 AM most nights, barkeeps who "whip up a mean martini" (including the chocolate house specialty) and "friendly, interesting servers"; the "dark", "trendy decor is great for late-night dining" – complete with "too much smoke."

Pete Miller's Steakhouse ◐[S] 21 19 20 $38

1557 Sherman Ave. (bet. Davis & Grove Sts.), Evanston, 847-328-0399

■ "Vegetarians need not apply" at this "clubby", "noisy and busy" "Evanston hangout", a "one-stop fun night out" with "fine", "upper-end steaks", "great chops", "the best garlic mashed potatoes in town", an "excellent liquor selection" and "good" "live jazz" that "adds a nice touch" six times a week; there's also a lighter lounge menu of "burgers and sandwiches, if you're on a budget."

Petterino's 18 20 20 $37

Goodman Theatre Bldg., 150 N. Dearborn St. (Randolph St.), 312-422-0150

◪ Stage buffs and business types cast this "classy joint" in the Goodman Theatre building as the "place to go before the show" and a "blessing in the Loop" for its "nice" Traditional American fare, the "polished" performances of its staffers and a setting that's a "throwback" to the "'40s supper club" genre; still, critics are less impressed by what they call an "expensive", "mundane" menu and dismiss the production as a "Sardi's wanna-be."

P.F. Chang's China Bistro [S] 19 20 18 $25

530 N. Wabash Ave. (Grand Ave.), 312-828-9977
2361 Fountain Square Dr. (Butterfield & Meyers Rds.), Lombard, 630-652-9977
1819 Lake Cook Rd. (east of I-94), Northbrook, 847-509-8844

◪ Fans "can't get enough of the eclectic", "tasty and adventurous" Chinese cuisine (lots of "hoorays" for the "amazing" lettuce wraps) at these "upscale" outposts of the "novel" national Sino chain; although purists pan the "gimmicky", "Americanized" cooking as "not authentic" and truly "average", these "trendy" spots are for many a "dependable" option offering "good value."

Phil Stefani's 437 Rush | 20 | 20 | 19 | $38 |
(fka 437 Rush)
437 N. Rush St. (Hubbard St.), 312-222-0101
◪ "It's fun to be a grown-up" at this Near North Italian steakhouse, a "favorite local after-work" "watering hole" and "biz-lunch" destination whose "handsome", "clubby decor" pays homage to the heyday of its applauded predecessor, popular Riccardo's; fans find the "consistently good food" "flavorful" (especially "the signature prime rib-eye" chop – "a must"), but the lukewarm lament it's "not Stefani's best."

Phoenix S | 22 | 12 | 16 | $23 |
2131 S. Archer Ave., 2nd fl. (Wentworth Ave.), 312-328-0848
◪ Champions of this Chinatown choice say its "fresh, creative" daily dim sum is "to die for", which helps explain why the "bright, airy space is always "bustling"; "slow service" prompts pleas to "get more carts on the floor", but aficionados agree the "great selection" of "delightful delicacies" is "worth the wait"; N.B. it serves Chinese dishes at lunch and dinner.

Piazza Bella S | ▽ 21 | 19 | 20 | $26 |
Roscoe Village, 2116 W. Roscoe St. (bet. Damen & Western Aves.), 773-477-7330
◼ Locals "love this little place" tucked away in Roscoe Village for its "true Italian-style" cooking, i.e. "simple dishes made with excellent ingredients" and served by a "friendly staff" that "makes you feel like you're visiting their home for dinner"; the setting is "festive" yet "cozy", prompting devotees to declare "we need more like this."

Piece ◖S | 18 | 16 | 15 | $18 |
1927 W. North Ave. (bet. Damen & Wolcott Aves.), 773-772-4422
◪ "Homemade pizza, homemade beer – what could be better?" say a slice of surveyors about this Bucktown yearling's "unique", New Haven–style thin-crust pies "done right", "many choices" of house microbrews and "cool" "hangout" setting (once featured on MTV's *Real World*); crusty contrarians "don't get" the "East Coast" allure, judging them "overrated."

Pie Hole ◖S | – | – | – | I |
606 N. Racine Ave. (Ogden Ave.), 312-666-6767
Who wants pie? – pizza pie, that is, served up with the sort of attitude you'd expect of this Near West spin-off from the Twisted Spoke folks; think premium thin-crust topped with standard stuff plus posher pile-ons like clams or capers

(and salads too), but don't think sit-down or even takeout –
we're talkin' phone-in delivery only, from a 'hole' in the
backside of Bone Daddy.

Pierrot Gourmet S — — — M
Peninsula Hotel, 108 E. Superior St. (Rush St.), 312-573-6749
A rustic Euro-style retreat in the Near North's Peninsula
Hotel, this combination cafe/bakery/wine bar is a casually
chic setting for sipping from an extensive wine list and
snacking from a limited menu of hearty housemade
sourdough tartines (stuffed savory pastries), fresh-baked
goods and artisanal cheeses; there's even a communal
table for gregarious guests, as well as a wine retail area.

Pine Yard Restaurant S ▽ 25 18 21 $19
1033 Davis St. (Oak St.), Evanston, 847-475-4940
■ Though "relocated" in the fall of 2000, this 20-year-
old "Chinese oasis" in the Northern Suburbs remains a
"classic" "local institution" that's still "always packed" with
fans of its "distinctive flavors" and "great, inexpensive
lunch specials"; some Evanstonians effuse that with Sino
fare this good so close at hand, there's "no need to go to
Chinatown"; N.B. beer and wine only.

Pizza Capri S 16 13 14 $18
964 W. Belmont Ave. (Sheffield Ave.), 773-296-6000
1501 E. 53rd St. (Harper Ave.), 773-324-7777
1733 N. Halsted St. (Willow St.), 312-280-5700
5139 Main St. (Curtiss St.), Downers Grove, 630-434-7777
☑ Usually "mobbed", these "bustling pizza joints" dish out
"tasty" "pizzas a cut above the ordinary" (in both "crispy
thin-crust" and "deep-dish" varieties) and "at reasonable
prices", as well as "a somewhat" "limited entrée menu"
and "interesting" salads that some say give the pies a
"run for their money"; homebodies hail them the "takeout-
and-delivery champions" of the city and suburbs, but that
could be because the "service is lacking."

Pizza D.O.C. S 21 14 16 $22
2251 W. Lawrence Ave. (Lincoln Ave.), 773-784-8777
☑ Fans of this Lincoln Square pizzeria attest that the "paper-
thin", "seriously authentic Italian" pies from its wood-
burning oven are the "next best thing to being in the Piazza
Navona"; few would mention the decor and Bernini in the
same breath, though, and the service can be "uneven", but
there's always "carryout"; P.S. "the name is misleading –
they have great pastas too."

Pizzeria Uno S 21 14 16 $19
29 E. Ohio St. (Wabash Ave.), 312-321-1000 ◗
Pizzeria Due ◗ S
619 N. Wabash Ave. (Ontario St.), 312-280-5110
(continued)

(continued)
Pizzeria Uno Chicago Bar & Grill
O'Hare Int'l Airport, 773-894-8667 ☽
986 Rte. 59 (Liberty Ave.), Aurora, 630-585-8075 ☽
4901 Cal-Sag Rd. (Cicero Ave.), Crestwood, 708-824-0700 ☽
6593 Grand Ave. (Hunt Club Rd.), Gurnee, 847-856-0000 ☽
Sportmart Plaza, 275 W. Roosevelt Rd. (Surrey Dr.), Lombard, 630-792-1400
1160 Plaza Dr. (Golf Rd.), Schaumburg, 847-413-0200 ☽
545 Lakeview Pkwy. (Fairway Dr.), Vernon Hills, 847-918-8667 ☽
■ "Sentimental favorites" "savored time and again", these Near North "classics" are "musts" for "original", "terrific deep-dish pizzas"; be "prepared to wait" for "hours", however, in a "dark, noisy" and "touristy" setting, unless weather permits sitting outside where you can "eat and watch the street"; N.B. numero Uno has spun off an international chain with links in the suburbs.

P.J. Clarke's ☽ S
18 | 15 | 17 | $21
1204 N. State St. (Division St.), 312-664-1650
■ Lettuce Entertain You's "local hangout" for a "mature" Gold Coast crowd serves a "great variety" of "solid", Traditional American "tavern fare" (from "awesome mini-burgers" to "tasty meatloaf") in a "dark", "pub-style" setting that's "always busy"; it's "not fancy", but it's a "good value" and its "late-night" kitchen cooks until 1:30 AM.

Pompei Bakery S
▽ 25 | 17 | 21 | $16
2955 N. Sheffield Ave. (Wellington St.), 773-325-1900
1531 W. Taylor St. (Ashland Ave.), 312-421-5179
17 W. 744 22nd St. (S. Summit Ave.), 630-620-0600
■ Descendents of a Taylor Street bakery opened in 1909, this family-owned triumvirate of "kid-friendly" Italian spots offers a "wide selection" of "quick and consistently good" fare at an "exceptional value"; the "cafeteria-style" presentation with "great counter service" makes it easy "to eat in or take out" "casual lunches or dinners."

Potbelly Sandwich Works
19 | 13 | 15 | $9
508 N. Clark St. (Hubbard St.), 312-644-9131 S
2264 N. Lincoln Ave. (bet. Belden & Webster Aves.), 773-528-1405 S
190 N. State St. (Lake St.), 312-683-1234 S
The Shops at North Bridge, 520 N. Michigan Ave. (Grand Ave.), 312-644-1068 S
303 W. Madison St. (Franklin St.), 312-346-1234
1422 W. Webster Ave. (Clybourn Ave.), 773-755-1234 S
Midway Airport, Terminal B-1, 773-582-1234
630 Davis St. (Sherman Ave.), Evanston, 847-328-1800 S
■ "There's always a line, but it moves fast" at this city and suburban chain where you can "choose your own ingredients" to create "tasty, custom-made subs and toasted sandwiches" and chase them with "old-fashioned

milkshakes"; it's an "absolute staple" for sammy savants "on the run" thanks to the staff's "ridiculous efficiency" and the "cheap prices."

Prairie S   22 | 22 | 22 | $41

Hyatt on Printer's Row, 500 S. Dearborn St. (Congress Pkwy.),
312-663-1143

■ "First-rate without pretension", this "solid" regional American, housed in on Hyatt on Printer's Row in the South Loop, is known for its "creative seasonal menus" of "Midwestern food with a gourmet twist" (including game in season); name notwithstanding, the "beautiful Arts and Crafts–style ambiance" of its Frank Lloyd Wright–inspired dining room is anything but plain.

Prego S   ▽ 19 | 15 | 19 | $26

2901 N. Ashland Ave. (bet. Diversey Pkwy. & Wellington Ave.),
773-472-9190

■ This "small and quaint" Lakeview yearling serves a "wonderful selection" of "lovely and simple Italian" "taste treats" (including "great risottos and tortellini") and now, having obtained a liquor license, alcoholic beverages as well; while boosters hail it as a "gem that's just being discovered", some anxious amici are praying that "it doesn't get overrun."

PRINTER'S ROW   25 | 21 | 23 | $46

550 S. Dearborn St. (bet. Congress Pkwy. & Harrison St.),
312-461-0780

■ Offering "innovative" New American fare in a "traditional setting", Michael Foley's South Loop production makes an indelible impression with its "creative menu", which takes advantage of the "freshest local ingredients", and its "knowledgeable" staff; cronies crow that its "unfailing commitment to food, wine and service" and its "quiet excellence" make for "quality dining."

P.S. Bangkok S   18 | 13 | 16 | $18

3345 N. Clark St. (bet. Addison St. & Belmont Ave.), 773-871-7777
2521 N. Halsted St. (bet. Fullerton Pkwy. & Wrightwood Ave.),
773-348-0072

◪ These separated Siamese twins in Wrigleyville and DePaul offer "huge menus" of "consistent" native fare including "fabulous curries" and "great crunchy pad Thai", and early-birds sing the praises of the Clark Street location's "wonderful Sunday brunch" ("worth getting up" for); cynics, though, sniff at the "predictable" eats and "so-so service"; N.B. the North Halsted branch is BYO.

Public Landing S   ▽ 23 | 22 | 22 | $34

200 W. Eighth St. (bet. Canal & State Sts.), Lockport, 815-838-6500

■ By all accounts, the change in ownership has been smooth sailing at this "charming oasis in a historic location" in the Southwest Suburbs, where the "excellent, simple" American cooking tempers the "traditional with a taste of inspiration"; paired with a "picturesque room" and "personable service", it continues to be many a fan's choice as "best meal for the price in the suburbs."

Puck's at the MCA S 20 19 17 $23
Museum of Contemporary Art, 220 E. Chicago Ave. (Mies van der Rohe Way), 312-397-4034
◪ "You can't beat the views in this jewel" pronounce peckish patrons of Wolfgang Puck's "hidden", "upscale" lunch-only spot installed in the Museum of Contemporary Art in Streeterville, where a "limited but well-prepared" New American menu is displayed in a "chic, arty setting" with "wonderful outdoor seating"; critics cavil that it's "understaffed", resulting in "iffy" service.

Pump Room, The S 21 25 21 $49
Omni Ambassador East Hotel, 1301 N. State St. (Goethe St.), 312-266-0360
◪ "The grand queen of the old dinner houses" continues to hold court at the Gold Coast's Omni Ambassador East Hotel, offering a "memorable" "dress-up" experience that includes "excellent" New French cuisine, "attentive, detail-oriented" service and "romantic dancing"; detractors, however, lament that it's merely "resting on its laurels" and say "the glamour is sadly gone, though Booth One remains."

Quincy Grille on the River 18 17 20 $36
200 S. Wacker Dr. (Adams St.), 312-627-1800
■ "A tucked-away treasure" for "pre-opera" and "power-lunching" in the Loop, this "clubby" spot combines an "innovative menu" featuring a "good variety" of New American dishes, service that "excels" and "below-street-level views overlooking the river" that create a "London-ish feel"; N.B lunch only, and early dinner during opera season.

Rainforest Cafe S 12 21 15 $21
605 N. Clark St. (bet. Ohio & Ontario Sts.), 312-787-1501
Woodfield Mall, 121 Woodfield Mall (bet. Golf & Higgins Rds.), Schaumburg, 847-619-1900
Gurnee Mills Mall, 6170 W. Grand Ave. (bet. I-94 & Hunt Club Rd.), Gurnee, 847-855-7800
◪ This trio of city and suburban links in a "novelty" chain are popular more for their "jungle" settings, complete with "thunder, lightning" and "moving animals", than their "average, overpriced" American eats, "long waits and poor service", but defenders declare it's "great for kids."

Rambutan S 22 17 19 $30
2049 W. Division St. (Damen Ave.), 773-772-2727
■ "Always an adventure" full of "visual delights and culinary surprises", this Wicker Parker is home to chef-owner

Jennifer Aranas' "fun" yet "sophisticated" tapas-style Filipino cuisine, which adds a touch of "exotic grazing" to "the new scene on West Division"; the "small portions are good for mixing 'n' matching" with friends, and the "high-energy" setting still remains "warm and comfortable."

Ranalli's 16 | 13 | 14 | $17

1925 N. Lincoln Ave. (bet. Armitage Ave. & Clark St.), 312-642-4700 ◐ [S]
1522 W. Montrose Ave. (Ashland Ave.), 773-506-8800 [S]
2301 N. Clark St. (Belden Ave.), 312-440-7000 ◐ [S]
343 W. Erie St. (Orleans St.), 312-932-0123

■ "Nothing spectacular" – just "good-quality" pizza and other "basic" eats with "a great selection of beers" – awaits at this "casual" "brew-and-a-bite" pizzeria chain; the Lincoln Avenue site has a "nice outdoor area", while the Montrose location is mainly takeout and serves no alcohol.

Ravinia Bistro [S] 21 | 17 | 20 | $31

581 Roger Williams Ave. (bet. Green Bay Rd. & St. Johns Ave.), Highland Park, 847-432-1033

■ "Small but elegant", this "solid bistro" in the Northern Suburbs "tries hard to please" and succeeds with "quality French cooking", "personal service" and "warm" ambiance; music lovers sing its praises as the "best place to go before concerts" at the annual Ravinia Festival; N.B. its wine list offers 35 by-the-glass selections.

Redfish [S] 16 | 16 | 17 | $26

400 N. State St. (Kinzie St.), 312-467-1600

◪ "Damn good" gumbo, jambalaya and "anything blackened (yum!)" highlight the seafood-focused Cajun-Creole menu at this "casual" River North "homage" to the Big Easy; foes, however, malign the "New Orleans–style" fare as a "poor try" "without any soul" served in a setting that's more "Disneyland" than bayou.

Red Light [S] 21 | 23 | 19 | $36

820 W. Randolph St. (Green St.), 312-733-8880

◪ Asiaphiles file into this "racy" purveyor of Pan-Asian fare in the Market District for its "excellent", "innovative" "fusion" featuring "incredible flavor combinations" (not to mention "must"-try mango martinis), while trendoids go for the "dramatic" decor and "hip", "bustling" setting that looks like an "*Alice in Wonderland* for beautiful people"; the "overpowering" decibel level and "pricey" tabs, though, give detractors pause.

Red Lion Pub [S] 15 | 18 | 18 | $19

2446 N. Lincoln Ave. (Fullerton Pkwy.), 773-348-2695

■ Britain boosters applaud this "dark", "charming" Lincoln Park taproom that "really evokes the atmosphere of a London pub", with a "bar cat and ghosts upstairs" and "typical English" grub such as "fish 'n' chips" and "Welsh rarebit and pasty"; noticeably absent is the "Bud-guzzling, football-brained crowd."

Red Tomato S
18 | 16 | 17 | $23

3417 N. Southport Ave. (Roscoe St.), 773-472-5300

◪ Some paesani plug this "convenient", "local Italian eatery" they say "serves a purpose" – providing Lakeview with "dependable" pastas, "a good variety of salads" and "delicious thin-crust pizzas" at "modest prices", as well as "family-style" service; naysayers sniff that it's "getting tired" and may have "lost its edge", dishing out eats that are "nothing innovative" and merely "adequate."

Restaurant on the Park
▽ 19 | 18 | 18 | $29

The Art Institute of Chicago, 111 S. Michigan Ave. (Monroe St.), 312-443-3600

■ A "touch of tranquility in the Loop", this "civilized" Continental is an "Art Institute masterpiece" exhibiting "artistically presented entrees" and "great service" in a "quiet" setting with "beautiful views" of Grant Park; patrons paint it as a "great little place" that's one of the neighborhood's "best spots for lunch", which just happens to be the only meal it serves.

RETRO BISTRO
26 | 19 | 23 | $35

Mt. Prospect Commons, 1746 W. Golf Rd. (Busse Rd.), Mt. Prospect, 847-439-2424

■ Mt. Prospect-ors panning for "excellent" French bistro fare that's a "good value" strike it rich at this "small", "intimate" spot, an "oasis" in a Northwest Suburban strip-mall "wasteland" that edges out its sibling, D & J Bistro, with the top-rated food for its category in our *Survey*; "happy, friendly service" and the transporting "feeling of being in Europe" round out the "memorable dining experience."

Reza's ◑S
19 | 15 | 17 | $22

5255 N. Clark St. (Berwyn Ave.), 773-561-1898
432 W. Ontario St. (Orleans St.), 312-664-4500

■ Partisans promise "you'll leave full" from these River North and Andersonville Middle Eastern stalwarts prized for their "fairly priced" and "large portions" of "consistently good", "healthy" choices from a "huge menu that aims to please", including "many vegetarian choices"; those who have trouble "getting the attention" of the "distracted" staff will be pleased to know they're "reliable for takeout too."

Rhapsody S
22 | 22 | 21 | $41

Symphony Ctr., 65 E. Adams St. (bet. Michigan & Wabash Aves.), 312-786-9911

◪ The cacophony in the kitchen at this New American in the Loop's Symphony Center seems to have reached its coda, with regulars reporting that the once "uneven" cooking "keeps getting better" since management "settled on a chef", maestro Romuald Jung, whose "sophisticated" cuisine has fans waxing rhapsodic; the "stunning" decor and "accommodating" staff score as well, though some say "spotty" service still sounds a sour note.

Rico's S 22 19 23 $30

626 S. Racine Ave. (Harrison St.), 312-421-7262

■ "More than just" your average "red-sauce Italian", this Little Italy "sleeper" is "one of the best" boast boosters of its "consistently good" "home cooking like no other", including "wonderful marinara sauce" and "meatballs to die for"; with an "unpretentious" setting and "warm, attentive" staffers who make "you feel welcome", it's "always a delight" and "perfect before the Pavilion or United Center."

Rinconcito Sudamericano S ▽ 21 11 18 $22

1954 W. Armitage Ave. (Damen Ave.), 773-489-3126

■ The "wonderful opportunity" to savor the "delicious", "out-of-the-ordinary flavors" of "real food from the Andes" gives Lake-level locals a natural mountain high at this "fabulous" Peruvian in Bucktown; regulars recommend you "get a Pisco sour" (a brandy-and-lime concoction) and "try" the national potato dish, "*papas huancaina* – a must"; given "bountiful portions" at "fair prices", few mind that the "storefront" space is "not very exciting."

Ringo ◗S ▽ 24 17 21 $21

2507 N. Lincoln Ave. (bet. Fullerton Pkwy. & Wrightwood Ave.), 773-248-5788

■ It's not a monument to the funny Beatle, but rather a "small" Lincoln Park Japanese BYO that gets by with a little help from "outstanding" sushi and other "unusual" fare served in its "simple" ocher interior bedecked with colorful kites; feel free, though, to order the signature Ringo Maki (tuna, salmon, scallions and smelt eggs) in honor of the mop-topped drummer.

Rise ◗ ▽ 21 20 15 $26

3401 N. Southport Ave. (Roscoe St.), 773-525-3535

■ While most folks Rise *then* Shine, the Zhang family did it the other way around, opening this "hip" new Wrigleyville Japanese and sake lounge after their Lincoln Park Asian hybrid was well established; its "yummy, different sushi rolls" are "priced right" and "don't disappoint", making it a "terrific new addition to Southport Avenue", though some find the "techno dance music" "annoying."

RITZ-CARLTON CAFÉ S 24 24 24 $36

Ritz-Carlton Hotel, 160 E. Pearson St. (Michigan Ave.), 312-573-5160

■ "You'll feel like a pampered tourist" at this "pleasant" cafe "overlooking a waterfall fountain" in the Streeterville hotel's lobby; "still beautiful" after more than 25 years, its "quiet-but-not-stuffy" room is the setting for meals marked by "consistently high-quality" American fare and "upscale service", making it a "great breakfast, luncheon or supper venue" and a "nice stopover from shopping"; yes, it's "pricey, but it's the Ritz."

RITZ-CARLTON DINING ROOM S | 28 | 27 | 28 | $68 |
Ritz-Carlton Hotel, 160 E. Pearson St. (Michigan Ave.), 312-573-5223
■ A "top dining experience" awaits at this "refined" New French in the Ritz-Carlton, a Four Seasons hotel; chef "Sarah Stegner is a treasure", and her "fantastic" food matches the "posh" yet "understated" surroundings; add in an "epic wine list", "absolutely fabulous cheese cart" and Sunday brunch that's a "food orgy with piano" and this is "the place to splurge" "when elegance, not money, is the object."

Riva S | 20 | 22 | 18 | $42 |
Navy Pier, 700 E. Grand Ave. (Lake Shore Dr.), 312-644-7482
■ One school of respondents rates Phil Stefani's "beautiful" American-Italian "fish specialist" as "the best on the Navy Pier", with "a great lake view" and "good seafood" that add up to "a delightful dinner before the Shakespeare Theatre" nearly "next door"; a rival retinue reacts reproachfully to what it calls "unenthusiastic service" and hints they hit a "captive audience with high prices."

Rivers | 19 | 18 | 18 | $33 |
Mercantile Bldg., 30 S. Wacker Dr. (bet. Madison & Monroe Sts.), 312-559-1515
■ In the ebb and flow of Chicago's fine-dining scene, this Loop New American has established itself as "the place for [Civic] Opera–goers", as well as a "great client-lunch spot" or "after-work stop" "for socializing", with "good fare" and a "serene view of the Chicago River" (you "can't beat the patio"); some, however, like the "location, not the food", which they say "misses the boat."

R.J. Grunts S | 18 | 16 | 18 | $19 |
2056 N. Lincoln Park W. (Dickens Ave.), 773-929-5363
■ "Thirty-plus years of greatness" mark Rich Melman's "legendary" first Lettuce Entertain You enterprise, a Lincoln Park "so-old-it's-new-again" "nostalgic treat" that's "stuck in the '70s and proud of it"; "bountiful burgers", a "gold-standard salad bar" and "humorous" decor (including the "wall of waitresses'" photos) make folks so "glad it hasn't closed" they don't even grunt that it's "small and crowded."

RL S | 21 | 26 | 22 | $44 |
115 E. Chicago Ave. (Michigan Ave.), 312-475-1100
■ Adjacent to his Michigan Avenue flagship, Ralph Lauren's maiden voyage into the victuals biz is now under the

management of the Gibsons folks, who've morphed this Near North changeling's menu from Italian to American 'club cuisine' more befitting the "terrific" "old-school decor", "a fashion statement all its own" with "lots of leather" and "impressive artwork"; P.S. you might want to "use the corporate card."

Robinson's No. 1 Ribs S — 20 | 11 | 15 | $18
225 S. Canal St. (Adams St.), 312-258-8477
655 W. Armitage Ave. (Orchard St.), 312-337-1399
77 W. Jackson Blvd. (bet. Clark & Federal Sts.), 312-431-1001
940 W. Madison Ave. (Clinton St.), Oak Park, 708-383-8452
◪ The secret to these city and suburban BBQ BYOs' success "is in the sauce" ("if you like sweet") that makes its "great ribs" "finger-lickin' good", as well as "unbeatably priced lunch specials" at some branches; several suggest, though, that these succulent satisfiers are best "for takeout, not eat-in", due in part to "spotty service" and decor that "leaves something to be desired."

Rock Bottom Brewery S — 15 | 15 | 15 | $21
1 W. Grand Ave. (State St.), 312-755-9339 ◑
28256 Diehl Rd. (Winfield Rd.), Warrenville, 630-836-1380
◪ "The beer is the reason to go" to any outpost of this "casual" national chain serving "mainstream" American fare with a Southwestern influence; some suds-lovers say they're "good for work gatherings", "happy hour" or to "catch a game", but uncharitable chuggers chide that they're "aptly named."

Roditys ◑S — 19 | 16 | 19 | $24
222 S. Halsted St. (bet. Adams St. & Jackson Blvd.), 312-454-0800
■ Since 1972, "good Greek hospitality" and an "extensive menu" of "standard", "old-fashioned food" that's "hot, fresh and well presented" – especially "great lamb dishes" "done exactly as you order" them – have kept constituents of this Greektown classic happy; "reasonable prices" and a "clean" environment add to its "fun, festive atmosphere."

Ron of Japan S — 20 | 18 | 20 | $33
230 E. Ontario St. (Fairbanks Ct.), 312-644-6500
633 Skokie Blvd. (Dundee Rd.), Northbrook, 847-564-5900
◪ "Great for a large group", this "classic" Downtown and Northbrook Japanese teppanyaki duo features "cook-at-the-table" chefs whose "showmanship at the grill" while slicing and dicing "excellent" chicken, lobster, shrimp and steak dishes makes for an "entertaining and tasty" evening; those who "love the preparation" say it "beats Benihana any day", but holdouts hint "the years are beginning to show" and hope for "better ventilation."

Room, The [S] 23 | 20 | 21 | $35

5900 N. Broadway (Rosedale Ave.), 773-989-7666

■ Room-mates regard this Eclectic New American in Andersonville as "the best high-end BYO" around, with "creative" chef Gil Langlois' "good food" and a "hip", "homey" and gay-friendly atmosphere within a "spacious setting" (some say "cavernous") of "exposed brick", leather banquettes and silk curtains; the menu may be "limited", but "fair prices" and "fun service" have fans saying Tomboy-owner "Jody [Andre] has done it again."

Roong [S] – | – | – | M

1633 N. Milwaukee Ave. (bet. Damen & North Aves.), 773-252-3488

Roong Petch

1828 W. Montrose Ave. (bet. Ashland & Damen Aves.), 773-989-0818

The long-standing, more downscale Roong Petch storefront standard in Lakeview has given birth to Roong, whose classic Thai dining room brings *lard nar, pad woon sen* and *satays* – as well as the clever signature "007 secret stir-fry" and sticky rice with mango dessert – to Wicker Park, along with stylish decor well suited to the trendy neighborhood.

RoSal's Cucina ◐ ▽ 21 | 17 | 22 | $27

1154 W. Taylor St. (Racine Ave.), 312-243-2357

■ A "classic gem on Taylor Street", this "friendly and filling" Italian in the heart of Little Italy is a "throwback" with "excellent home-cooked food" (and "shopping bags of leftovers"), "real charm" and an "adorable", "homey atmosphere"; on the last Tuesday of the month, its upstairs dining room hosts prix fixe *Big Night* dinners for 15 or more that pay homage to the Stanley Tucci movie.

Rose & Crown [S] ▽ 16 | 15 | 18 | $18

420 W. Belmont Ave. (Sheridan Rd.), 773-248-6654

◪ While few are buying this "fun", "smoke-filled" Lakeview "neighborhood place" as authentically "British" ("good fish 'n' chips" and "wall posters aside"), it's still well received as an "upbeat", "undiscovered" spot with an "excellent beer selection" and "relatively well-done standard pub grub."

Rose Angelis [S] 23 | 20 | 21 | $26

1314 W. Wrightwood Ave. (bet. Racine & Southport Aves.), 773-296-0081

■ Legions of Lincoln Parkers are loyal to this "charming" "favorite" "date place" "cozily set" within the "meandering rooms" of "a great brownstone", insisting it's "always worth the wait" for its "mouthwatering", "rich" Italian fare smothered in "divine sauces" and delivered with "down-to-earth service" in "portions large enough for a linebacker" ("get ready for" "the inevitable doggy bag").

Rosebud, The S   21   18   19 $33
1500 W. Taylor St. (Laflin St.), 312-942-1117
Rosebud on Rush S
720 N. Rush St. (Superior St.), 312-266-6444
Rosebud of Naperville S
48 W. Chicago Ave. (Washington St.), Naperville, 630-548-9800
Rosebud of Highland Park S
1850 Second St. (Central Ave.), Highland Park, 847-926-4800
◪ Alex Dana's "expanding" group of "real Chicago Italians"
furthers the "formula" of his "crowded" Taylor Street
original, "a favorite" for "ridiculously large portions" of
"honest, old-fashioned food" from a "consistent" kitchen,
consumed "under the watchful eye of the Frank Sinatra
portrait"; not everyone agrees "these roses have no thorns",
though, with protesters pointing to "predictable food",
"spotty service" and "too much noise."

Rosebud Steakhouse ◕ S   23   21   20 $45
192 E. Walton Pl. (Mies van der Rohe Way), 312-397-1000
◪ "They snuck a great little steakhouse east of Michigan
Avenue" – so say supporters of this "excellent" example
of "Alex Dana branching out" from his Italian roots; a
"sophisticated crowd" of converts considers it "a keeper"
for its "classy", "clublike" "neighborhood feel", its "juicy
steaks" and its "very good wine list", and even adversaries
who say the "price is high" admit it's "one to watch."

Roy's S   –   –   –   E
720 N. State St. (Superior St.), 312-787-7599
"You can almost feel the tropical breezes" at this River
North branch of Roy Yamaguchi's national haute Hawaiian
chain, "a winner from the start" thanks to an exhibition
kitchen turning out "exceptionally tasty food" "you don't
see everywhere" ("mostly seafood with unexpected flair")
served amid "sophisticated" decor – not a tiki torch in sight.

Ruby of Siam S   –   –   –   M
1125 Emerson St. (Ridge Ave.), Evanston, 847-492-1008
Skokie Fashion Sq., 9420 Skokie Blvd. (Foster Ave.), Skokie,
847-675-7008
Sizzling rice soups, brightly flavored glass-noodle salads,
chicken and pork satay and a variety of curry dishes make
these Suburban North Thais popular for both dine-in and
takeout (or a bargain buffet lunch); both are family-friendly
and tastefully decorated with Siamese artifacts, but the
Evanston strip-mall location serves beer and wine, whereas
the Skokie storefront BYO offers no alcohol.

Rudi Fazuli's S   19   18   18 $25
2442 N. Clark St. (bet. Arlington Pl. & Fullerton Pkwy.),
773-388-0100
■ "Mix 'n' match pastas and sauces" and other Italian
"favorites" like "baked chicken Alfredo to die for" "always

deliver a great meal" and "good value" at this "fun"
Lincoln Park spot owned by "Rudi [Melchiorre, who] is
related to Mama Celeste"; there's "cozy decor" within and
a "great patio" "for summer people-watching" without, as
well as all-you-can-eat "family-style meals on Sunday."

Rushmore

| 23 | 19 | 20 | $43 |

1023 W. Lake St. (Carpenter St.), 312-421-8845

⬛ "A fantastic find" in a "quirky location" ("under the El"
in the Market District), this "hip" New American harbors
"innovative" chef-owner Michael Dean Hazen, whose
"exciting menu" is a "mix of haute cuisine and comfort
food" ("try the lobster pot pie") served with "lots of attitude"
in an "austere but romantic" space; most say the "food's so
good you forget the sound" of the "train overhead."

Russell's Barbecue S⊄

| 18 | 11 | 14 | $14 |

1621 N. Thatcher Ave. (North Ave.), Elmwood Park, 708-453-7065

⬛ "It's not BBQ – it's a religion" posit parishioners of this
West Suburban "institution" packing the pews since 1930
thanks to "old-time good" stuff like "tasty beef sandwiches"
and "fall-off-the-bone ribs" slathered in "sauce you could
drink from the bottle"; though a "sentimental favorite" of the
"over-60" set, it's also a "great place for kids" to "be noisy
and messy" while making "lots of memories" of their own.

Russian Tea Time S

| 20 | 20 | 20 | $32 |

77 E. Adams St. (bet. Michigan & Wabash Aves.), 312-360-0000

⬛ For a "novel" and "nice change of pace", fans of
"Eastern European food" "love the samovars" full of
"strong tea", "great" "flavored vodkas" and "authentic"
"Russian specialties" (including "lots of choices for
vegetarians") at this "civilized" Loop "treasure" "convenient
to the Art Institute and Symphony Center"; with its "quiet,
intimate", "old-world" air, it strikes lovers as "the place to
have a passionate affair."

RUTH'S CHRIS STEAK HOUSE S

| 24 | 20 | 22 | $45 |

431 N. Dearborn St. (Hubbard St.), 312-321-2725
933 Skokie Blvd. (Dundee Rd.), Northbrook, 847-498-6889

⬛ "Beef with butter . . . I love America!" belt out boosters of
these "comfortable and consistent" chophouses, saying
they're "always a good choice" (albeit an "expensive" one)
and a "favorite place to escalate the cholesterol level" via
"tender fillets you can cut with a fork"; even those who
prefer to "support local" "hometown steakhouses" admit
they're "excellent, despite being part of a chain."

Sabatino's ●S

| 22 | 17 | 21 | $28 |

4441 W. Irving Park Rd. (bet. Cicero & Kostner Aves.),
773-283-8331

⬛ "Old-fashioned Italian – and proud of it!" characterizes
the bill of fare at this "dependable" Northwest Side "Chicago

classic" that "hasn't changed in years (and that's good)";
"you get a lot" of "delicious food" "for a little", and strolling
musicians every night (and a piano player on weekends)
add to its "dark, crowded", "romantic" atmosphere.

Sabor S　　　　　　　– | – | – | M
Schaumburg's Town Square Ctr., 160E S. Roselle Rd.
(Schaumburg Rd.), Schaumburg, 847-301-1470
Young chef-owner Christina Hernandez's innovative use of
Nuevo Latino flavors from Caribbean, Spanish and South
American sources – as evidenced in her signature plantain-
crusted mahi-mahi with mango-pepper salsa – does her
proud at this vibrant, casually upscale newcomer in the
Northwest Suburbs, with a colorful South Beach deco
ambiance and complementary wine list.

Sai Cafe S　　　　　　23 | 15 | 18 | $29
2010 N. Sheffield Ave. (Armitage Ave.), 773-472-8080
■ "When good fish die, they don't go to heaven – they go to"
this "noisy and busy" Lincoln Park Japanese "favorite" to
be turned into "fresh, generous portions" of "consistent-
quality" sushi; its "homey" setting may be a bit "lacking"
in the decor department, but "interesting specials" and
"helpful", "smiling" servers make it "a must" for novices
and a "mainstay" for "experts."

SALBUTE　　　　　　25 | 17 | 20 | $30
20 E. First St. (bet. Garfield & Washington Sts.), Hinsdale,
630-920-8077
■ "Worth the wait at twice the drive", this West Suburban
Hinsdale haven "deserves its raves" for the "wonderful
flavors" of "inventive" chef-owner Edgar Rodriguez's
"thrilling, complex, delicious" "gourmet Mexican cuisine"
and its "knowledgeable" staff; remember, "reservations are
a must", especially since the "wait" for "the long-promised
liquor license" has ended – now "all it needs is more space."

Saloon, The S　　　　　21 | 18 | 21 | $41
Seneca Hotel, 200 E. Chestnut St. (Michigan Ave.), 312-280-5454
■ Pardners praise this "solid" Streeterville "hideaway
from Michigan Avenue" for rustlin' up "excellent" cuts of
beef, "great fish" dishes and "perfect cocktails" "without all
the fuss of the better-known joints in town"; still "something
of a secret", it's "a manly place" with "personable and
friendly service" and a "comfortable", "stylish setting"
that can get "smoky and noisy" at times.

Salpicón S　　　　　　22 | 18 | 20 | $36
1252 N. Wells St. (bet. Division & Goethe Sts.), 312-988-7811
■ Mexican-lovers say "*muy bueno*" about this "loud,
happy" and "crowded" Old Towner and the "innovative",
"intriguing options" on chef-owner-"magician" Priscila
Satkoff's menu of "authentic regional" dishes coupled

with a "superior wine list" (overseen by her husband, sommelier-proprietor Vincent) and an "amazing selection" of "top-shelf tequilas", all served in a "brightly colored room" that "accentuates the brightly flavored food."

Salt & Pepper Diner 🖪⇗   16 | 15 | 16 | $12

3537 N. Clark St. (Addison St.), 773-883-9800
2575 N. Lincoln Ave. (Sheffield Ave.), 773-525-8788
■ You "get what you expect" at this Lincoln Park and Wrigleyville paired set that seasons "cheap", "classic diner food" "with '50s decor", "blaring" jukeboxes and some of the "best milkshakes in Chicago"; rock-around-the-clockers also report it's "fun" "to roll out of bed and into S&P on Saturday mornings" (or afternoons), since breakfasts here are "good for a hangover."

Salvatore's Ristorante 🖪   19 | 22 | 19 | $31

525 W. Arlington Pl. (Clark St.), 773-528-1200
■ "Tucked" into "a vintage building" in Lincoln Park, this "timeless" "gem" boasts a "dark, elegant", "old-world" "supper-club setting" (plus a "wonderful outdoor garden" for "alfresco summertime" dining) and "quality" Northern Italian cooking; the "romantic atmosphere" of this "big date spot" is further enhanced on weekends by a professional ivory tickler; P.S. since it sometimes "closes for private parties, call ahead."

Samba Room 🖪   ▽ 20 | 20 | 18 | $32

22 E. Chicago Ave. (Washington St.), Naperville, 630-753-0985
◪ It's "never boring" at this "trendy" cafe (with six siblings in several states) that locals laud as "a good reason to stay in Naperville" thanks to "tasty food" showcasing "creative" "combinations" of "great Cuban" classics with "wonderful *neuvo* Latin" influences; "don't plan on having much conversation", though, as the "fun", "festive" setting can get "so noisy you can't even talk."

San Soo Gap San ◖🖪   – | – | – | M

5247 N. Western Ave. (Foster Ave.), 773-334-1589
It's always packed at this Uptown Korean BBQ eatery – sometimes even at its ungodly 6 AM closing time – and the harried staff is always hustling out heavy platters holding a vast array of specialties, including tabletop-grilled octopus and seafood, marinated skirt steak and huge, spicy hot pots of tofu and vegetables with noodles.

Santorini ◖🖪   20 | 19 | 19 | $31

800 W. Adams St. (Halsted St.), 312-829-8820
■ "Be transported to a Greek village" via this "beautiful taverna", an "island namesake" "in the heart of Greektown" specializing in "excellent seafood" such as "great whole" red "snapper or [black] sea bass" "from the grill"; "more subdued than some" of its counterparts, it has "charming",

"cozy decor" and a "lovely fireplace", but remember your options – "go early, have reservations or wait a long time!"

Sarkis Grill S⊄　　　　　18 | 9 | 19 | $12
2632 Gross Point Rd. (Crawford St.), Evanston, 847-328-9703
◪ "A North Shore relic" circa 1970, this "classic" "hole-in-the-wall" serves up "eggs with an attitude" as well as other "old-fashioned diner" fare; "regulars ranging from denim-clad kids to businessmen" report that though founder Sarkis Tashjian "sold his grill", this "joy of a man" known for his "welcoming personality" "still comes in every day" and remains "the main attraction."

Saussy　　　　　　　▽ 21 | 18 | 19 | $39
1156 W. Grand Ave. (Racine Ave.), 312-491-1122
■ "Well-presented" and "good American" cuisine "with inventive touches" and a "tasting menu [that's] a bargain" satisfy supporters of this "conversation-friendly" Near North eatery; "great service" from a "friendly, reliable" staff, a "nice chef" who sometimes "stops by to check" on customers and a "sleek", "romantic" atmosphere round out its appeal; P.S. it's no longer "BYO."

Scoozi! S　　　　　　　20 | 20 | 19 | $30
410 W. Huron St. (bet. Kingsbury & Orleans Sts.), 312-943-5900
■ Striking "a balance between food and fun", Lettuce Entertain You's "informal", "loftlike" River North Italian is a "dependable" choice for "affordable, good" fare (folks "love the butternut squash ravioli" and "crispy, paper-thin pizza"); the "lively", "casual" atmosphere is "good for singles and families" alike, helping make this a "favorite" for "happy hour" and "celebrations"; in short, young and old agree "Scoozi! is a doozi!"

SEASONS S　　　　　　28 | 27 | 27 | $65
Four Seasons Hotel, 120 E. Delaware Pl., 7th fl.
(bet. Michigan Ave. & Rush St.), 312-649-2349
■ Clients coo that the Four Seasons Hotel's "culinary magician", "Mark Baker, is truly a chef for *all* seasons", and his "classic yet contemporary" "crème-de-la-crème" New American "creations" are rated No. 1 for Food in our *Survey*; they also covet being "coddled by the loving staff" for whom "the customer is king" within the cosseting confines of its "classy" accommodations; P.S. its "lunch buffet is wonderful", and the "Sunday brunch is spectacular."

SEASONS CAFÉ ◕S　　　24 | 26 | 25 | $38
Four Seasons Hotel, 120 E. Delaware Pl., 7th fl.
(bet. Michigan Ave. & Rush St.), 312-649-2349
■ Cafe society settles into this "small, intimate" "treat" on the Four Seasons Hotel's seventh floor then tucks into "wonderful" Traditional American dishes offered with "the same great service" as at its superior sibling and "at

reasonable rates" (considering it's like "dining in a millionaire's home"); it's "the perfect antidote to shopping-weary feet" and "great for a pre-theater" repast, too.

Seoul Dook Bae Gee ⌀
_ _ _ M

3737 W. Lawrence Ave. (bet. Lawndale & Ridgeway Aves.), 773-583-5353

Nestled in a small strip mall on the Northwest Side, this authentic Korean eatery offers a broad menu of authentic fare – with options like seafood pancakes, cuttlefish and bibimbop alongside classic tabletop cook-your-own *kalbi* (short ribs) and *bulgoki* (beef) – complete with English menu descriptions and a patient, polite staff.

Settimana Café S
20 17 19 $31

2056 W. Divison St. (Hoyne Ave.), 773-394-1629

◪ When it comes to this Wicker Park one-year-old, the ayes appreciate its "very good" "authentic Italian dishes" served by a "friendly" staff "in a festive" and "comfortable" "city atmosphere" (including "excellent patios" both front and back) "without the city prices"; the nays nonetheless knock it as "noisy" and having "hit-or-miss" service and food, saying "it seems they still have kinks to work out."

1776
∇ 23 15 22 $32

397 Virginia St. (bet. Dole & McHenry Aves.), Crystal Lake, 815-356-1776

■ There's "always a little something unusual" at this "innovative", independent New American in the Northwest Suburbs, where the "seasonal cuisine" is "a treat" for "wild-game" lovers and the "excellent planked" salmon is cooked like it was in 1776; owner "Andy [Andresky]'s hospitality" warms the "homey" space, but it's his "great wine knowledge" – and "huge" 550-label, 7,200-bottle collection – that really gets revolutionaries fired up.

Shabu-ya S
_ _ _ M

3475 N. Clark St. (bet. Cornelia & Newport Aves.), 773-388-9203

Those who like to work for their supper will love the healthful if high-maintenance shabu-shabu at this small, laid-back Japanese BYO newcomer in Wrigleyville; various meats, seafood and vegetables are cooked in broth bubbling on built-in hot plates (forgoing any oil or MSG in the process); special sauces complete the savory, self-cheffed results, and the broth is then eaten with rice or noodles.

Shallots S
22 19 21 $44

2324 N. Clark St. (bet. Belden Ave. & Fullerton Pkwy.), 773-755-5205

◪ Lincoln Park is home to this "first [of its kind] in Chicago" – an "upscale", "top-notch restaurant that just happens to be kosher" (and "could succeed even if it weren't"), turning out "creative", "gourmet" Mediterranean fare the faithful feel is "well-done" and "luscious"; other kashruth-keeping critics concede it "fills a niche" but caution that its "small portions" are "not equal to" its "golden-calf prices."

Shanghai Terrace ◐ [S] ▽ 26 | 25 | 26 | $51

Peninsula Hotel, 108 E. Superior St., 4th fl. (bet. Michigan Ave. & Rush St.), 312-573-6754

■ Pamper yourself with some posh Pan-Asian in this "beautiful and blessedly quiet" refuge on the fourth floor of the Near North's Peninsula Hotel; you may "pay big for the upscale room" reminiscent of 1930s Shanghai and the "attentive service", but the "gourmet" cuisine is "excellent", and the "five-spice duck will blow your mind"; N.B. outdoor terrace seating is available in warm weather.

Shaw's Crab House & Blue Crab Lounge [S] 22 | 19 | 20 | $38

21 E. Hubbard St. (bet. State St. & Wabash Ave.), 312-527-2722

Shaw's Crab House & Red Shell Lounge [S]

1900 E. Higgins Rd. (Rte. 53), Schaumburg, 847-517-2722

■ "They wrote the book on steakhouse-style seafooders" at these "great Lettuce Entertain You" "landmarks", "old standbys" for "fun 'n' fish" that supplement "classy" main dining rooms with "more casual" lounges (the River North's Blue Crab "is the place to go" for "fresh oysters", and the Suburban Northwest's Red Shell is shrimp-centric); they may be "expensive", but they bring "the Atlantic shore to the Midwest."

She She 21 | 17 | 20 | $35

4539 N. Lincoln Ave. (bet. Sunnyside & Wilson Aves.), 773-293-3690

◪ "Flamboyant servers" in "leopard-print pants" present plates of "diverse and creative" Eclectic New American fare at this "adorable, tiny" Lincoln Square spot (owned by Dana Hechtman and chef Nicole Parthemore – she and she, respectively) with a "loud, hip, gay-dominated" scene and "a pretty back-garden area"; a few she-devils declare the kitchen "uneven", but most maintain its "sometimes surprising combinations usually work."

Shine & Morida [S] 20 | 17 | 19 | $24

901 W. Armitage Ave. (Fremont St.), 773-296-0101

■ Fans of these fraternal Lincoln Parkers tout the "trendy" twin-set as a "don't-miss" treat, saying "what a great idea" – "good Chinese and Japanese" in a one-stop shop; Shine serves "fresh" Hunan, Mandarin and Szechuan dishes "in a pleasant and serene" setting while next-door Morida slices "yummy sushi" in a "hip", "clubby atmosphere" with "pretty lighting"; N.B. you can order from either menu on either side.

Shiroi Hana [S] ▽ 21 | 11 | 16 | $19

3242 N. Clark St. (Belmont Ave.), 773-477-1652

■ "An extensive, well-executed Japanese menu" including "tasty" "sushi without the attitude" tempts the crowds into the "tight seating" of this "small, friendly" Lakeview "standby"; true, it's also "without all the glitz of some newer spots", but it's "good for carryout", the "great lunch specials" are a "fantastic bargain" and "you can't beat the party trays"; N.B. wine and beer only.

Shula's Steakhouse [S] 18 | 18 | 18 | $48

Sheraton Chicago, 301 E. North Water St. (Columbus Dr.), 312-670-0788

Wyndham Northwest Chicago, 400 Park Blvd. (Thorndale Ave.), Itasca, 630-775-1499

◪ Not surprising, these "workhorse steakhouse joints" in Streeterville and the Northwest Suburbs (part of a national chain owned by legendary NFL coach Don Shula) serve "mammoth-size steaks" that fans say are not only "big enough for a football player" but "good too"; still, some spoilsports are stymied by the "strange contrast" of a "sports-bar feel" and a "pricey", "upscale setting."

SIGNATURE ROOM AT THE 95TH [S] 18 | 26 | 19 | $45

John Hancock Ctr., 875 N. Michigan Ave., 95th fl. (bet. Chestnut St. & Delaware Pl.), 312-787-9596

◪ Like the song says, "on a clear day you can see forever" from this "romantic" New American perched high atop Streeterville's John Hancock Building, a "memorable" "must for visitors" with a "great, economical lunchtime buffet"; loyalists are "never disappointed", but others bemoan the "overpriced", "run-of-the-mill" meals, noting that while "you can't beat the view", you also "can't *eat* the view."

Silver Cloud Bar & Grill [S] 18 | 15 | 17 | $19

1700 N. Damen Ave. (Wabansia Ave.), 773-489-6212

■ "Just-plain-good" American "comfort-food favorites" – from "amazing sloppy joes" and "delicious pot roast" to "the mother of all grilled-cheese" sandwiches – as well as "lots of good beer on tap" (mostly microbrews) lure the "young and old alike" to this "cozy" "neighborhood sit-down" with a "fun, funky" atmosphere (complete with "rotating art exhibitions") that simply "screams Bucktown."

Silver Seafood ◐ [S] – | – | – | I

4829 N. Broadway (Lawrence Ave.), 773-784-0668

A new seafood sleeper in Uptown, this colorfully decorated Chinese BYO will steam you a whole fish that may have been swimming (in a small tank in the rear) when you walked in the door; fin fare aside, roasted birds such as pigeon and duck are a specialty; insiders bypass the English menu for the Chinese version with translations and more interesting offerings, including bubble teas and fruit shakes.

Sinibar ●S
▽ 15 | 21 | 17 | $29

1540 N. Milwaukee Ave. (North Ave.), 773-278-7797

☑ A light Eclectic menu of spring rolls, quesadillas, satays, panini, pastas and desserts is designed to appeal to the "see-and-be-seen" crowd that loves to lounge at this "too-cool" Moroccan-accented Wicker Park spot with a "snazzy downstairs for drinks" and DJ-driven grooving; the jury is still out, though, on the revamped menu – some see it as "above-average", others as "disappointing."

Sixty-Five S
15 | 8 | 11 | $16

201 W. Madison St. (bet. Clark & La Salle Sts.), 312-782-6565
Union Station, 225 S. Canal St. (bet. Adams St. & Jackson Blvd.), 312-474-0065
336 N. Michigan Ave. (Wacker Dr.), 312-372-0306
176 N. Wells St. (bet. Lake & Randolph Sts.), 312-346-6565

☑ The "good reputation" of this once-venerated group of Chinese fish specialists seems to be "on the way down"; while hopefuls still like the "large portions", "fast service" and "cheap prices", almost all concede that the "good seafood" is "not what it used to be" while the "dumpy atmosphere", unfortunately, is.

Slice of Life/Hy Life Bistro S⊄
14 | 12 | 15 | $23

4120 W. Dempster St. (Crawford Ave.), Skokie, 847-674-2021

☑ Set in the North Suburbs, this "interesting place" is actually two kosher restaurants with "separate dining rooms" and kitchens under one roof – one a "casual" "vegetarian" (Slice of Life), the other serving meat (Hy Life Bistro) and both "family-friendly"; but what strikes some as "cheerful service" and "orthodox Jewish soul food" "leaves something to be desired" according to others.

Smith & Wollensky S
21 | 20 | 20 | $46

318 N. State St. (bet. Kinzie St. & Wacker Dr.), 312-670-9900

☑ A "New York steakhouse tradition brought to Chicago", this River Norther in a "romantic riverfront location" is "always jumping with an after-work crowd" that gathers in its "great watering hole downstairs" or one of its handsome dining rooms for "beautiful steaks"; not surprisingly, some say it's not quite "up to the standards of" "its namesake" in Manhattan despite its "NYC prices."

Smoke Daddy ●S
20 | 14 | 16 | $18

1804 W. Division St. (bet. Ashland & Damen Aves.), 773-772-6656

■ 'Cue cravers queue up for the "melt-in-your-mouth ribs", "fabulous pulled-pork and brisket" sandwiches and "amazing" "greasy fries" at this "offbeat", "no-frills roadhouse" in Wicker Park, the "perfect neighborhood dive" where the "cool vibe" from a "laid-back" staff and "fun" crowd enjoying "great live music" (blues and jazz nightly excluding Wednesdays, rockabilly on Sundays) more than makes up for the "hole-in-the-wall decor."

Soju – | – | – | M

1745 W. North Ave. (bet. Hermitage Ave. & Wood St.), 773-782-9000

Upscale urban decor is a hallmark of this hip *bulgoki* headquarters whose slightly Americanized menu of tasty Korean (and some Japanese) dishes is divided into Western courses; also aiding in accessibility is its Wicker Park location, much closer to most city-dwellers than Lawrence Avenue; N.B. the unusual namesake liquor (a sweet-potato vodka) makes for a different sort of cocktailing.

Sorriso ▽ 16 | 21 | 18 | $32

321 N. Clark St. (Kinzie St.), 312-644-0283

◪ For those who see "the Chicago River as the Grand Canal in Venice", the chance to "eat right on it is the real draw" of this River North Italian with "nice views" from both its dining room and large outdoor seating area; "an awesome summer place" and "great lunch spot", it offers fare that some find "solid", others "uninteresting", and service that's "ok."

Souk 18 | 20 | 18 | $34

1552 N. Milwaukee Ave. (bet. Damen & North Aves.), 773-227-1818

◪ Adventurous diners "love the decor and spices" at this "cool, modern", "funky" spot "in the heart of Wicker Park" serving "good Middle Eastern" and Mediterranean fare in an "exotic" environment complete with bands and belly-dancing on weekends – "they even provide the pipes" (hookah, that is, filled with fruit-flavored tobaccos); despite "lots of potential", though, infidels insist the "novelty-act aspects overshadow the food."

Soul Kitchen [S] 21 | 20 | 19 | $31

1576 N. Milwaukee Ave. (bet. Damen & North Aves.), 773-342-9742

■ An "original" "interpretation of soul food" featuring "fascinating flavor blends" and "awesome spices" combines with "funky", "colorful decor" and an "offbeat", "upbeat scene" that's "great for people-watching" to make this Regional American a Wicker Park "favorite" of a "painfully hip, attractive clientele"; P.S. there's a "great weekend brunch menu", but "go early or wait a long time."

South Gate Cafe [S] 17 | 18 | 18 | $28

655 Forest Ave. (Deerpath Rd.), Lake Forest, 847-234-8800

◪ Fresh-air fiends favor this Lake Forest "standby" as much for its "lovely, scenic outdoor patio" with "pretty views of the market square" as its "basic", "consistently good" Traditional American fare; grouchy gate-crashers grouse that it's only "busy because it's convenient", though, grumbling that it "needs improvement in food and service."

Southport City Saloon S   14   14   16 $21
2548 N. Southport Ave. (bet. Altgeld St. & Wrightwood Ave.), 773-975-6110
■ "Great burgers" stand out on an otherwise "average" menu of Traditional American pub grub at this local "staple" in Lincoln Park where a "fun", "clublike" ambiance pervades; the enclosed patio is not only "great in summer" but is heated by a fireplace in the winter, making it "truly delightful" anytime of the year.

Spago   22   22   21 $47
520 N. Dearborn St. (Grand Ave.), 312-527-3700
☑ "Chicago goes Hollywood" at River North's "trendy", "noisy" satellite of the LA original, where "beautiful people eat beautiful [New American] food"; aficionados applaud the menu's "wonderful eclecticism" – "pizzas, Wiener schnitzel, Chinois chicken salad" – and the room's "warmer look", the result of a recent face-lift, but critics slam it as "overpriced", "overrated" and "losing its edge."

Sparacino Ristorante   –   –   –   M
6966 W. North Ave. (bet. Harlem & Oak Park Aves.), 773-836-2089
A sophisticated slant on traditional Italian cuisine comes to the Far West side via this one-year-old that takes its inspiration from multiple regions; run by brother and sister Mark and Steffania Sparacino, its intimate coffee-and-cream-colored dining room is set in a space that it shares with its sibling, a catering concern called Traveling Fare; there's also a vintage bar and a sidewalk cafe offering seasonal outdoor dining.

SPIAGGIA S   27   27   26 $62
One Magnificent Mile Bldg., 980 N. Michigan Ave., 2nd fl. (Oak St.), 312-280-2750
■ "You know you've arrived when you enter the gorgeous dining room" of this "wildly expensive" "romantic splurge spot" in the Gold Coast, ranked No. 1 for Decor by surveyors who also laud "talented chef" Tony Mantuano's "refined", "innovative" Italian cuisine as the "best [of its kind] in the city"; "attentive" service and "awesome views" from its "grand" setting contribute to a "special" experience; P.S. it's nearby "cafe is wonderful and less" costly too.

SPRING S   26   25   25 $53
2039 W. North Ave. (Damen Ave.), 773-395-7100
■ An "excellent addition" that's already a "favorite" of the "chic" set, this "hot", "hip" New American in Wicker Park

"lives up to its hype" on the strength of "magnificent"
chef-owner Shawn McClain (formerly of Trio) and his
"gorgeous", "sublime" "Asian-influenced" cuisine
(including "swimmingly fresh seafood") "professionally"
served in a "stark", "stylish", "tranquil" space graced with
a Zen garden; it's "pricey" but "worth springing for."

Stained Glass Wine Bar Bistro S

24 20 23 $40

*1735 Benson Ave. (bet. Church & Clark Sts.), Evanston,
847-864-8600*

■ "A sparkling treasure" to bacchic boosters, this Evanston
enoteca/bistro entices oenophiles with its "fun, flight-
oriented approach" and "terrific selection", but many who
first "go for the wine" later "come back for the [Eclectic]
food", which fans describe as "top-notch", "appropriately
complex" and "fabulously creative"; "enjoyable service"
helps make this "a welcome addition to Chicago's limited
wine bar scene."

Standard India S

▽ 21 11 17 $18

917 W. Belmont Ave. (Clark St.), 773-929-1123

◪ Supporters of this Lakeview Indian counsel "go on an
empty stomach", for "you'll be tempted to try every dish" on
the "superb buffet" that's a "must" for its "excellent value";
cynics, however, find "no charm" in fare they feel is, well,
"standard", not to mention decor that's even less than that.

Stanley's Kitchen & Tap S

18 14 16 $18

1970 N. Lincoln Ave. (Armitage Ave.), 312-642-0007

■ "Tasty homestyle cooking" and "family atmosphere"
make this Traditional American eatery in Lincoln Park
"good" for a "casual brunch on Sundays" "with the kids",
but it's also nice for a "bar buddies'" or "girls' night out";
just remember you may "need a wheelbarrow to get"
yourself home; P.S. "they've got Tater Tots!"

Star of Siam S

19 15 17 $18

11 E. Illinois St. (State St.), 312-670-0100

■ "Amazing value", "consistent" cooking and a "comfy
atmosphere" keep 'em coming to this "old Thai favorite"
in River North offering "plenty of variety" at "reasonable
prices in an area where everything else is expensive";
some find the "fast service" "mind-blowing" (in a good
way), while others say it's "too quick", but most agree the
place is "great for eat-in or takeaway."

Stefani's S

20 16 20 $29

1418 W. Fullerton Ave. (Southport Ave.), 773-348-0111

■ *Amici* of Phil Stefani's "reliable" DePaul-area Northern
Italian (including the husband of NY's Chicago-born junior
senator) appreciate the "huge portions" of "consistently
good", "basic" fare ("plentiful pasta, no paltry poultry") at

"reasonable prices"; the decor may need "sprucing up", but the "nice outdoor area" offers "alfresco in the summer."

Stevie B's ⦿S ▽ 19 8 14 $19
1401 N. Ashland Ave. (Blackhawk St.), 773-486-7427
■ "Good ribs fast – 'nuff said" gush grandiloquent groupies of this casual Wicker Park BBQ, who also pen poems to its "great sandwiches", compose arias in honor of its "fine chicken" and give glory to its "good sides"; as reflected by the single-digit Decor score, "no atmosphere" might help explain why insiders rely on it "strictly for takeout."

Stir Crazy Cafe S 19 17 17 $20
1186 N. Northbrook Court Mall (bet. Skokie Blvd. &
Waukegan Rd.), Northbrook, 847-562-4800
Oakbrook Center Mall, 105 Oakbrook Ctr. (Rte. 83), Oak Brook,
630-575-0155
Woodfield Mall, 5 Woodfield Mall (Perimeter Dr.),
Schaumburg, 847-330-1200
■ "Eating by the numbers has never been so fun" exclaim enthusiasts of these "attractive", mall-based "build-your-own" Asian stir-fry spots that are "good places to experiment"; "delicious, fresh ingredients" including "a large selection of vegetables and sauces" are "cooked fast" by a "friendly staff" that "handles crowds well"; it has to, as the "always-busy" scene is no wok in the park.

Strega Nona S 17 17 17 $29
3747 N. Southport Ave. (bet. Grace St. & Waveland Ave.),
773-244-0990
◪ A "solid performer in the crowded Italian scene" is how pros portray this Lakeview paesano offering "dependable" cooking and a "comfortable, low-lit setting" (with "nice outdoor seating") in a location that's handy for pre- or post- "movie or theater" dining; detractors contend that it "manages to lower the bar" with "so-so" eats and "spotty service", opting for it "only when in a hurry."

Su Casa S 16 16 16 $24
49 E. Ontario St. (bet. Rush St. & Wabash Ave.), 312-943-4041
◪ Friends of this "well-located" Near North Mexican vet say *si* to its "ample portions" of "authentic", "basic" south-of-the-border fare, "great margaritas" and "cute" environs, but enemigos insist that the "average" eats "fill the stomach but leave something to be desired", saying this old-timer "needs upgrading" across the board.

Sullivan's Steakhouse S 21 20 20 $43
415 N. Dearborn St. (Hubbard St.), 312-527-3510
244 S. Main St. (bet. Jackson & Jefferson Aves.), Naperville,
630-305-0230
■ It takes a lot to "survive in this steak town", and these links of a national chophouse chain "stand tall" ("yes,

sir!") with "consistently" "great steaks" accompanied by "quality sides" such as "mushrooms to die for" served by "enthusiastic" staffers in a "dark", "clubby" setting brightened by the strains of "live jazz"; they're "pricey", but they "don't disappoint."

Suparossa 🖪   17 | 14 | 16 | $22
210 E. Ohio St. (St. Clair St.), 312-587-0030
4256 N. Central Ave. (Cullom Ave.), 773-736-5828
7319 W. Lawrence Ave. (bet. Harlem & Oketo Aves.),
Harwood Heights, 708-867-4641 ⬤
6301 Purchase Dr. (Rte. 53), Woodridge, 630-852-1000
■ Although it's a chain, this city and suburban Italian quartet of "friendly and casual" "neighborhood" spots earns props as "favorite stops" serving "good pizzas" (both thick and thin) and other "standards"; "excellent delivery" is another plus.

Superdawg Drive-In ⬤🖪⇗   22 | 18 | 18 | $9
6363 N. Milwaukee Ave. (Devon Ave.), 773-763-0660
■ "As much a part of Chicago as the Bears and the Daleys", this "kitschy, retro" Northwest Side "top dawg" is the No. 1 Bang for the Buck in our *Survey* and "has been there forever [actually, since 1948] for a reason": "the Rolls-Royce of hot dogs" is "hung on your window" by carhops (so "the decor depends on your car"); P.S. loyalists love the "dancing mascots on the roof."

Sushi Naniwa 🖪   23 | 15 | 20 | $28
607 N. Wells St. (bet. Ohio & Ontario Sts.), 312-255-8555
■ "No nonsense", "no attitude" – "just excellent", "creative and colorful" raw fish in "generous portions"; that's what keeps this River North Japanese joint jumping and makes "sitting at the sushi bar" with the "hip crowd" "a joy" (by the way, the "great specials" and "friendly service" don't hurt either); P.S. a planned expansion at press time may outdate the "blah" Decor score.

Sushi Wabi ⬤🖪   24 | 19 | 18 | $33
842 W. Randolph St. (Green St.), 312-563-1224
◪ A "real scene" awaits at this "so-cool-even-the-fish-wear-black" Market District raw-fin-fare affair where "fresh, high-end" seafood that's "a cut above" is sliced by knife-wielding "artists" then served in a "loud", "austere, industrial" setting resembling "an after-hours club" – "complete with DJ"; if you can "ignore the attitude" from the "know-it-all staff", this place will "make you fall in love with sushi again."

Takkatsu 🖪   – | – | – | M
45 Green Bay Rd. (Scott Ave.), Winnetka, 847-784-9031
Distinguishing itself from the tidal wave of sushi spots, this North Shore newcomer specializes in tonkatsu, a breaded

pork cutlet popular in its native Japan but less-known stateside, as well as beef, chicken, shrimp and cheese versions of its signature dish, curried pork and pork skewers, and more recognizable Japanese fare such as, yes, the ubiquitous raw fish.

TALLGRASS [S] 27 25 27 $63

1006 S. State St. (10th St.), Lockport, 815-838-5566

■ Intrepid diners deem it "worth the trip" to this "small", "romantic" Southwest Suburban New French in the "lovely canal town" of Lockport, where chef Robert Burcenski "continues to amaze" with his prix fixe menus of "creative", "serious" fare highlighted by "innovative pairings" and "gorgeous presentations"; the "reserved, understated space" and "excellent" service contribute to the "world-class" experience; N.B. jacket required.

Tanglewood 20 20 20 $36

Laundry Mall, 566 Chestnut St. (Spruce St.), Winnetka, 847-441-4600

■ A "great North Suburban choice" that "works" "for all occasions" – from simple dinners to "private parties" to groups "going to [the annual] Ravinia" Festival – this "creative" New American offers "well-presented" dishes at "reasonable prices"; a "fireplace in the winter" and a patio where you can "eat outside in nice weather" during the warmer months add year-round allure.

Tango Sur [S] 20 14 17 $24

3763 N. Southport Ave. (Grace St.), 773-477-5466

■ "In a city known for great steakhouses", the "excellent Argentinean beef" served at this "Lakeview hideaway" BYO cow palace is "something different" that "aims to please" with "cattle-ranch-size portions" of "awesome" meat, "don't-miss empanadas and flan"; "friendly, helpful" service and "great prices" are added bonuses and help excuse the "intimate" digs (read: "close quarters") and "long waits"; N.B. live tango music on Wednesdays.

Tapas Barcelona [S] 19 18 17 $26

1615 Chicago Ave. (bet. Church & Davis Sts.), Evanston, 847-866-9900

■ "So many choices" of "good cheap eats" are a "fun way to try new things" at Evanston's "authentically Spanish" tapas "hot spot" and "great date place"; though sometimes a bit "noisy", its transporting Iberian ambiance nevertheless provides a "relaxing atmosphere in which to enjoy your meal", whether inside or out in the "wonderful garden."

Tarantino's [S] 20 19 20 $32

1112 W. Armitage Ave. (Seminary St.), 773-871-2929

■ Hitting the Lincoln Park "trifecta of food, atmosphere and service", this "classy" "joint" wins praise from loyal locals for its "light", "flavorful" Northern Italian fare, and its "cozy", "romantic" ambiance makes it a popular "date place"; P.S. the staff is "knowledgeable", and it shows.

Tasting Room, The ▽ 19 22 21 $28
1415 W. Randolph St. (Ogden Ave.), 312-942-1212
■ Aficionados aver "you can't beat" this Market District wine bar for an "impressive list" of vintages (including 110 by-the-glass pours) complemented by "great cheese and charcuterie plates" and a "limited menu" of New American appetizers and desserts; the "comfortable", "loftlike" setting ("love the sofas") offers "romantic skyline views", creating a "cozy environment."

Tavern ▽ 20 22 23 $40
(fka Tavern in the Town)
519 N. Milwaukee Ave. (bet. Cook Ave. & Lake St.), Libertyville, 847-367-5755
■ "A little gem of a place on a busy street" in Northwest Suburban Libertyville, this "lovely", "popular" Contemporary American "continues to please consistently" with "excellent food" and a "good selection of wines by the glass" in a "gorgeous room" with "wonderful atmosphere"; N.B. next door, the casual, unrated Firkin offers live blues and a more Eclectic menu.

Tavern on Rush ●⬤ 19 20 18 $41
1031 N. Rush St. (Bellevue Pl.), 312-664-9600
◪ A popular "people-watching" "meet market", this Gold Coast steakhouse has a "happening bar" and a "busy outdoor cafe" that tend to upstage the "lovely" upstairs dining room, as well as its "friendly" service and signature steaks, which garner only mixed reviews ("great" vs. "just ok"); detractors dismiss it as a "noisy tourist trap."

Taza ⬤≠ 16 10 11 $11
39 S. Wabash Ave. (Monroe St.), 312-425-9988
◪ A "popular lunch place", this Loop Eclectic serves "quick, cheap eats", including a Middle Eastern–influenced charcoal-grilled clucker that some poultry pundits praise as the "best fast-food chicken ever" and "fresh salads" worth crossing the road for; perturbed patrons, however, cry foul, pecking at the "lousy" decor and "terrible" service.

Tecalitlan ●⬤ 19 14 16 $18
1814 W. Chicago Ave. (Wood St.), 773-384-4285
■ "Consistently good" "down-home, authentic" Mexican cooking "you can't get anywhere else" – including "burritos as big as your head" and "high-quality steaks" – and "dangerous margaritas" help explain why this Ukrainian Village Mexican is "always busy"; while a few banditos bellyache that it's "cheap, and you get what you pay for", defenders counter "value, value, value."

Technicolor Kitchen S   19 | 21 | 19 | $31
3210 N. Lincoln Ave. (Ashland & Belmont Aves.),
773-665-2111
◪ A panoramic palette punches up the "welcoming",
"colorful" interior of this "electric, stylish" Lakeview spot,
but the New American fare leaves palates ambivalent –
proponents paint the "tempting menu" of "feel-good food"
as "contemporary" and "unusual", while critics color it
"disappointing", claiming its cooking is "more technicolor
than kitchen"; "attentive" service completes the picture.

Tempo ●S⬠   18 | 12 | 16 | $15
6 E. Chestnut St. (State St.), 312-943-4373
■ "Everyone goes" to this Gold Coast "Greek coffee shop"
for breakfast at "any time of day", so "be prepared to wait
in line" for "excellent omelets", "huevos rancheros that
rock" and other "good, basic, cheap eats"; its "trendy
location" and 24/7 hours make it "a great place to refuel
after clubbing", though hopeful hangover healers won't hit
upon hair-of-the-dog here – no liquor is served.

Thai Classic S   ▽ 21 | 15 | 20 | $18
3332 N. Clark St. (bet. Belmont Ave. & Roscoe St.),
773-404-2000
■ "The name says it all" crow cronies who clamor for the
"consistently reliable", "moderately priced" fare on offer at
this Thai pad in the heart of Lakeview, including "fabulous
curries" and one of the "best buffets in Chicago"; "kind,
relaxed service" complements the "cozy atmosphere",
which jurists gingerly suggest "could be slightly enhanced
by better decor"; N.B. it's BYO.

Thai Little Home Cafe S   ▽ 22 | 12 | 19 | $18
4747 N. Kedzie Ave. (Lawrence Ave.), 773-478-3944
■ A "dependable" "favorite" on the Northwest Side, this
"consistent" BYO performer offers "wonderful", inexpensive
Thai dishes, and regulars recommend the "lunch buffet
feast" (which doubles as weekend brunch) as a "great
way to taste different dishes"; it may not be much in the
looks department, but "friendly service" makes it feel like
a little home of your own.

Thai Pastry S   22 | 13 | 18 | $17
4925 N. Broadway (bet. Argyle St. & Lawrence Ave.),
773-784-5399
■ "Top-notch", "authentic and fresh" Thai dishes exhibiting
"flavor and creativity" are the draw at this "friendly",
"delightful", "inexpensive little gem" in Uptown; some say
"the name is deceiving" (though there is a pastry case,
"they are not known for it"), others that the "storefront"
setting and "bright dining room" are "bleak", but advocates
argue "what it lacks in ambiance it more than makes up for
in the kitchen."

Thai Star Cafe S
17 | 9 | 14 | $17
660 N. State St. (Erie St.), 312-951-1196
☑ Star-gazers who favor this River North "hole-in-the-wall" say they "don't go for" the venue but for the "good-value", "reliable Thai" cooking; foes, however, can't "ignore" the "drab exterior", "cramped", "tired-looking" and housekeeping-challenged interior, "unbearably slow service" and "unappetizingly served" "boring fare."

Three Happiness ● S
– | – | – | M
209 W. Cermak Rd. (Wentworth Ave.), 312-842-1964
"Adventurous offerings" of dim sum from the "rolling tables" are a daily draw at this small Chinatown storefront, as well as "very good", "cheap" Szechuan seafood; cognoscenti counsel "disregard the decor" – or "take it to go"; N.B. no relation to New Three Happiness (its former sibling) on South Wentworth Avenue.

302 WEST
25 | 25 | 24 | $49
302 W. State St. (3rd St.), Geneva, 630-232-9302
■ "If this place were on the Near North Side, you wouldn't be able to get in" boast boosters of Joel Findlay's "first-class" New American in the Western Suburbs, a "longtime favorite" for its "wonderful, inventive, always-changing menu" and "great selection of small-provider wines" "served with care" in a "beautiful, gracious dining room" set in a former bank; P.S. "they understand that desserts are supposed to be fun."

312 Chicago S
20 | 18 | 19 | $36
Hotel Allegro, 136 N. La Salle St. (Randolph St.), 312-696-2420
☑ Named after the city's area code, this "jewel" in the Loop's Hotel Allegro connects with many surveyors thanks to chef Dean Zanella's "damn good", "interesting" Italian-inspired American cuisine, served in a "pleasant" setting suitable for "power breakfasts", "business lunches" or "pre-theater dining"; critics, however, are hung up on the "inattentive" service and "noisy, frenetic" scene.

Thyme S
22 | 21 | 20 | $42
464 N. Halsted St. (Grand Ave.), 312-226-4300
☑ Fans rave over this "trendy", "out-of-the-way" Near West New American–French production thanks to chef-owner John Bubala's "creative" and "consistent" cooking seasoned with "subtle and sensuous flavor infusions", as well as its "lovely" interior and "romantic courtyard" that's "fabulous" in the summer; foes, however, have no time for the "noisy" scene and "overpriced" menu.

Tiffin S
22 | 17 | 18 | $23
2536 W. Devon Ave. (Maplewood Ave.), 773-338-2143
■ It's "Indian at its best" declare devotees describing this "elegant" establishment on the Northwest Side, where an

"abundant" selection of "authentic", "flavorful" dishes is served in "classy", "fancy" digs; the "attentive and friendly" owner's "pride in his restaurant is a joy for patrons" and a big reason why many say it's the "clearly superior choice on the Devon strip."

Tilli's 🟥　　　　16　19　17　$22
1952 N. Halsted St. (bet. Armitage Ave. & Willow St.), 773-325-0044

☑ It gets "loud and crowded" at this "friendly, casual" Lincoln Park "after-work" spot that's "great for drinks" and "people-watching", sporting a "cozy" setting, complete with fireplace, patio and window seats that are "ideal for couples"; the "diverse" Eclectic menu elicits mixed responses ("decent", "different", "blah"), which is why some skeptics just "get drinks and skip the food."

Tizi Melloul 🟥　　　　21　25　21　$35
531 N. Wells St. (Grand Ave.), 312-670-4338

■ You "feel like you've stepped into another world" upon entering this "sultry", "spectacular" River North Med specialist (don't miss the "round room" with "pillow seating" that's "wonderful for groups of friends"); after a gradual cuisine shift, the menu still shows signs of its original Moroccan influences, offering "distinctive flavors" that are "a playground for your taste buds"; N.B. the Sunday-night belly dancer survived the concept change.

Toast 🟥　　　　20　15　15　$15
2046 N. Damen Ave. (Dickens Ave.), 773-772-5600
746 W. Webster Ave. (Halsted St.), 773-935-5600

☑ The toast of the town for its "large portions and crazy combinations", including the "don't-miss mascarpone-stuffed French toast" and "mouthwatering 'crabby eggs Benedict'", this "funky" duo of "urban" "breakfast and lunch joints" is "worth getting up and standing in line" for declare diurnal devotees; "hour-long waits" and "cranky service", though, burn crusty critics.

Tokyo Marina 🟥　　　▽ 22　12　16　$21
5058 N. Clark St. (Carmen Ave.), 773-878-2900

■ There's "never a wait" for a slip at the dock of this Andersonville "sushi dive" where finatics moor themselves at the bar then plunge into "fresh, yummy" fish, as well as other "reliable and tasty" Japanese dishes on the menu; "the price is right", with "generous portions" ensuring "good value", and the "chefs will accommodate fussy diners", which is typical of the "friendly service."

Tomboy 🟥　　　　20　18　18　$32
5402 N. Clark St. (Balmoral Ave.), 773-907-0636

☑ "Interesting" Eclectic fare, "pleasant decor" and "fun", "accommodating" service draw a "hip crowd" to this "urban", "gay-friendly" spot in Andersonville; while critics throw up their hands at some "hit-or-miss" cooking and a "crowded" dining room that "offers charm but is noisy", stalwarts hang in there for the ambiance and "great value"; P.S. folks "love being able to bring their own wine."

Tommy Nevin's Pub ◐ S 17 | 16 | 17 | $21
1450 Sherman Ave. (Lake St.), Evanston, 847-869-0450
☑ "Northwestern students and locals" alike hie to this "casual" Evanston pub whenever "they're feeling Irish" or just in the mood for "beers by the pint and bar food"; still, the "authenticity" of this Gaelic-American spot is questioned by purists who would prefer "a little more [of the former] and a little less [of the latter]."

Topo Gigio Ristorante S 21 | 18 | 19 | $31
1516 N. Wells St. (bet. Division St. & North Ave.), 312-266-9355
■ Advocates avow there's nothing mousy about this "tried and true" Old Town "Chicago tradition", a "cozy" yet "high-energy" stop for "satisfying, good Italian food" ("splendid osso buco", "yummy pastas"), served in a "busy and boisterous room" and a "great outdoor area" that's a "must in summer"; while most approve of the "no-nonsense" service, a few find it borderline "rude."

TOPOLOBAMPO 27 | 24 | 25 | $50
445 N. Clark St. (bet. Hubbard & Illinois Sts.), 312-661-1434
■ A "real star in a big food town", this River North Mexican (Frontera Grill's "upscale cousin") "continues to shine" thanks to "serious", "daring" cuisine admirers insist is "better than any in Mexico"; chef Rick Bayless dazzles fans with his "exciting treatment" of "the best ingredients", while "professional service", "beautifully artistic decor" and a "good tequila selection and wine list" contribute to an "all-around outstanding" experience.

Tournesol S – | – | – | M
4343 N. Lincoln Ave. (bet. Cullom & Montrose Aves.), 773-477-8820
Paris-born Eric Aubriot, a partner at this new storefront bistro in Lincoln Square, designed its menu in keeping with the casual yet traditional decor, placing the emphasis on classic dishes at moderate prices, such as salade niçoise, steak frites and braised rabbit; as befits a restaurant named for the sunflowers that dot the Gallic countryside, its accessible wine list focuses on French country vintages.

Trader Vic's S 17 | 20 | 18 | $33
Palmer House Hilton, 17 E. Monroe St. (bet. State St. & Wabash Ave.), 312-917-7317
☑ "Where's the Rat Pack?" wonder wags about this "retro-funk" Polynesian in the Loop's Palmer House Hilton, where the "hokey '50s decor and drinks" are "so unhip they're hip";

while pros protest "don't pupu" the "unappreciated fantasy food" that's "much better than its reputation", hecklers hiss at the "hodgepodge" of "hotel-ish fare"; N.B. no longer serving lunch.

Trattoria Dinotto 🅂   21 | 19 | 22 | $31
163 W. North Ave. (Wells St.), 312-787-3345
■ "Terrific waiters" provide "friendly, well-informed service", not to mention "fresh", "well-prepared" and "tasty" Italian fare, at this "dependable" Old Towner that longtime lovers laud as "one of the neighborhood greats"; the "cute", storefront setting is "quaint" and "cozy", even if the "tiny" interior is somewhat "cramped"; N.B. the new, nearby ristorante (serving the same menu) is unrated.

Trattoria Gianni 🅂   20 | 16 | 21 | $32
1711 N. Halsted St. (bet. North Ave. & Willow St.), 312-266-1976
■ "Never a disappointment", this "unassuming" Lincoln Park "sleeper" reminds regulars of "a lovely little trattoria in Rome" with its "fresh, simple, unpretentious Italian fare"; "convenient to the North Side theater row", it's a natural for "pre-Steppenwolf" dining, and though it offers a "fabulous brunch" on Sundays, some pastaphiles "wish it were open for lunch" during the week.

Trattoria No. 10   22 | 20 | 21 | $36
10 N. Dearborn St. (bet. Madison St. & Washington Blvd.), 312-984-1718
■ Surveyors say this "basement beauty" of an "efficient trattoria" is "a staple in the Loop business and theater district" for "tasty" "classic Italian, done well" and served in a "comfortable cave atmosphere" that's "a refuge for romance and rotini" ("try the homemade butternut squash ravioli"); P.S. boosters say *bene* to the "bargain bar buffet."

Trattoria Pizzeria Roma 🅂   ▽ 20 | 16 | 20 | $29
1535 N. Wells St. (bet. North Ave. & Schiller St.), 312-664-7907
■ While loyalists of this "quaint", time-honored Old Town Italian lament the passing of the late owner, Franco Zalloni, most are confident that his widow, Laura, will preserve the "quality" of its "delicious" fare with "classic flavors", as well as its "down-home feel" and "informal" service; it's "not pretentious or overpriced", which is why it's been a "favorite" "through the years."

Tre Kronor 🅂   23 | 17 | 21 | $18
3258 W. Foster Ave. (bet. Kedzie & Kimball Aves.), 773-267-9888
■ "You'll think you're in Sweden" at this "bright, sunny" storefront BYO spot on the Northwest Side serving "a variety of Scandinavian specialties" at "reasonable prices"; admirers muse "this is what they mean when they say 'a

cozy little place'", with "homestyle" "comfort food", a "family atmosphere" and "wonderful service"; P.S. "the trolls dancing on the walls are not to be missed."

TRIO [S] 28 | 25 | 28 | $74

Homestead Hotel, 1625 Hinman Ave. (Davis St.), Evanston, 847-733-8746

■ "The French Laundry comes to Evanston" in the person of toque Grant Achatz (ex Thomas Keller's California legend), whose "finesse, bravado and quality" make him "as original a [chef] as you'll ever find"; his "exceptional cuisine" is "as serious as the setting" of this "true foodies' restaurant", while "inspired wine pairings" and "knowledgeable service" add to the "near-perfect experience", after which "all you can think about is doing it again."

TRU 27 | 27 | 27 | $85

676 N. St. Clair St. (bet. Erie & Huron Sts.), 312-202-0001

■ Rick Tramonto and Gale Gand "add humor and surprise to elegant cuisine" in their Streeterville Lettuce Entertain You partnership, a haven "for serious foodies" voted No. 1 for Popularity in our *Survey* where "splendid [New French] food and synchronized service" are showcased in a "spartan setting" and at a "leisurely pace" (with "dinner lasting two to four hours", depending on your choice of prix-fixe or "collection" menus); even "demanding diners" concede its "excellence" is "worth the astronomical price."

Tsunami [S] 20 | 18 | 18 | $33

1160 N. Dearborn St. (Division St.), 312-642-9911

◪ Bucking the tide of "average Japanese restaurants", this "classy" Gold Coaster does "sexy sushi" served in a "dark", "clublike" setting with a "swanky sake lounge" upstairs; champions praise the "consistently good" seafood that "can make anyone a [raw-fish] eater", but boat-rockers retort it's really "for those looking to be seen", and wallet-watchers are wiped out by tabs that are "way too high."

Tucci Benucch [S] 17 | 18 | 18 | $26

900 N. Michigan Ave., 5th fl. (Walton St.), 312-266-2500

◪ In the Bloomie's building, this "cute", "rustic" Gold Coast Italian eatery serves "consistent" "standard Italian fare" that's "better than average mall food"; although the digs look a bit "tired" and are often "crowded", the "casual" vibe and "fast" service make it an attractive stop "after a movie or shopping" to "escape the Michigan Avenue madness."

Tufano's Vernon Park Tap [S] ⊘ 21 | 15 | 19 | $23

1073 W. Vernon Park Pl. (Taylor St.), 312-733-3393

■ "Hidden" away in Tri-Taylor, this timeless "favorite of locals and politicians" is a "fun, raucous, truly family-style" Southern Italian "joint" serving "inexpensive, no-frills" red-sauce fare "as old-school as can be" in a "noisy" room adorned with "celebrity pictures"; "brisk service" and "low prices" enhance the classic "Chicago atmosphere."

Tuscany 🄂 | 21 | 19 | 20 | $33 |

3700 N. Clark St. (Waveland Ave.), 773-404-7700
1014 W. Taylor St. (Morgan St.), 312-829-1990
1415 W. 22nd St. (Rte. 83), Oak Brook, 630-990-1993
550 S. Milwaukee Ave. (bet. Hintz Rd. & Manchester Dr.), Wheeling, 847-465-9988

Tuscany Café 🄂

Shops at North Bridge, 520 N. Michigan Ave. (bet. Grand Ave. & Ohio St.), 312-595-9090

☑ Phil Stefani's "tried-and-true" Little Italy original and its spin-offs "consistently" deliver "robust dining" and "a good variety" of Northern Italian fare that's "not fancy but reliable"; the convivial proceedings can get "noisy" when the room gets "crowded", and some penne-pinchers pan the "pricey" tabs; P.S. the cafe's "fast-food" offerings "don't reflect the full-scale restaurant."

Twelve 12 | 24 | 22 | 21 | $51 |

1212 N. State Pkwy. (Division St.), 312-951-1212

■ At this "dazzling" Gold Coast New American, David Shea's "terrific balanced menu" of "imaginative dishes" (with an "excellent-bargain prix fixe"), enhanced by "beautiful presentations", "an impressive wine list", "chic", "well-appointed" decor and a "friendly, knowledgeable" staff, has fans hoping it enjoys a "long, happy run."

Twin Anchors 🄂 | 21 | 14 | 17 | $25 |

1655 N. Sedgwick St. (Concord Pl.), 312-266-1616

■ "Chicago's best ribs" ("huge, tender slabs" with "zesty sauce") continue to make this "fun, retro" stalwart in Old Town a "family tradition" ("my parents went there as kids"); the "homey", "classic tavern setting" is "quintessentially 'local'", and while there's "always a wait", service that's "surprisingly good, given the crowds", keeps things on an even keel; still, cagey connoisseurs prefer to "take out."

Twist 🄂 | ▽ 22 | 19 | 18 | $25 |

3412 N. Sheffield Ave. (Clark St.), 773-388-2727

■ "Killer tapas" and "tasty sangria" make this "cute" Lakeview yearling a "new favorite" of in-the-know worshipers who warrant "everything on the [Spanish-International] menu is great" and wonder "why everyone doesn't know about this place"; still, they advise "getting there early", as the space is "tight" and "there's no waiting area"; N.B. outdoor seating is an added twist.

Twisted Lizard, The 🄂 | 17 | 15 | 16 | $19 |

1964 N. Sheffield Ave. (Armitage Ave.), 773-929-1414

☑ Fans flock to this "noisy", "local" Lincoln Park "basement" (with tables outside too) for "fresh, fun Mexican" eats, including "holy *mole*" and "righteous margaritas" (try the "worthwhile cranberry version"); cynics snipe at the "so-so" sustenance, however, and sneer "go for the drinks and the scene" then "leave when you want to eat."

Twisted Spoke ◐ [S] 18 16 16 $16

501 N. Ogden Ave. (Grand Ave.), 312-666-1500

■ For "yuppies who like to live dangerously", this "safe" but "grungy" Near West hog heaven with a "biker-bar motif" and an American pub-grub menu "reflects a sassy attitude"; while some warn it's "not for the faint of heart", a few wild ones dismiss the "faux" scene with "stick-on tattoos in a vending machine" as "'trendy meets Harley'"; P.S. road warriors rave about the "rooftop picnic tables."

Udupi Palace [S] ▽ 25 11 18 $16

2543 W. Devon Ave. (bet. Maplewood Ave. & Rockwell St.), 773-338-2152

■ "Dive" digs on Devon don't deter diehards from delighting in the "delicious Indian vegetarian fare" that's "cheap and really great" at this "no-frills" storefront sibling of the more elegant top-rated Tiffin; the mostly "conventional" cuisine contains "a few innovations", and the kitchen is accommodating to spice girls and boys – "if you ask for it hot, they provide."

Uncle Julio's Hacienda [S] 17 16 15 $21

855 W. North Ave. (Clybourn Ave.), 312-266-4222

◪ "Big portions" of "cheap", "consistently good" Mexican fare served in a "loud, fun atmosphere" have supporters saying this Lincoln Park link in a national chain is "great for kids" and big folks alike; still, snipers snort it's "*nada especial*", sneering at what they say is "Americanized food" "for the undiscriminating", while the impatient cry uncle over the "long waits."

Uncommon Ground [S] ▽ 17 16 16 $14

1214 W. Grace St. (Clark St.), 773-929-3680

■ With its "good, healthy" Eclectic menu full of "vegetarian options", this "cool, casual" Wrigleyville local has grown beyond its coffeehouse roots into a "perfect hangout" for the "granola crowd" (though java junkies advise "don't pass up the bowl of latte"); "great live musicians" add allure to the "fantastic, warm atmosphere"; N.B. outdoor seating in summer.

Va Pensiero [S] 24 22 23 $44

Margarita Inn, 1566 Oak Ave. (Davis St.), Evanston, 847-475-7779

■ A "special place" in Evanston's Margarita Inn, this "relaxing" "elegant eatery" pairs "outstanding", "creative", "contemporary fare" from The Boot with a "top-notch" "all-Italian wine list", "sophisticated decor" and "impeccable service"; better still, despite the somewhat "formal" feel there's "virtually no snob factor"; P.S. "don't miss" the "terrific monthly wine dinners."

Via Carducci [S] — 23 | 18 | 20 | $25

1419 W. Fullerton Ave. (Southport Ave.), 773-665-1981

■ A "great Italian" in Lincoln Park, this "casual dining favorite" "keeps getting better" at serving "big portions" of "fresh", "good, basic" fare such as "wonderful pastas" and "gnocchi like silk" that taste like they were made from someone's "mother's recipes"; the prices are "reasonable", and the setting is as "romantic" as a "hole-in-the-wall" can be (it's handy for takeout too).

Via Emilia Ristorante [S] — ▽ 20 | 18 | 18 | $31

2119 N. Clark St. (bet. Dickens & Webster Aves.), 773-248-6283

◪ Specializing in the cuisine of the under-exposed Emilia-Romagna region, this "cozy" Lincoln Park Italian offers "tasty, affordable" fare, including "excellent pastas" and "wonderful salads", with an emphasis on seafood (both in its specials and its risottos); the "enthusiastic" staff of native paesani enhances the "authentic" ambiance, but opinions of the service range from "ok" to "spotty."

Via Veneto [S] — 20 | 15 | 20 | $29

3449 W. Peterson Ave. (Kimball Ave.), 773-267-0888

■ At this "authentic and rustic" "neighborhood favorite" on the Northwest Side, "big portions" of "consistently good" and "well-prepared" "classic Italian" dishes (including "outstanding pastas" and "great risottos") offered with "warm service" from an "attentive" staff make up for the "tight seating" in a "small dining room" that clearly "needs work"; N.B. a relocation was being planned at press time, so phone first.

Viceroy of India [S] — 20 | 15 | 17 | $22

2520 W. Devon Ave. (bet. Campbell & Maplewood Aves.), 773-743-4100

555 Roosevelt Rd. (Highland Ave.), Lombard, 630-627-4411

■ "Delicious Indian" dishes delight diners at these "great" Northwest Side and West Suburban "standbys" that stand out with their "authentic" "tandoori cooking", "superb vindaloos made to order" and "fast, bountiful lunch buffets"; though a trifle dated, the city location's decor is slightly more "upscale" than the Devon Avenue standard, and insiders warn that both can "get crowded on weekends."

Victory's Banner ◐ — ▽ 19 | 13 | 17 | $13

2100 W. Roscoe St. (Hoyne Ave.), 773-665-0227

■ "Don't let the Midwestern waitresses in saris scare you away from" this "soulful" Roscoe Village vegetarian advise advocates; while the "meditative atmosphere" can be "annoying" to the unconverted, "pure, tasty, healthful fare that's served with spirit" (though not with spirits – there's no alcohol or BYO) makes this "crazy little place" a winner in the eyes of many.

Village, The ●S

20 | 20 | 20 | $28

71 W. Monroe St., 2nd fl. (bet. Clark & Dearborn Sts.), 312-332-7005

■ A "vintage Chicago" landmark, this namesake located on the second floor of the Loop's venerable Italian Village (with Vivere at ground level and La Cantina Enoteca underneath) is "still an old favorite" for "solid, traditional" Northern cuisine and "professional", "take-the-shirt-off-my-back service"; also, the "cozy", "quirky decor is always a hit with first-timers."

Vinci S

22 | 21 | 20 | $36

1732 N. Halsted St. (Willow St.), 312-266-1199

■ "A longtime, reliable pre- or post-theater" spot in Lincoln Park's Halsted corridor, this "quiet", "classic Italian" owned by chef Paul LoDuca (who also helms Adobo Grill) is "romantic and refined", with "reliably delicious", "unadorned food" that's "not overly expensive"; "Royal George and Steppenwolf"–matinee mavens recommend you "request a coveted window table" for its "great, uncrowded brunch" on Sundays.

Vinh Phat BBQ S≠

⌐ | ⌐ | ⌐ | I

4940 N. Sheridan Rd. (bet. Ainslie & Argyle Sts.), 773-878-8688

Mahogany-hued crisp-roasted ducks, quail and chickens hang in the window of this casual Uptown Chinese where a bountiful steam table features trays of duck feet, pork intestines and other stewed-until-ultra-tender vittles; there are only a few tables within its small space, so it's most popular as a place to pick up provender for a picnic or outdoor concert in the park.

Vivere

23 | 23 | 22 | $43

71 W. Monroe St. (bet. Clark & Dearborn Sts.), 312-332-4040

■ The more contemporary counterpart of the Italian Village's old-guard dining duo (The Village above and La Cantina Enoteca below), this "beautiful" "surprise" is a "wine lover's paradise", combining chef "Jonathan Harootunian's playful and tantalizing food" with an "exceptional" 1,000-bottle list; Jordan Mozer's "cosmic-trip decor" and a "knowledgeable" staff are also important players in this "fine-dining drama."

Vivo S

20 | 20 | 19 | $36

838 W. Randolph St. (bet. Green & Peoria Sts.), 312-733-3379

◪ A pioneer of "the Randolph Street restaurant row", this "trendy" "hipsters' Italian" serves "good", "straightforward food" amid a "dark and mysterious" "scene"; it's "a great place to be alone with the one you love (or like)", unless you agree with those who find its fare "uninteresting" and its "crammed" room "too noisy"; P.S. the "outdoor summer seating offers a great view of the city."

Volare S   22 17 21 $32

201 E. Grand Ave. (St. Clair St.), 312-410-9900

■ The "reasonably priced", "solid offerings" of "classic" Italian fare at this "wonderful neighborhood restaurant" in Streeterville may be "nothing novel", but they are "hearty and tasty"; in fact, testifiers tout them as "red-sauce and garlic done with flair and sophistication" (and the "creamy pasta dishes are cholesterol heaven!"); it's considered a "good date place" even though it "gets loud and crowded."

Vong's Thai Kitchen S   21 22 20 $40
(fka Vong)

6 W. Hubbard St. (State St.), 312-644-8664

◪ The recent "reinterpretation" of this River North Lettuce Entertain You import, originally a spin-off of Jean-Georges Vongerichten's New York Vong, has surveyors seesawing: some "love the revamp", praising the "more accessible prices" of its still–"exotic and imaginative" New French–Thai fusion menu and the "great makeover" of its "dramatic" but now "cozier setting"; fans of the first version feel "disappointed", though, and wonder "why does everything have to be dumbed down?"

Walker Bros. S   23 18 19 $15

825 W. Dundee Rd. (bet. Arlington Hts. Rd. & Rte. 53), Arlington Heights, 847-392-6600
1615 Waukegan Rd. (bet. Chestnut & Lake Aves.), Glenview, 847-724-0220
620 Central Ave. (bet. Green Bay Rd. & 2nd St.), Highland Park, 847-432-0660
Lake Zurich Theatre Development, 767 S. Rand Rd. (Rte. 22), Lake Zurich, 847-550-0006
200 Marriott Dr. (Milwaukee Ave.), Lincolnshire, 847-634-2220
153 Green Bay Rd. (bet. Central & Lake Aves.), Wilmette, 847-251-6000

■ For a "great breakfast any time of day", these North and Northwest Suburban "family"-"favorite" "institutions" "never disappoint", with "wonderful, filling and inexpensive treats" that are "worth the wait"; not only does their "legendary apple pancake live up to its rep" – "calling it a 'pancake' is like calling champagne a 'drink'" – but "there's real cream" for "your always-full cup" of "heavenly coffee."

Watusi ●S   21 20 20 $34

1540 W. North Ave. (Ashland Ave.), 773-862-1540

◪ The "high-design" home of a "hipster crowd", this Wicker Parker puts "a creative, crazy mix" of "Caribbean flavors" into its New American cuisine; fans say the "daring menu works surprisingly well", but those who "can't comprehend the approach" propose that the "pricey" and "overly bizarre drinks" "are better than" the "too-inventive" food; N.B. name and DJs notwithstanding, there's no dance floor.

Wave ●◗S   ▽ 20 22 17 $41

W Chicago Lakeshore, 644 N. Lake Shore Dr. (Ontario St.), 312-255-4460

☒ Streeterville's "vibrant", "loud" "new hot spot" in the W Chicago Lakeshore is a "way-cool scene with lots of beautiful people" in "terrific booths" surrounded by "hip", "modern decor" and eating "beautiful food" – namely, Jason Paskewitz's mod Med cuisine (some surfers say it's "wonderful", some suggest it "sounds better than it is"); for others, pluses are wiped out by a wave of service minuses.

We S   ▽ 16 18 16 $41

W Chicago City Ctr., 172 W. Adams St. (La Salle St.), 312-917-5608

☒ The "W Hotel [chain] has done it again" – but what exactly it's done at this "upscale New French"–American newcomer in its "hip" City Center hostelry is a subject of debate; a ration of raters approves of the "cool" "design-your-own-meal" idea and its "beautiful" results, but others reprove it as a "bizarre concept" that "doesn't make any sense", saying the "sauces don't match the food."

Weber Grill S   18 16 17 $30

Hilton Garden Inn, 10 E. Grand Ave. (State St.), 312-595-0000
2331 Fountain Sq. Dr. (Meyers Rd.), Lombard, 630-953-8880
920 N. Milwaukee Ave. (Lake Cook Rd.), Wheeling, 847-215-0996

☒ It's "fun to watch the chefs at work on the giant Webers" at these "relaxed" Suburban bastions of barbecuing backed by the business behind those ubiquitous backyard bowl-bottomed briquette-burning braziers; still, many meat mavens maintain you might "do better" to "stay home and grill" such "standard fare" "yourself"; N.B. the new Near North location is unrated.

Webster's Wine Bar ●◗S   18 20 19 $24

1480 W. Webster Ave. (bet. Ashland Ave. & Clybourn St.), 773-868-0608

■ A "sexy, cozy" haven in Lincoln Park's Clybourn corridor, this "unpretentious", "wonderful wine bar" is a "great date place" and a "favorite" "choice for meeting with friends after a long day"; "knowledgeable staffers" serve an "expanded appetizer menu" of "good" International fare "complementing" "fun flights" from the cellar; P.S. night-owls should note it's "open late."

White Fence Farm S   19 17 19 $20

Joliet Rd. (2 mi. south of I-55), Lemont, 630-739-1720

■ "Americana at its best", this Southwest "Suburban legend" remains a "classic" "family gathering place" for "comfort food" like "out-of-this-world fried chicken and corn fritters"; you get "so much for the price" and "sincere service" too, and if "no reservations" for parties under a dozen means "long waits", at least there are "interesting things to see", such as a "museum with cars and a small zoo out back."

Wiener's Circle, The ☽ [S] ≠ 21 | 8 | 13 | $9

2622 N. Clark St. (Wrightwood Ave.), 773-477-7444

■ Dogged devotees worry it "would be an empty world without" this "classic" Lincoln Parker where "great char dogs and cheese fries" draw an "eclectic crowd of yuppies and street people"; the "tacky decor is part of the fun", but wags "warn" beware its "hilarious" "late-night" "shtick" – "deliberately rude staffers" serving up "four-letter words", "insults and fried food."

WILDFIRE [S] 23 | 21 | 20 | $33

159 W. Erie St. (bet. La Salle & Wells Sts.), 312-787-9000
235 Parkway Dr. (Milwaukee Ave.), Lincolnshire, 847-279-7900
Oakbrook Center Mall, 232 Oakbrook Ctr. (Rte. 83), Oak Brook, 630-586-9000

■ A Lettuce Entertain You River North success that's spread to the North and West Suburbs, these "casual, clubby" American steakhouses keep the "crowds waiting" for "great, hearty food" "cooked in a wood-burning oven" then "accompanied by wine" and "beer flights", "varied martinis" and "better-than-sex desserts"; it can be "tough to get reservations", but the memories, like the "wildfire smell" "in your clothes", will linger.

Wild Onion [S] 17 | 15 | 17 | $28

3500 N. Lincoln Ave. (Cornelia Ave.), 773-871-5555

■ Given its moniker (the translation of the Native American word 'Chicago'), it's no wonder the namesake bulb and its cloven cousin are well represented in the form of "excellent onion soup", "nice roasted garlic" and other "nutritious" Traditional American fare at this "comfortable spot" in Lakeview, an "airy, conversation-friendly space" with "white tablecloths"; P.S. it's "convenient for the pre- and post-theater crowd."

Wishbone [S] 20 | 15 | 17 | $19

3300 N. Lincoln Ave. (School St.), 773-549-2663
1001 W. Washington Blvd. (Morgan St.), 312-850-2663

■ "There's always something comforting to eat" at these "casual-but-trendy" chowhouses in the West Loop and Lakeview, where "integrated, happy crowds gorge on" "homey" "Southern- and Cajun-influenced" "diner food with a twist" served at "reasonable prices" amid "funky decor" featuring "crazy artwork" by chef Joel Nickson's talented mother, Lia; weekends are "hectic" – "everyone goes there" – so "be ready to wait."

Wolfgang Puck's Grand Café [S] 19 | 19 | 18 | $28

Century Theatre Complex, 1701 Maple Ave. (Church St.), Evanston, 847-869-9653

◪ Proffered by the prolific Puck, this "casual" North Suburban New American in "the Century theater" complex is deemed an "enjoyable spot before or after the movies" by a contingent of Evanston eaters who enjoy its "unique menu items" (no surprise, "the pizzas are the winners") and "amusing", "eye-catching decor"; those who find it less than grand complain it's "more hype" and "high prices" "than substance."

Yoshi's Café [S] 23 | 18 | 22 | $38

3257 N. Halsted St. (Belmont Ave.), 773-248-6160

■ Still "a favorite" after 20 years in its Lakeview locale, this French-Asian "fusion-accented bistro" "continues" to be "a perfect blend of East and West"; "inventive" chef Yoshi Katsumura's "innovative preparations" (regulars "love the tofu steak" with brie and basil) and "delectable desserts" like "great chocolate espresso crème brûlée" are "served with flair" by a "gracious" staff in a "homey" and "comfortable", if "not elegant", setting.

Zaven's ▽ 23 | 21 | 24 | $47

260 E. Chestnut St. (bet. DeWitt Pl. & Lake Shore Dr.), 312-787-8260

■ Still "such a secret place", even after 27 years in its "small" Streeterville setting, this largely "undiscovered treasure" remains a "romantic" and "intimate winner"; meals commence with a "warm welcome" from the "superior host", "congenial and caring" "Zaven [Kodjayan] himself", followed by "well-prepared and -presented" traditional Continental cuisine served by a "seasoned staff."

Zealous 22 | 23 | 21 | $62

419 W. Superior St. (Chicago Ave.), 312-475-9112

◪ The "hushed" "elegance" of its "gorgeous, tranquil space" has all agreeing this River North New American "is one beautiful restaurant", but there accord ends; fans rate chef-owner Michael Taus "a real genius" for the "daring mix of ingredients" in his "complex menu" of "exciting cuisine", but the "unimpressed" say the "overzealous kitchen" "tries too hard" with "off-the-wall recipes", adding the "astronomical prices" "are extreme" for such "small portions."

Zest [S] – | – | – | E

Hotel Inter-Continental, 525 N. Michigan Ave. (Grand Ave.), 312-321-8766

New to the Near North, this "sophisticated" spot at the Hotel Inter-Continental serves up a "winning combination" of "excellent service" and "expertly done", "picturesque dishes" – Spanish-, Portuguese- and Moroccan-inflected

Mediterranean, including "fabulous seafood" and tapas – at "great prices"; with floor-to-ceiling windows overlooking Michigan Avenue, its sleek bi-level space is a "quiet place to people-watch."

Zia's Trattoria ☒　　　　24 | 20 | 22 | $32

6699 N. Northwest Hwy. (bet. Harlem & Touhy Aves.), 773-775-0808

■ The "memorable sauces" of its "creative pasta dishes" and the "vibrant flavors" of its "wonderful selection of fresh fish" plates render this "friendly, casual" Edison Park Italian a "shining light" that's "worth the trip from Downtown"; they still don't take reservations on weekends for fewer than five folks, but "the waits are more comfortable since the recent expansion"; P.S. it "won't break the bank."

Zinfandel　　　　　　　22 | 20 | 21 | $39

59 W. Grand Ave. (bet. Clark & Dearborn Sts.), 312-527-1818

■ Zin-heads hoist their glasses high and tender a tenth-anniversary "toast to the monthly menu" at this "warm, hospitable" River North "favorite" celebrating a different Regional American cuisine every new moon; chef-owner Susan Goss fashions "zestful, original cuisine" from "fresh ingredients" and pairs it with her co-proprietor husband Drew's "knockout" Zinfandel-centric domestic wine list in a "colorful", "funky atmosphere."

Zoom Kitchen　　　　　17 | 12 | 14 | $13

1646 N. Damen Ave. (Milwaukee & North Aves.), 773-278-7000 ☒
923 N. Rush St. (bet. Delaware Pl. & Walton St.), 312-440-3500 ☒
620 W. Belmont Ave. (Broadway), 773-325-1400 ☒
247 S. State St. (Jackson Blvd.), 312-377-9666

■ "When you want fresh and fast", zoom to one of these "casual" and "affordable" American eateries for "good food" done "your way" by "cheerful" staffers then served up "cafeteria-style"; "fantastic sandwiches", "fabulous salads" and "mom's meatloaf and mashed potatoes" are topped off by "great chocolate-chunk cookies" – after all, "even Gen-Xers need comfort food sometimes."

Indexes

CUISINES
LOCATIONS
SPECIAL FEATURES

Indexes list the best of many within each category.

CUISINES

Afghan
Kabul House

American (New)
Atwater's
Bandera
Bank Lane Bistro
Bin 36
Bistro Marbuzet
Blackbird
Black Duck Tavern
Brett's Café Americain
Cab's Wine Bar
Café Absinthe
Cafe Selmarie
Caliterra Bar & Grille
Charlie Trotter's
Chef's Station
Christophe
Cielo
Cité
Courtright's
Deleece
D'Vine Rest./Wine Bar
Elaine
Entre Nous
erwin, an american cafe
Feast
Flavor
Green Dolphin St.
Harry's Velvet Room
Harvest on Huron
Jack's on Halsted
Jane's
Jilly's Cafe
Karizma
Kevin
Kit Kat Lounge/Supper Club
Leo's Lunchroom
Lovells of Lake Forest
Magnolia Café
Masck

Meritage Cafe/Wine Bar
mk
mk North
MOD.
Molive
Naha
Napa Valley Grille
Next Door Bistro
North Pond
Oceanique
one sixtyblue
120 Ocean Place
Outpost
Pangea
Park Ave. Cafe
Pepper Lounge
Printer's Row
Puck's at the MCA
Quincy Grille on River
Rhapsody
Ritz-Carlton Café
Riva
Rivers
RL
Room, The
Rushmore
Saussy
Seasons
1776
She She
Signature Rm. at 95th
Spago
Spring
Tanglewood
Tasting Room
Tavern
Technicolor Kitchen
302 West
Thyme
Tomboy
Twelve 12

Pappadeaux Seafood
Redfish
Wishbone

Caribbean
Calypso Cafe
Ezuli
Julio's Cocina Latina
Watusi

Chinese
Ben Pao
Best Hunan
Dee's Mandarin
Emperor's Choice
Evergreen
Furama
Hai Yen
Happy Chef Dim Sum
Hong Min
Jia's
Lao Sze Chuan
Mars
New Three Happiness
Papajin
P.F. Chang's
Phoenix
Pine Yard
Shine & Morida
Silver Seafood
Sixty-Five
Three Happiness
Vinh Phat BBQ

Coffee Shops/Diners
Dearborn Diner
Lou Mitchell's
Manny's Coffee Shop
Nookies
Pauline's
Pompei Bakery
Salt & Pepper Diner
Sarkis Grill
Tempo

Colombian
Flying Chicken
Las Tablas

Continental
Café La Cave
Lutnia
Lutz Cafe & Pastry Shop
Narcisse
Restaurant on the Park
Trader Vic's
Zaven's

Cuban
Cafe Bolero
Cafe 28
Copa Cubana
Samba Room

Czech
Czech Plaza

Delis/Sandwich Shops
Bagel, The
Chicago Flat Sammies
Cold Comfort Cafe
Corner Bakery
Cosí
5 Boroughs Deli
Max's
Mrs. Levy's Deli
Panera Bread
Potbelly Sandwich

Dim Sum
Furama
Happy Chef Dim Sum
Hong Min
LuLu's Dim Sum
New Three Happiness
Phoenix
Sixty-Five
Three Happiness

Eclectic/International
Big Bowl
Bite

Blind Faith Café
Cafe Nordstrom
CHIC Cafe
Chinoiserie
Corner Bakery
Cru Wine Bar
Deleece
Eclectic
Feast
foodlife
Hilary's Urban Eatery
Iggy's
Jane's
John's Place
Kitsch'n on Roscoe
La Mora
Lobby, The
Lucky Platter
Lula Café
Mosaic
Mysore Woodland
Narcisse
Orange
Pangea
Room, The
She She
Sinibar
Stained Glass Wine Bar
Taza
Tilli's
Toast
Tomboy
Twist
Uncommon Ground
Webster's Wine Bar

Ecuadoran
La Peña

English
Red Lion Pub
Rose & Crown

Ethiopian
Addis Abeba
Ethiopian Diamond
Ethiopian Village
Mama Desta's Red Sea

Filipino
Rambutan

Fondue
Fondue Stube
Geja's Cafe

French (Bistro)
Albert's Café & Patiss.
Bank Lane Bistro
Barrington Ctry. Bistro
Bêtise
Bistro Banlieue
Bistro Marbuzet
Bistro 110
Bistrot Margot
Bistrot Zinc
Bistro Ultra
Brasserie Jo
Café Bernard
Cafe Central
Café Le Loup
Cafe Matou
Cafe Pyrenees
Café 36
Cerise
Chez François
Chez Joel
Clark St. Bistro
Cochon Sauvage
Cyrano's Bistrot/Wine Bar
D & J Bistro
David's Bistro
Fond de la Tour
Froggy's French Cafe
KiKi's Bistro
La Crêperie
La Sardine
Le Bouchon
Le Passage
Mon Ami Gabi
Mossant Bistro

Ravinia Bistro
Retro Bistro
Tournesol
Yoshi's Café

French (Classic)
La Petite Folie
Les Deux Gros
Le Titi de Paris
Le Vichyssois
Oceanique

French (New)
Ambria
Atwater's
Aubriot
Avenues
Brasserie Jo
Carlos'
CHIC Cafe
Cité
D'Vine Rest./Wine Bar
Everest
Gabriel's
Jacky's Bistro
Jilly's Cafe
L'anne
Le Colonial
Le Français
Les Nomades
Le Titi de Paris
Maison
Marché
Mimosa
Mossant Bistro
Napa Valley Grille
NoMI
Oceanique
Pasha
Pasteur
Pump Room
Ritz-Carlton Din. Rm.
Tallgrass
Thyme

Trio
Tru
Vong's Thai Kitchen
We

German
Berghoff
Edelweiss
Lutz Cafe & Pastry Shop
Metro Club
Mirabell

Greek
Artopolis Bakery
Athena
Athenian Room
Costa's
Cross-Rhodes
Greek Islands
Noyes St. Café
Papagus Taverna
Parthenon
Pegasus
Roditys
Santorini

Hamburgers
Billy Goat Tavern
Boston Blackie's
Goose Island
Green Door Tavern
Hackney's
Johnny Rockets
Pete Miller's Steakhse.
P.J. Clarke's
R.J. Grunts
Superdawg Drive-In
Twisted Spoke
Wiener's Circle

Hawaiian
Roy's

Hot Dogs
Fluky's
Gold Coast Dogs

Leona's (S)
Lexi's (N&S)
Lino's Rist. (N)
Maggiano's Little Italy (S)
Mario's Gold Coast (N&S)
Merlo Rist. (N)
Mia Cucina (N&S)
Mia Francesca (N&S)
Millennium Steaks (N&S)
Mimosa (N&S)
Misto (N&S)
Next Door Bistro (N&S)
Nick & Tony's (N&S)
Nicolinas Cucina (N&S)
Noyes St. Café (N&S)
O'Fame (N&S)
O'Neil's (N)
Palaggi's (N&S)
Pane Caldo (N)
Papa Milano (S)
Pasha (N&S)
Pasta Palazzo (N&S)
Phil Stefani's 437 Rush (N&S)
Piazza Bella (N&S)
Pizza Capri (N)
Pompei Bakery (N&S)
Prego (N&S)
Red Tomato (N&S)
Rico's (N&S)
Riva (N&S)
RoSal's Cucina (N&S)
Rose Angelis (N&S)
Rosebud (N&S)
Rudi Fazuli's (N&S)
Sabatino's (N)
Salvatore's Rist. (N)
Scoozi! (N&S)
Settimana Café (N&S)
Sorriso (N&S)
Sparacino Rist. (N&S)
Spiaggia (N&S)
Stefani's (N)
Strega Nona (N&S)

Suparossa (N&S)
Tarantino's (N)
Topo Gigio Rist. (N&S)
Trattoria Dinotto (N&S)
Trattoria Gianni (N&S)
Trattoria No. 10 (N&S)
Trattoria Pizzeria (N&S)
Tucci Benucch (N&S)
Tufano's Vernon Pk. Tap (S)
Tuscany (N&S)
Va Pensiero (N&S)
Via Carducci (S)
Via Emilia Rist. (N)
Via Veneto (N&S)
Village, The (N)
Vinci (N&S)
Vivere (N&S)
Vivo (N&S)
Volare (N&S)
Zia's Trattoria (N&S)

Japanese
Akai Hana
Benihana
Bluefin
Bob San
CoCoRo/East
Dozu Sushi & Lobster
Hatsuhana
Heat
Itto Sushi
Jia's
Kamehachi
Kuni's
Kyoto
Matsuya
Midori
Mirai Sushi
New Japan
Ringo
Rise
Ron of Japan
Sai Cafe
Shabu-ya

Cuisine Index

Arun's
Bangkok
Bangkok Star
Erawan Royal Thai
Mama Thai
P.S. Bangkok
Roong
Ruby of Siam
Star of Siam
Thai Classic
Thai Little Home Cafe
Thai Pastry
Thai Star Cafe
Vong's Thai Kitchen

Turkish
A La Turka
Cousin's

Vegetarian
Blind Faith Café
Chicago Diner
Ethiopian Diamond
Ethiopian Village
Heartland Cafe
Mysore Woodland
Potbelly Sandwich
Reza's
Slice of Life/Hy Life Bistro
Udupi Palace
Victory's Banner

Vietnamese
Hai Yen
Le Colonial
Pasteur

West African
Ofie

LOCATIONS

DOWNTOWN

Loop
Atwood Cafe
Bacino's
Berghoff
Billy Goat Tavern
Catch 35
Chipotle Mexican Grill
Corner Bakery
Cosí
Entre Nous
Everest
Giordano's
Gold Coast Dogs
Grillroom, The
Hackney's
Heaven on Seven
La Cantina Enoteca
La Rosetta
La Strada Rist.
Miller's Pub
Mossant Bistro
Mrs. Levy's Deli
Nick & Tony's
Nick's Fishmarket
Palm
Petterino's
Potbelly Sandwich
Quincy Grille on River
Restaurant on the Park
Rhapsody
Rivers
Robinson's No. 1 Ribs
Russian Tea Time
Sixty-Five
Taza
312 Chicago
Trader Vic's
Trattoria No. 10
Village, The

Vivere
We

River North
Ben Pao
Big Bowl
Bin 36
Brasserie Jo
BUtterfield 8
Café Iberico
Carson's Ribs
Chicago Chop Hse.
CHIC Cafe
Chilpancingo
Coco Pazzo
CoCoRo/East
Corner Bakery
Creole
Crofton on Wells
Cyrano's Bistrot/Wine Bar
Dearborn Diner
Erawan Royal Thai
Erie Cafe
ESPN Zone
Fadó Irish Pub
5 Boroughs Deli
Freddy's Ribhse.
Frontera Grill
Gaylord India
Gene & Georgetti
Green Door Tavern
Hard Rock Cafe
Harry Caray's
Harry's Velvet Room
Harvest on Huron
House of Blues
Isaac Hayes
Jaipur Palace
Keefer's
Kevin

GOLD COAST/NEAR NORTH AREA

Potbelly Sandwich
RL
Rosebud
Seasons
Seasons Café
Su Casa
Tuscany
Weber Grill
Zest

Old Town
Adobo Grill
Bar Louie
Bistrot Margot

Cucina Bella
Father & Son Pizza
Fireplace Inn
Flat Top Grill
Heat
Kamehachi
Nookies
Old Jerusalem
Salpicón
Topo Gigio Rist.
Trattoria Dinotto
Trattoria Pizzeria
Twin Anchors

CITY NORTH

Andersonville/Edgewater
Andies
Ann Sather
Atlantique
Ethiopian Diamond
Francesca's
Hai Yen
Jin Ju
La Donna
Moody's Pub
Pasteur
Pauline's
Reza's
Room, The
Tokyo Marina
Tomboy

Lakeview/Wrigleyville
Addis Abeba
A La Turka
Always Thai
Angelina Rist.
Anna Maria Pasteria
Ann Sather
Arco de Cuchilleros
Art of Pizza
Bagel, The
Bangkok

Bar Louie
BD's Mongolian BBQ
Billy Goat Tavern
Brett's Café Americain
Buca di Beppo
Café Le Loup
Cafe 28
Chicago Diner
Chipotle Mexican Grill
Cornelia's
Cousin's
Cullen's B&G
Cy's Crab Hse.
Deleece
Diosa Red
Duke of Perth
Du Yee
El Jardin
erwin, an american cafe
Ethiopian Village
Flat Top Grill
Flying Chicken
Genesee Depot
Goose Island
Half Shell
Heaven on Seven
Hi Ricky

CITY SOUTH

Chinatown
Emperor's Choice
Evergreen
Furama
Happy Chef Dim Sum
Hong Min
Joy Yee's Noodle Shop
Lao Sze Chuan
New Three Happiness
Penang
Phoenix
Three Happiness

Far South Side
BJ's Market & Bakery
Lem's BBQ

Hyde Park/Kenwood
Calypso Cafe
Dixie Kitchen & Bait
Edwardo's
Giordano's
Gladys Luncheonette
La Petite Folie
Leona's

Original Pancake Hse.
Pizza Capri

Near South Side
Corner Bakery
Lem's BBQ
Original Pancake Hse.

Pilsen
Nuevo Leon

South Shore
Army & Lou's
Jackson Harbor Grill

Southwest Side
Bacchanalia
Bruna's Rist.
Giordano's
Harry Caray's
Leona's
Lou Malnati's Pizzeria
Potbelly Sandwich

Tri-Taylor
Gold Coast Dogs

CITY WEST

Far West
Amarind's
Edna's
Flavor
Sparacino Rist.

Greektown
Artopolis Bakery
Athena
Costa's
Greek Islands
Parthenon
Pegasus
Roditys
Santorini

Little Italy/University Village
Chez Joel
Francesca's
Lao Sze Chuan
Leona's
Pompei Bakery
Rico's
RoSal's Cucina
Rosebud
Tufano's Vernon Pk. Tap
Tuscany

Market District
Bar Louie
Bluepoint Oyster Bar

Flat Top Grill
Hi Ricky
Ina's
La Sardine
Marché
Millennium Steaks
one sixtyblue
Red Light
Rushmore
Sushi Wabi
Tasting Room
Vivo

Near West
Bar Louie
Bella Notte
Billy Goat Tavern
Bone Daddy
Breakfast Club
Cannella's on Grand
Como
Iggy's
La Borsa
La Scarola
Misto

Pie Hole
Robinson's No. 1 Ribs
Saussy
Thyme
Twisted Spoke

Ukrainian Village
a tavola
Bite
Fortunato
Leona's
Mac's
Tecalitlan

West Loop
Bacino's
Blackbird
Carmichael's Steak Hse.
Corner Bakery
Crab St. Saloon
Gold Coast Dogs
Lexi's
Lou Mitchell's
Nine
Wishbone

SUBURBS

Suburban North
Akai Hana
Bacaro da Nino
Bagel, The
Bank Lane Bistro
Bar Louie
Bêtise
Bice Grill
Bice Rist.
Big Bowl
Blind Faith Café
Cafe Central
Café Luciano
Cafe Nordstrom
Campagnola
Carlos'

Carson's Ribs
Chef's Station
Chicago Diner
Chinoiserie
Chipotle Mexican Grill
Convito Italiano
Corner Bakery
Cross-Rhodes
Dave's Italian Kit.
Davis St. Fishmarket
Del Rio
Dixie Kitchen & Bait
Don's Fishmarket & Tav.
Edwardo's
EJ's Place
Flat Top Grill

Suburban Northwest

Location Index

Location Index

SPECIAL FEATURES

Breakfast
(See also Hotel Dining)
Albert's Café & Patiss.
Ann Sather†
Bin 36
Bite
Blind Faith Café
Bongo Room
Breakfast Club
Cafe Selmarie
Chicago Diner
Corner Bakery
David's Bistro
Fox & Obel Cafe
Heartland Cafe
Ina's
John's Place
Lou Mitchell's
Nookies
Oak Tree
Original Pancake Hse.†
Pauline's
Salt & Pepper Diner
Sarkis Grill
Tempo
Toast
Tre Kronor
Victory's Banner
Walker Bros.†
Wishbone

Brunch
Adobo Grill
Atwood Cafe
Avenues
Barn of Barrington
Bêtise
Bistro 110
Bistrot Margot
Bistrot Zinc
Bite
Bongo Room

Brett's Café Americain
Cafe Selmarie
Cafe 28
Caliterra Bar & Grille
Charlie's Ale House
Chef's Station
CHIC Cafe
Cité
Cochon Sauvage
Deleece
erwin, an american cafe
Four Farthings
Frontera Grill
Heaven on Seven
House of Blues
Ina's
Jackson Harbor Grill
Jane's
John's Place
Kitsch'n on Roscoe
Las Bellas Artes
Lobby, The
Lula Café
Magnolia Café
Mosaic
Mossant Bistro
North Pond
Northside Cafe
Noyes St. Café
Oak Terrace
Orange
Park Ave. Cafe
P.J. Clarke's
Pump Room
Ritz-Carlton Din. Rm.
R.J. Grunts
Salpicón
Seasons
Signature Rm. at 95th
Soul Kitchen
Tavern on Rush

312 Chicago
Thyme
Twisted Spoke
Vinci
Wishbone
Zinfandel

Buffet Served
(Check availability)
American Smokehse.
Bangkok
Barn of Barrington
Bukhara
Clark St. Bistro
Dell Rhea's Chicken
Dick's Last Resort
Edwardo's†
El Jardin
Ethiopian Village
Flat Top Grill
Furama†
Gaylord India
Giannotti Steak Hse.
Hackney's†
Hilary's Urban Eatery
Indian Garden
Jaipur Palace
John Barleycorn†
Klay Oven
Leona's†
Mesón Sabika†
Moti Mahal
Oak Terrace
Ritz-Carlton Din. Rm.
Seasons
Signature Rm. at 95th
Standard India
Stanley's Kitchen & Tap
Thai Classic
Thai Little Home Cafe
Tiffin
Trader Vic's
Trattoria Dinotto
Viceroy of India

Wild Onion
Zoom Kitchen†

Business Dining
Atwood Cafe
Avenues
Bacaro da Nino
Balagio
Ben Pao
Bice Rist.
Blackbird
Bluepoint Oyster Bar
Brasserie Jo
Cafe Pyrenees
Café 36
Caliterra Bar & Grille
Cantare
Capital Grille
Carlucci
Carmichael's Steak Hse.
Catch 35
Charlie Trotter's
Chez François
Chicago Chop Hse.
Coco Pazzo
Crofton on Wells
David's Bistro
Entre Nous
Erie Cafe
Everest
Gene & Georgetti
Gibsons Steakhse.
Grill on the Alley
Grillroom, The
Harry Caray's†
Joe's Seafood, Steak/Crab
Karma
Keefer's
Kevin
Lawry's Prime Rib
Le Colonial
Les Nomades
Le Titi de Paris
Magnum's Steakhse.

McCormick & Schmick's
Mike Ditka's
Millennium Steaks†
mk
mk North
Morton's†
Mossant Bistro
Mrs. Park's Tavern
Naha
Napa Valley Grille
Nick's Fishmarket
Nine
NoMI
one sixtyblue
120 Ocean Place
Palm
Park Ave. Cafe
Petterino's
Phil Stefani's 437 Rush
Prairie
Printer's Row
Quincy Grille on River
Rhapsody
Ritz-Carlton Din. Rm.
Rivers
RL
Roy's
Ruth's Chris
Saloon
Seasons
Shaw's Crab House
Smith & Wollensky
Spago
Spiaggia
Sullivan's Steakhse.
Takkatsu
312 Chicago
Topolobampo
Tuscany†
Vivere
Vivo
Vong's Thai Kitchen

BYO

Always Thai
Amitabul
Ann Sather†
Bite
CHIC Cafe
Chinoiserie
Cold Comfort Cafe
Dozu Sushi & Lobster
El Presidente
Flavor
Genesee Depot
Giordano's†
Happy Chef Dim Sum
Hashalom
Hilary's Urban Eatery
Hong Min†
Izalco
Joy Yee's Noodle Shop
Kabul House
Kismet
La Cazuela Mariscos
Lao Sze Chuan†
Las Tablas
Leo's Lunchroom
Lincoln Noodle Hse.
Moti Mahal
Mysore Woodland
Nancy's Stuffed Pizza†
Nookies†
Noon-O-Kabab
Nuevo Leon†
Old Jerusalem
Orange
Original Gino's East†
Penny's Noodle Shop†
Pizza Capri†
P.S. Bangkok†
Ranalli's†
Robinson's No. 1 Ribs†
Room, The
Ruby of Siam
Shabu-ya

Silver Seafood
Standard India
Tango Sur
Thai Classic
Thai Little Home Cafe
Thai Pastry
Thai Star Cafe
Tomboy
Tournesol
Tre Kronor

Catering
Antico Posto
Artopolis Bakery
a tavola
Bagel, The
Bella Notte
Biloxi Grill
Bistro 110
Cafe Ba-Ba-Reeba!
Cafe 28
Caliterra Bar & Grille
Carlucci†
Carmine's
CHIC Cafe
Cosí
Cyrano's Bistrot/Wine Bar
Don Juan on Halsted
EJ's Place
Emilio's Tapas†
Erie Cafe
erwin, an american cafe
Feast
Filippo's
Francesca's†
Froggy's French Cafe
Gaylord India
Gilardi's
Gioco
Greek Islands†
Harry Caray's†
Harvest on Huron
Hatsuhana
Heaven on Seven†

Hong Min†
Indian Garden†
Itto Sushi
Ixcapuzalco
Jacky's Bistro
Kamehachi†
Karizma
Keefer's
KiKi's Bistro
Kinzie Chophouse
Klay Oven
La Donna
La Petite Folie
La Scarola
Les Deux Gros
Le Vichyssois
Lino's Rist.
Lou Malnati's Pizzeria†
Lou Mitchell's
Lucca's
Lupita's
Magnum's Steakhse.†
Manny's Coffee Shop
Margie's Candies
Merle's Smokehse.
Mesón Sabika
Millennium Steaks†
Molive
Mon Ami Gabi†
My Pie Pizza†
Nacional 27
Napa Valley Grille
Nuevo Leon†
Original Gino's East†
Papagus Taverna†
Pasteur
Pegasus
Phil Stefani's 437 Rush
Phoenix
Puck's at the MCA
Ravinia Bistro
Rhapsody
Robinson's No. 1 Ribs†

Twelve 12, *David Shea*
Wave, *Jason Paskewitz*
Zealous, *Michael Taus*
Zinfandel, *Susan Goss*

Child-Friendly
(Besides the normal fast-food places; * children's menu available)
American Girl Pl.
Ann Sather†
Athenian Room
Aurelio's Pizza
Bacino's†
Big Bowl*
Bob Chinn's Crab Hse.*
Bricks
Bubba Gump Shrimp*
California Pizza Kit.
Cheesecake Factory
Chicago Flat Sammies
Chicago Pizza/Oven Grinder
Chipotle Mexican Grill†
Dave & Buster's*
Edwardo's*
El Jardin
ESPN Zone*
Famous Dave's*
Father & Son Pizza†
Flat Top Grill†
Fluky's
foodlife
Giordano's
Gold Coast Dogs†
Hackney's†
Hard Rock Cafe*
Heartland Cafe
Hot Doug's
Johnny Rockets*
John's Place*
Leona's*
Lindo Mexico
Lou Malnati's Pizzeria†
Lou Mitchell's†

Max's*
Merle's Smokehse.*
Mity Nice Grill*
My Pie Pizza†
Nancy's Stuffed Pizza
Nookies
Original Gino's East†
Original Pancake Hse.†
Pizzeria Uno†
Potbelly Sandwich
Rainforest Cafe†
Ranalli's
R.J. Grunts*
Robinson's No. 1 Ribs†
Rock Bottom Brewery†
Russell's BBQ*
Sarkis Grill
Stir Crazy Cafe*
Superdawg Drive-In
Tempo
Toast*
Tucci Benucch*
Walker Bros.†
Wiener's Circle
Wishbone*

Cigars Welcome
Avenue Ale House
Berghoff†
Biloxi Grill
Bistro 110
BUtterfield 8
Café Luciano†
Caliterra Bar & Grille
Capital Grille
Carlucci†
Carmichael's Steak Hse.
Carmine's
Carson's Ribs†
Chicago Chop Hse.
Cité
Clubhouse
Coco Pazzo
Como

Courtright's
Crab St. Saloon
Cru Wine Bar
D & J Bistro
El Nandu
Erie Cafe
ESPN Zone
Gale St. Inn†
Gibsons Steakhse.
Gilardi's
Gino's Steak Hse.
Green Dolphin St.
Green Door Tavern
Grillroom, The
Hackney's†
Harry Caray's†
Harry's Velvet Room
Harvest on Huron
Hugo's Frog Bar
Karma
Keefer's
Kinzie Chophouse
La Borsa
La Cantina Enoteca
Las Tablas
La Strada Rist.
Le Vichyssois
Lino's Rist.
Lovells of Lake Forest
Magnum's Steakhse.
McCormick & Schmick's
Metro Club
Mike Ditka's
Millennium Steaks†
Mill Race Inn
Millrose Brewing Co.
Morton's†
Mosaic
Myron & Phil's Steakhse.
Nick's Fishmarket†
Nine
120 Ocean Place
Parker's Ocean Grill

Pasha
Pete Miller's Steakhse.
P.J. Clarke's
Pompei Bakery†
Pump Room
Retro Bistro
Riva
Rock Bottom Brewery†
Rosebud Steakhse.
Sabatino's
Sabor
Saloon
Samba Room
Shula's Steakhouse†
Signature Rm. at 95th
Sinibar
Smith & Wollensky
Stefani's
Sullivan's Steakhse.
Tavern on Rush
Tommy Nevin's Pub
Tuscany†
Twelve 12
Village, The
Volare
Zaven's

Critic-Proof
(Get lots of business, despite
so-so food)
Bar Louie†
Billy Goat Tavern
Bubba Gump Shrimp
Dave & Buster's
Dick's Last Resort
Fadó Irish Pub
John Barleycorn
Rainforest Cafe†

Dancing
Barn of Barrington
Bone Daddy
Gale St. Inn†
Giannotti Steak Hse.

Salbute (D,T)
Shallots (D,T)
She She (T)
Smith & Wollensky (T)
Spiaggia (T)
Stained Glass Wine Bar (T)
Sullivan's Steakhse.†
Superdawg Drive-In (T)
Sushi Naniwa (D,T)
Thai Pastry (D,T)
Tiffin (T)
Tizi Melloul (T)
Topo Gigio Rist. (T)
Trattoria Dinotto (D,T)
Tre Kronor (T)
Tufano's Vernon Pk. Tap (T)
Twin Anchors (T)
Va Pensiero (T)
Via Carducci (D,T)
Vong's Thai Kitchen (T)
Walker Bros.†
Watusi (T)
Wiener's Circle (T)
Wildfire†
Yoshi's Café (T)
Zia's Trattoria (T)

Dessert

Albert's Café & Patiss.
Ambria
Aubriot
Avenues
Carlos'
Charlie Trotter's
Courtright's
Crofton on Wells
erwin, an american cafe
Everest
Gabriel's
Jacky's Bistro
La Crêperie
Le Français
Les Nomades
Le Titi de Paris

Lutz Cafe & Pastry Shop
mk
Mon Ami Gabi
North Pond
one sixtyblue
Printer's Row
Rhapsody
Ritz-Carlton Din. Rm.
Seasons
Spiaggia
Spring
Tallgrass
302 West
Thyme
Topolobampo
Trio
Tru
Twelve 12
Va Pensiero
Zealous

Dining Alone

(Other than hotels and places
with counter service)
Amitabul
Ann Sather†
Bar Louie†
Bite
Blind Faith Café
Breakfast Club
Cafe Nordstrom†
Chicago Diner
Chipotle Mexican Grill†
Corner Bakery
Cosí†
Flat Top Grill
Fluky's
foodlife
Fox & Obel Cafe
Gold Coast Dogs†
Heartland Cafe
Hilary's Urban Eatery
Hi Ricky†
Johnny Rockets

Leo's Lunchroom
Lula Café
Manny's Coffee Shop
Moody's Pub
Nookies
Noyes St. Café
Oak Tree
Penny's Noodle Shop†
Pierrot Gourmet
Puck's at the MCA
Reza's
Salt & Pepper Diner
Taza
Toast
Wiener's Circle
Zoom Kitchen

Entertainment

(Call for days and times of performances)
A La Turka (belly dancing)
American Girl Pl. (show)
Andies†
Avenue Ale House (jazz/top 40)
Balagio (piano)
Barn of Barrington (piano)
Bistro 110 (jazz)
Bistro Ultra (jazz)
Bone Daddy (varies)
Carmichael's Steak Hse. (piano)
Carmine's (piano)
Chef's Station (jazz duo)
Chicago Chop Hse. (piano)
Chief O'Neill's Pub (Irish)
Crawdaddy (blues & zydeco)
Cyrano's Bistrot (cabaret)
Dick's Last Resort (varies)
Diosa Red (Chinese musicians)
Dover Straits (bands)
D'Vine Rest./Wine Bar (DJ)
Edelweiss (German)
Eli's Place for Steaks (piano bar)
El Nandu (guitarist)
Entre Nous (jazz trio)

Ethiopian Village (DJ)
Ezuli (DJ)
Fadó Irish Pub (varies)
Fond de la Tour (piano)
Gale St. Inn†
Geja's Cafe (guitar)
Gibsons Steakhse. (piano)
Gilardi's (piano)
Gino's Steak Hse. (jazz pianist)
Green Dolphin St. (jazz)
Hackney's†
Hard Rock Cafe (varies)
Harry's Velvet (DJ/singers)
Hot Tamales†
House of Blues (band)
Hugo's Frog Bar (piano)
Irish Oak (Irish)
Isaac Hayes (bands/comedy/
    open mic)
Jackson Harbor Grill (jazz)
Joe's Be-Bop Cafe (varies)
Julio's Cocina (Brazilian/jazz)
Karizma (jazz)
Kit Kat (female impersonators)
Lambay Island/Abbey (Irish)
La Peña (Latin)
La Strada Rist. (piano)
Le Passage (DJ)
Lino's Rist. (piano)
Little Bucharest (minstrels)
Lucca's (guitarist)
Lula Café (varies)
Lutnia (piano)
Magnum's Steakhse. (piano)
McCormick & Schmick's (piano)
Mesón Sabika†
Mia Cucina (jazz/pop)
Midori (karaoke)
Mill Race Inn (varies)
Millrose Brewing Co. (piano)
Myron & Phil's Steak. (piano)
Nacional 27 (DJ)
Nine (DJ)

Palaggi's (jazz)
Parker's Ocean Grill (jazz/piano)
Pasha (Flamingo)
Pete Miller's Steakhse. (jazz)
Piece (DJ)
Public Landing (jazz)
Pump Room (piano/singer)
Redfish (blues/jazz)
Ritz-Carlton Din. Rm. (piano)
Rudi Fazuli's (jazz)
Sabatino's (guitar/piano/violin)
Salvatore's Rist. (piano)
Shaw's Crab House (blues/jazz)
Signature Rm. at 95th (jazz)
Sinibar (DJ)
Smoke Daddy (blues/jazz)
Sorriso (piano/singer)
Souk (band/belly dancing)
Sullivan's Steakhse.†
Sushi Wabi (DJ)
Tango Sur (tango)
302 West (jazz)
Tizi Melloul (belly dancing)
Tommy Nevin's Pub (folk/Irish)
Uncommon Ground (acoustic)
Watusi (DJ)
Wave (DJ)
We (DJ)
Zaven's (guitar/violin)

Fireplaces

Andies†
Atwater's
Barn of Barrington
Bêtise
Café La Cave
Cantare
Carlucci†
Clubhouse
Cochon Sauvage
Costa's
Courtright's
Crawdaddy Bayou
Cru Wine Bar
Cy's Crab Hse.†

Dell Rhea's Chicken
Don Roth's Blackhawk
Don's Fishmarket & Tav.
Dover Straits†
Edelweiss
Erie Cafe
Ezuli
Famous Dave's†
Fireplace Inn
Francesca's†
Gale St. Inn†
Gene & Georgetti
Giannotti Steak Hse.
Gibsons Steakhse.
Gino's Steak Hse.
Greek Islands
Half Shell
John's Place
La Borsa
Les Nomades
Lovells of Lake Forest
Magnum's Steakhse.†
Maison
McCormick & Schmick's
Mill Race Inn
Millrose Brewing Co.
Misto
Napa Valley Grille
Narcisse
Nick & Tony's†
Northside Cafe
Reza's†
RL
Rudi Fazuli's
Sai Cafe
Salbute
Santorini
Shallots
Smith & Wollensky
South Gate Cafe
Southport City Saloon
Spago
Tanglewood
Tecalitlan
Tilli's
Trio
Tsunami

Special Feature Index

Va Pensiero
Via Carducci
Walker Bros.†
Webster's Wine Bar

Historic Places
(Year opened; * building)
1874 Atwater's*
1888 Bricks*
1890 John Barleycorn†
1893 Tavern*
1898 Berghoff*
1916 Del Rio*
1921 Green Door Tavern
1921 Margie's Candies
1922 Salvatore's Rist.*
1923 Lou Mitchell's
1924 302 West*
1927 Village, The
1930 Russell's BBQ
1930 Tufano's Vernon Pk. Tap*
1932 Twin Anchors*
1933 Bruna's Rist.
1933 Cape Cod Room
1933 Mill Race Inn
1938 Pump Room
1939 Hackney's
1941 Gene & Georgetti
1943 Pizzeria Uno
1945 Ann Sather*
1948 Superdawg Drive-In
1949 Miller's Pub

Hotel Dining
Belden Stratford Hotel
  Ambria
Crowne Plaza Hotel
  Karma
Doubletree Guest Suites Hotel
  Mrs. Park's Tavern
  Park Ave. Cafe
Doubletree Hotel
  Gibsons Steakhse.†
Drake Hotel
  Cape Cod Room
  Oak Terrace

Embassy Suites Hotel
  Papagus Taverna†
Fairmont, The
  Entre Nous
Fitzpatrick Hotel
  Benihana†
Four Seasons Hotel
  Seasons
  Seasons Café
Homestead Hotel
  Trio
Hotel Allegro
  312 Chicago
Hotel Burnham
  Atwood Cafe
Hotel Inter-Continental
  Zest
Hotel Monaco
  Mossant Bistro
Le Meridien Hotel
  Cerise
Omni Ambassador East Hotel
  Pump Room
Omni Chicago Hotel
  Cielo
Park Hyatt Chicago
  NoMI
Peninsula Hotel
  Avenues
  Lobby, The
  Pierrot Gourmet
  Shanghai Terrace
Radisson Hotel & Suites
  Becco d'Oro
Ritz-Carlton Hotel
  Ritz-Carlton Café
  Ritz-Carlton Din. Rm.
Seneca Hotel
  Saloon
Sheraton Chicago
  Shula's Steakhouse
Swissôtel
  Palm

Tremont Hotel
  Mike Ditka's
W Chicago - City Center
  We
W Chicago - Lakeshore
  Wave
Westin Hotel
  Grill on the Alley
Whitehall Hotel
  Molive
Wyndham Hotel
  Caliterra Bar & Grille
Wyndham Northwest
  Shula's Steakhouse

"In" Places

Adobo Grill
Bin 36
Bistrot Margot
Blackbird
Bob San
Bongo Room
Café Iberico
Fortunato
Frontera Grill
Gibsons Steakhse.†
Gioco
Heat
Jin Ju
Joe's Seafood, Steak/Crab
Keefer's
Kevin
Marché
Mas
Mia Francesca
Mirai Sushi
mk
mk North
MOD.
Naha
Nine
NoMI
one sixtyblue
Otro Mas

Red Light
Roy's
Shaw's Crab House†
Soul Kitchen
Spring
Sushi Wabi
Tavern on Rush
Tournesol
Trio
Tru
Twelve 12
Wave

Jacket Required

Ambria
Cape Cod Room
Carlos'
Charlie Trotter's
Cité
Everest
Fond de la Tour
Le Français
Les Nomades
Little Bucharest
Ritz-Carlton Din. Rm.
Seasons
Spiaggia
Tallgrass
Trio
Tru

Late Dining

(Weekday closing hour)
Bar Louie†
Billy Goat Tavern†
Bistro 110 (1 AM)
Bone Daddy (2 AM)
Father & Son Pizza†
Gibsons Steakhse.†
Happy Chef Dim Sum (2 AM)
Harry's Velvet Room (3 AM)
Hong Min†
Hugo's Frog Bar (1 AM)
Kit Kat Lounge (1:30 AM)

Billy Goat Tavern
Bone Daddy
Bongo Room
BUtterfield 8
CHIC Cafe
Chief O'Neill's Pub
Cold Comfort Cafe
Como
Crab St. Saloon
Eclectic
Erawan Royal Thai
Evergreen
Ezuli
5 Boroughs Deli
Flavor
Fortunato
Hai Yen
Hilary's Urban Eatery
Hot Doug's
Iggy's
Jin Ju
Karma
Keefer's
Kevin
Kismet
L'anne
Lobby, The
Lula Café
Mac's
Magnolia Café
Margie's Candies
Masck
Mi Sueño, Su Realidad
mk North
Napa Valley Grille
Orange
Pangea
Piece
Pierrot Gourmet
Prego
Restaurant on the Park
Roong
Roy's

Sabor
Shabu-ya
Shanghai Terrace
Shine & Morida
Silver Seafood
Spring
Stained Glass Wine Bar
Sushi Naniwa
Takkatsu
Tasting Room
Thai Pastry
Tournesol
Wave
We
Zest

Offbeat

Billy Goat Tavern
Bite
Bone Daddy
CHIC Cafe
Dell Rhea's Chicken
Edna's
Gladys Luncheonette
Heat
Kabul House
Kismet
Kit Kat Lounge/Supper Club
Kitsch'n on Roscoe
Leo's Lunchroom
Little Bucharest
MOD.
Mt. Everest
Narcisse
Shabu-ya
Superdawg Drive-In
Technicolor Kitchen
Twisted Spoke
Victory's Banner
Vinh Phat BBQ
White Fence Farm
Wiener's Circle
Zoom Kitchen†

Napa Valley Grille (P)
Nick & Tony'st
Nicolinas Cucina (P)
NoMI (T,W)
Northside Cafe (G)
O'Neil's (S)
120 Ocean Place (P)
Otro Mas (P)
Papagus Taverna (S)
Parker's Ocean Grill (P)
Pasha (S)
Pegasus (T)
Petterino's (S)
Phil Stefani's 437 Rush (S)
Pizzeria Unot
Prego (G)
Public Landing (T)
Puck's at the MCA (P,W)
Quincy Grille on River (G,W)
Rambutan (P)
Ranalli'st
Red Light (P)
Retro Bistro (S)
Reza'st
Rhapsody (P)
Riva (P,W)
Rivers (P,W)
Robinson's No. 1 Ribst
Rock Bottom Breweryt
Room, The (S)
Rose Angelis (P)
Rosebudt
Roy's (P)
Rudi Fazuli's (P)
Sabor (P)
Salvatore's Rist. (G,P)
Sarkis Grill (P)
Settimana Café (P,S)
Shaw's Crab Houset
She She (P)
Silver Cloud B&G (P)
Smith & Wollensky (P,T,W)
Sorriso (P,W)

South Gate Cafe (P,S)
Southport City Saloon (P)
Stained Glass Wine Bar (S)
Star of Siam (P)
Stefani's (P)
Strega Nona (S)
Sullivan's Steakhse.t
Sushi Naniwa (P)
Takkatsu (S)
Tanglewood (P)
Tango Sur (P,S)
Tapas Barcelona (G,P)
Tarantino's (P)
Tavern on Rush (P,S)
Tempo (P)
Thyme (G,P,T)
Tilli's (P)
Tommy Nevin's Pub (P)
Topo Gigio Rist. (G,S)
Topolobampo (S)
Trattoria Pizzeria (S)
Tre Kronor (G,S)
Tsunami (P,S)
Tufano's Vernon Pk. Tap (S)
Tuscanyt
Twist (S)
Twisted Lizard (P,S)
Twisted Spoke (P)
Uncommon Ground (S)
Va Pensiero (T)
Via Veneto (S)
Vinci (S,T)
Vivo (S)
Volare (S)
Watusi (P)
Wave (S)
Wild Onion (P)
Yoshi's Café (P)

People-Watching
Adobo Grill
Berghoff
Bice Rist.t
Bin 36

Blackbird
Brasserie Jo
Carmine's
Chicago Chop Hse.
Coco Pazzo
Gibsons Steakhse.†
Grill on the Alley
Harry Caray's†
Harry's Velvet Room
Iggy's
Keefer's
Le Colonial
Le Passage
Marché
Mirai Sushi
mk
MOD.
Naha
Narcisse
Nine
NoMI
one sixtyblue
Pasha
Rosebud†
Rosebud Steakhse.
Scoozi!
Sinibar
Spring
Tavern on Rush
Wave

Power Scenes
Ambria
Avenues
Bice Rist.
Capital Grille
Catch 35
Charlie Trotter's
Chicago Chop Hse.
Coco Pazzo
Everest
Gene & Georgetti
Gibsons Steakhse.
Grill on the Alley

Keefer's
Le Français
Les Nomades
mk
Morton's†
Naha
NoMI
Ritz-Carlton Café
Ritz-Carlton Din. Rm.
RL
Ruth's Chris
Seasons
Smith & Wollensky
Spago
Spiaggia
Spring
Tru
Zealous

Private Rooms Available
(Restaurants charge less at off times; call for capacity)
Ambria
Arun's
a tavola
Aubriot
Avenues
Bagel, The†
Barrington Ctry. Bistro
Bistro Marbuzet
Bistrot Margot
Bob San
Café La Cave
Cafe Pyrenees
Café Spiaggia
Caliterra Bar & Grille
Campagnola
Cape Cod Room
Capital Grille
Carlos'
Carmichael's Steak Hse.
Catch 35
Charlie Trotter's
Chicago Chop Hse.

Costa's

Courtright's

Crofton on Wells

D & J Bistro

Don Roth's Blackhawk

Entre Nous

Erie Cafe

Everest

Fond de la Tour

Francesca's†

Froggy's French Cafe

Frontera Grill

Gabriel's

Gene & Georgetti

Giannotti Steak Hse.

Gibsons Steakhse.

Gioco

Goose Island

Harvest on Huron

Hatsuhana

Ixcapuzalco

Jack's on Halsted

Jacky's Bistro

Kamehachi†

Keefer's

Lawry's Prime Rib

Le Colonial

Le Français

Les Deux Gros

Le Titi de Paris

Le Vichyssois

Lou Malnati's Pizzeria†

Magnum's Steakhse.

Marché

Mesón Sabika†

Mia Francesca

Midori

mk

MOD.

Mon Ami Gabi†

Morton's†

Naha

Nick's Fishmarket

Nine

NoMI

Oceanique

one sixtyblue

120 Ocean Place

Original Gino's East†

Palm

Park Ave. Cafe

Parker's Ocean Grill

Pasteur

Phoenix

Printer's Row

Rhapsody

Rock Bottom Brewery

Rose Angelis

Ruth's Chris†

Sabatino's

Seasons

Shaw's Crab House

Spago

Spiaggia

Tallgrass

Thyme

Topolobampo

Trattoria Dinotto

Trattoria No. 10

Trio

Tru

Tuscany†

Twelve 12

Va Pensiero

Via Carducci

Vinci

Vivere

Walker Bros.†

Wildfire

Zealous

Zia's Trattoria

Zinfandel

Prix Fixe Menus
(Call for prices and times)

Ambria

American Girl Pl.

American Smokehse.
Arun's
Aubriot
Bin 36
Café Le Loup
Cafe Pyrenees
Caliterra Bar & Grille
Campagnola
Carlos'
Charlie Trotter's
CHIC Cafe
Cielo
Clark St. Bistro
Cyrano's Bistrot/Wine Bar
D & J Bistro
Dick's Last Resort
Diosa Red
Dozu Sushi & Lobster
El Jardin
Erawan Royal Thai
Ethiopian Village
Everest
Froggy's French Cafe
Jilly's Cafe
Kismet
La Petite Folie
La Sardine
Las Bellas Artes
La Strada Rist.
Le Français
Les Deux Gros
Les Nomades
Le Titi de Paris
Le Vichyssois
Lexi's
Lino's Rist.
Lobby, The
L'Olive
Marché
Mossant Bistro
one sixtyblue
Papagus Taverna†
Pump Room

Retro Bistro
Reza's†
Ritz-Carlton Din. Rm.
Riva
Rudi Fazuli's
Rushmore
Seasons
Sorriso
Spiaggia
Sushi Naniwa
Tallgrass
Thyme
Tizi Melloul
Trio
Tru
Twelve 12

Quick Fix

Albert's Café & Patiss.
Art of Pizza
Artopolis Bakery
Bagel, The
Bar Louie
BD's Mongolian BBQ
Berghoff†
Bice Grill†
Big Bowl
Billy Goat Tavern
Bin 36
Cafe Nordstrom
Cafe Selmarie
Chicago Flat Sammies
Chicago Pizza/Oven Grinder
Chipotle Mexican Grill†
Cold Comfort Cafe
Corner Bakery
Cosí†
Cru Wine Bar
El Presidente
5 Boroughs Deli
Flat Top Grill
Fluky's
Flying Chicken
foodlife

Fox & Obel Cafe
Gold Coast Dogs†
Hi Ricky†
Hot Doug's
Johnny Rockets
Lem's BBQ
Lincoln Noodle Hse.
Manny's Coffee Shop
Max's
Mrs. Levy's Deli
Noon-O-Kabab
Oak Tree
Old Jerusalem
Panera Bread
Penny's Noodle Shop†
Pierrot Gourmet
Pompei Bakery†
Potbelly Sandwich
Puck's at the MCA
Russell's BBQ
Salt & Pepper Diner
Sarkis Grill
Stained Glass Wine Bar
Stevie B's
Stir Crazy Cafe
Superdawg Drive-In
Tasting Room
Taza
Tempo
Uncommon Ground
Vinh Phat BBQ
Webster's Wine Bar
Wiener's Circle
Zoom Kitchen

Quiet Conversation
Akai Hana†
Albert's Café & Patiss.
Amitabul
Arun's
Bank Lane Bistro
Barn of Barrington
Barrington Ctry. Bistro
Best Hunan

Bêtise
Bistro Banlieue
Bukhara
Café Bernard
Café La Cave
Cafe Matou
Cafe Pyrenees
Cafe Selmarie
Café Spiaggia
Caliterra Bar & Grille
Cape Cod Room
Carlos'
Charlie Trotter's
Chinoiserie
Christophe
Cité
CoCoRo/East
Convito Italiano
D & J Bistro
Don Roth's Blackhawk
Dover Straits†
Eli's Place for Steaks
erwin, an american cafe
Everest
Fond de la Tour
Fondue Stube
Gale St. Inn†
Gaylord India
Geja's Cafe
Genesee Depot
Hashalom
Hatsuhana
Hong Min
Itto Sushi
Jaipur Palace
Jilly's Cafe
Kevin
Klay Oven
Kyoto
La Crêperie
La Gondola
Las Bellas Artes
Lawry's Prime Rib

Romantic Places

KiKi's Bistro
La Crêperie
La Sardine
Le Bouchon
Le Colonial
Le Français
Le Passage
Les Deux Gros
Les Nomades
Le Titi de Paris
Le Vichyssois
Meritage Cafe/Wine Bar
Mill Race Inn
mk
Mon Ami Gabi
Nacional 27
Naha
Narcisse
NoMI
Oceanique
Pane Caldo
Pasteur
Pump Room
Ravinia Bistro
Rhapsody
Ritz-Carlton Din. Rm.
RL
RoSal's Cucina
Rushmore
Seasons
1776
Shanghai Terrace
Signature Rm. at 95th
Sinibar
Souk
South Gate Cafe
Spring
Stained Glass Wine Bar
Tallgrass
Tanglewood
Tasting Room
Tavern
302 West

Tizi Melloul
Topo Gigio Rist.
Tru
Twelve 12
Va Pensiero
Vinci
Webster's Wine Bar

Senior Appeal
Albert's Café & Patiss.
Andies†
Ann Sather†
Army & Lou's
Berghoff†
Biaggio's
Bogart's Charhse.
Bruna's Rist.
Buca di Beppo
Café Luciano
Cannella's on Grand
Cape Cod Room
Carson's Ribs†
Czech Plaza
Dave's Italian Kit.
Davis St. Fishmarket
Don Roth's Blackhawk
Don's Fishmarket & Tav.
Dover Straits
Edelweiss
Father & Son Pizza†
Fireplace Inn
Francesco's Hole in Wall
Gale St. Inn
Genesee Depot
La Bella Winnetka
La Cantina Enoteca
La Gondola
Las Tablas
La Strada Rist.
Lawry's Prime Rib
Leona's†
Little Bucharest
Lou Mitchell's†
Lutnia

Special Feature Index

Wine Vintage Chart 1985–2000

This chart is designed to help you select wine to go with your meal. It is based on the same 0 to 30 scale used throughout this *Survey*. The ratings (prepared by our friend **Howard Stravitz**, a law professor at the University of South Carolina) reflect both the quality of the vintage and the wine's readiness for present consumption. Thus, if a wine is not fully mature or is over the hill, its rating has been reduced. We do not include 1987, 1991–1993 vintages because they are not especially recommended for most areas.

	'85	'86	'88	'89	'90	'94	'95	'96	'97	'98	'99	'00
WHITES												
French:												
Alsace	24	18	22	28	28	26	25	23	23	25	23	25
Burgundy	24	24	18	26	21	22	27	28	25	24	25	–
Loire Valley	–	–	–	26	25	22	24	26	23	22	24	–
Champagne	28	25	24	26	29	–	24	27	24	24	–	–
Sauternes	22	28	29	25	27	–	22	23	24	24	–	20
California:												
Chardonnay	–	–	–	–	–	21	26	22	25	24	25	–
REDS												
French:												
Bordeaux	26	27	25	28	29	24	26	25	23	24	22	25
Burgundy	23	–	22	26	29	20	26	27	25	23	26	–
Rhône	25	19	26	29	28	23	25	22	24	28	26	–
Beaujolais	–	–	–	–	–	–	22	20	24	22	24	–
California:												
Cab./Merlot	26	26	–	21	28	27	26	24	28	23	26	–
Zinfandel	–	–	–	–	–	26	24	25	23	24	25	–
Italian:												
Tuscany	26	–	24	–	26	23	25	19	28	24	25	–
Piedmont	25	–	25	28	28	–	24	26	28	26	25	–